Covenant:
The Basis of God's Self-Disclosure

Covenant:
The Basis of God's Self-Disclosure

*A Comprehensive Guide to the Essentiality
of Covenant as the Foundation for Christians
in their Relating to God and to Each Other*

CHRIS WOODALL

WIPF & STOCK · Eugene, Oregon

COVENANT: THE BASIS OF GOD'S SELF-DISCLOSURE
A Comprehensive Guide to the Essentiality of Covenant as the Foundation for Christians in their Relating to God and to Each Other

Copyright © 2011 Chris Woodall. All rights reserved. Except for brief quotations in critical publications or reviews, no part of this book may be reproduced in any manner without prior written permission from the publisher. Write: Permissions, Wipf and Stock Publishers, 199 W. 8th Ave., Suite 3, Eugene, OR 97401.

Wipf & Stock
An Imprint of Wipf and Stock Publishers
199 W. 8th Ave., Suite 3
Eugene, OR 97401
www.wipfandstock.com

ISBN 13: 978-1-61097-358-8

Manufactured in the U.S.A.

All scripture quotations, unless otherwise indicated, are taken from the Holy Bible, New International Version®, NIV®. Copyright ©1973, 1978, 1984 by Biblica, Inc.™ Used by permission of Zondervan. All rights reserved worldwide.

Contents

Foreword vii
Acknowledgments ix
Introduction xi

1 The Old Covenants 1

2 The New Covenant 41

3 Covenant Law, Covenant Grace 79

4 The Covenant Meal 117

5 Covenant Expressed 155

Conclusion 191
Bibliography 195

Foreword

Dr. Woodall's apposite book on the important theme of the covenant in the Bible, and in the lives of believers today, appears at a time when churches all over the world are thinking about the scriptural basis of their existence and of their task in the modern world.

Covenant: The Basis of God's Self-Disclosure is very well structured. After the Introduction, the author discusses the six major covenants of the Old Testament, namely those of God with Adam, Noah, Abraham, Phinehas, and David, as well as the Mosaic covenant. A covenant can be defined as an agreement between two parties and, as in the case of the covenants herein described, between two unequal parties: God and his covenant people. In such a relationship, the initiative belongs exclusively in God's hands.

Chris summarizes the main contents of each of these covenants in the subsections of Chapter 1 with, for example, the covenant with Abraham labeled "The Covenant of Promise," and the one with David identified as "The Covenant of the Kingdom." He demonstrates how these covenants are linked in the progression of God's revelation in the Old Testament, before explaining the fulfillment of each in the new covenant in Christ. He argues against the description of the Old Testament as law and the New Testament as grace, since each of the covenants of the former is a sign of God's grace for those who would obediently embrace it. The same is true of the new covenant that was established in and through Christ, and the example of the covenant meal is explored in terms of its importance for the church today. The partakers of this meal must be aware of their responsibilities in this regard—that they may thereby avoid the covenant curses and anticipate its blessings.

In the final chapter, Chris discusses the meaning of the covenant for believers in the twenty-first century, looking especially at mutual honor, potential confrontation, forgiveness, and reciprocal provision.

The concept of the covenant must play an important part in the lives of believers and in their growth in faith.

I have no hesitation in recommending this book to all for whom the church is important as an instrument in the kingdom of God, and for those who want to place their faith and their development in that faith on a firm footing.

Herrie van Rooy
Professor of Old Testament Studies
North-West University
Potchefstroom
South Africa

Acknowledgments

THE LIST OF THOSE to whom I owe a colossal debt of gratitude in making this work possible is far too long to include here. The following names are, therefore, only a sample.

I remain eternally grateful to my mother, Pat, for introducing me to the wonderful person of Jesus Christ almost forty years ago. Jude Thurlow, my Religious Education teacher at Selby Grammar School, is also worthy of mention for sowing the seeds some four years earlier. My very first pastor and lifelong friend, David Wilson, has continually challenged, provoked, and encouraged in just the right proportions.

My thanks must also go to all those people whose spiritual instruction and godly inspiration have helped to shape my thinking over the years. Included among these are Richard Maton, Merrill Mauk, Jeff Cox, David Matthew, Russ Andrews, Roger Grainger, Ben Rees, and Byron and Peg Evans. Thanks for so readily agreeing to provide the Foreword must also go to Professor Herrie van Rooy, someone I have found to be not only a man of God, but also a godly man.

I am particularly appreciative of my late grandparents, Horace and Annie Green, not only for bringing me up as their own from a young age and for providing me with a framework of support that is becoming increasingly less common, but also for the financial help that eventually allowed me to pursue my passion.

Finally, I am especially indebted to my wife, Barbara. She is a helpmeet, a source of encouragement, and truly my best friend: "Let her works bring her praise at the city gate" (Prov 31:10–31).

Introduction

Given the emphasis that Scripture accords the concept of covenant, it is perhaps a sad indictment that the word itself does not figure more prominently in the Christian vocabulary. Even the way the Bible is divided illustrates the word's status: God has graciously entrusted us with his self-disclosure under the Old and New Covenants, but the term "Testaments" is probably far more familiar to many of us.

A covenant, or testament, is essentially an agreement between two parties—not necessarily of equal stature—the principal features of which include obligations, rewards, and penalties. These are determined and agreed to in advance, so that each party is fully aware of its responsibilities toward the other, i.e., the blessings that obedience might produce, and the sanctions that may be invoked should the commitment be neglected. Once these are agreed, a final feature comes into play that binds both parties to the terms and conditions of the covenant. In modern language, they effectively become joint signatories; biblically, the binding was usually sealed by the shedding of blood.[1]

The fundamental nature of divine covenants is that they are established solely by the prerogative of Almighty God. Their conditions are presented for acceptance or rejection; they are never the subject of negotiation. Such is the nature of God's covenants with mankind, seen in those with Adam, Noah, Abraham, Moses, Phinehas, and David in the Old Testament—and in the promise of the new covenant, which was to fulfill all the obligations of its predecessors as the final step in God's progressive self-revelation (see Jer 31:31–33). It must be noted, however, that although the divine covenants are necessarily monopleuric in their initiation, they are vitally reciprocal in their execution.

It might reasonably be argued that the covenants entered into by the Old Testament representatives mentioned above were not separate, but rather successive expressions of the same covenant, their thematic

---

1. See Robertson, *Christ of the Covenants*, 11.

unity characterized by the constant underlying thought—"I will be your God and you will be my people" (Jer 7:23). Each of the agreements in the Old Testament after that with Adam is consequently to be regarded as a development of its predecessor. Thus, the Noahic covenant was substantially one of grace, expressed through preservation, while at the same time it reaffirmed the twin creational commands given to Adam: expansion and dominion, fruitfulness and authority (see Gen 6:17–19; 9:8–17). The Patriarchal covenant, given to Abraham, embraced the promise that Yahweh would be his God and would bless the territorial inheritance through Abraham's "seed" (Gen 22:18). The Sinaitic covenant through Moses was structured around the law in such a way that Jacob's tribal descendants would represent God's kingdom on earth as a nation of priests (Exod 19:5–6). Later still, the priesthood was instituted specifically through Phinehas (cf. Num 3:12; Mal 2:4–8), kingship being assigned principally through David's line in the divine continuum (Ps 89:3–4).

Grace is the common thread that seems to unite the divine covenants of the Old Testament. God can only be known by virtue of the fact that he chooses to make himself known and, in the Old Testament, God continually and sequentially reveals himself as one who chooses a people for relationship, not out of obligation or need, but purely due to sovereign choice. The fact that God takes the initiative to do so is further testimony to his self-disclosure, for Israel was not chosen to represent him as a reward for its righteousness: it, too, was an act of God's gracious favor.

Each successive covenant agreement effectively and progressively unfolded throughout the course of history towards the original intention of the Father's heart, fulfilled in the new covenant as God's final revelation, Jesus Christ. The commands given to Adam were not scrapped, when he fell, in favor of some divine rescue operation code-named "Plan B." The anticipation of a new beginning for God's elect under Abraham, similar to the promise enjoyed by Noah, bears all the features of God's unfailing—though utterly undeserved—love. And the promises given to Abraham were not cancelled and replaced by the legal code. Even the law of Moses was not invalidated as an expression of God's grace toward his people. How much more gracious could God possibly be than to draw men and women into a relationship with him—best summed up as loving him with all of one's heart, all of one's soul, all of one's mind, and all of one's strength—and then to allow that grace to flow through us in expressions of love toward our neighbor (see Mark 12:30–31)? The nature of the covenants with Phinehas and David were those of priesthood and kingdom, respectively. But they, too, were founded upon the Lord's everlasting kindness, their purpose being to proclaim God's delegated rule as witness of a radical lifestyle ordained by him and maintained by his supernatural provision.

The evidence seems to suggest, therefore, that the basis of God's self-disclosure is exclusively and consistently one of covenant. The soteriological inferences to be drawn from this fact are obvious, for, as Thomas McComiskey points out:

> The great redemptive eras are not simply initiated by covenant; they are governed by it. Covenant is the key to the understanding of redemptive history.[2]

If this is so—and I must first of all demonstrate that it is—then the church of the twenty-first century can ill afford to remain ignorant of its truth and associated practical implications.

In essence, then, the argument this book will make is that God's self-disclosure is inextricably linked to covenant—this coming together (from the Latin *con venire*) of two parties. In other words, from man's perspective at least, purity of religion is commensurate with pursuit of relationship. The extent to which we honor God, in accordance with our understanding of his righteous standards, determines the integrity of our claim to sonship. As in the Garden of Eden, man has always found revelation of God to be a prerequisite to living in relationship with God. It is perhaps, therefore, legitimate to suggest that the design of revelation through covenant is meant to accomplish the very objective of creation.

---

2. McComiskey, *Covenants of Promise*, 176.

1

The Old Covenants

THE ADAMIC COVENANT—A COVENANT OF SONSHIP

As a prelude to all that follows, it may be helpful to introduce some basic terms. We have already seen in the Introduction that the English word "covenant" derives from the Latin *con venire* (come together). On the other hand, the Hebrew concept of covenant is encapsulated in the word *berith*, which includes the idea of eating together in celebration of being bound in unity. Scripture treats such a bond as eminently serious; it can only be severed by the death of one of the parties. Of the divine covenants, therefore, Palmer Robertson notes that "[w]hen God enters into a covenantal relationship with men, he sovereignly institutes a life-and-death bond. A covenant is a bond in blood, or a bond of life and death, sovereignly administered."[1]

Covenant Established . . . and Broken

The first covenant recorded in Scripture is between God and Adam. Some have challenged this assertion on the grounds that the word "covenant" does not actually appear in the biblical text until it is used to describe God's dealings with Noah, but this objection is somewhat irrelevant. As Louis Berkhof rightly points out, "[o]ne would hardly infer from the absence of the term 'Trinity' that the doctrine of the Trinity is not found in the Bible," adding that "all the elements of a covenant are indicated in Scripture."[2] Peter Golding also comments: "There is such a thing as

---

1. Robertson, *Christ of the Covenants*, 4.
2. Berkhof, *Systematic Theology*, 213.

inferential theology."[3] Moreover, it must be observed that Adam's rebellion is described by the prophets as his having "broken the covenant" (Hos 6:7).

There are two other major indicators that a covenant was present between God and Adam. First, a relationship manifestly existed between them as Creator and pinnacle of creation, respectively. Indeed, if there is any truth in Calvin's claim that "creation is the theatre of God's glory," then surely Adam is its principal character. Second, the conditions of their continued fellowship were clearly spelled out in terms of benefits for obedience and penalties for unfaithfulness (see Gen 1:29; 2:16–17). In establishing a covenant with Adam, God revealed himself to be personal, and fellowship with God is pivotal to all other relationships. Through obedience to God in honoring the Sabbath, man was to express primary allegiance toward the initiator of the Sabbath principle (Gen 2:3). The root of the command to be fruitful and fill the earth was the requirement to be productive within the legitimate confines of the marriage relationship (Gen 1:28), and the work ethic (a prelapsarian requirement) was coupled with a mandate for caring stewardship, so that man would learn to rule for the common benefit of the created order (Gen 2:15).

Arguments associated with the problem of evil aside, Adam's disobedience became the immediate and irreversible gateway between original righteousness and original sin. Those who suggest that the gateway was the principle determining his action, rather than the action itself, must distinguish between *sin* and *evil*. Evil is essentially a principle diametrically opposed to good. The forbidden fruit of Eden was not excluded from Adam's reach because it illuminated the distinction between *good* and *sin*, but because it enabled our covenant representative to discern between *good* and *evil*. Sin, on the other hand, is not so much a principle as it is a condition of human nature. In other words, if sin is fundamentally an abrogation of moral responsibility, then it must, *ipso facto*, be confined to morally responsible beings. Furthermore, it might even be argued that sinful acts are not merely those deeds that are overtly harmful, or that contravene perceived laws, or that are necessarily less than considerate toward others. Rather, *all* actions that emanate from a sinful nature are, by definition, sinful deeds. As the prophet Isaiah proclaimed: "All of us have become like one who is unclean, and all our righteous acts are like filthy rags" (Isa 64:6).

3. Golding, *Covenant Theology*, 109.

T. C. Hammond is correct to conclude that "the Bible is 'a chronicle of redemption' and not a textbook on sin."[4] However, because Adam did sin, we only know the consequences of his having broken the terms and conditions of his covenant with God. What might have happened had he not succumbed to temptation can only ever be a matter for speculation. What we do know is that his call to obedience was a call to honor his relational commitments on three levels:

- Toward his God
- Toward his wife (and, by extension, toward others); and
- Toward the created order.

Relating to God

The essence of all relationships is trust. Or, to put it another way, to whatever degree trust is absent from a relationship, the perfection of that relationship—in relative terms—is commensurately marred. Although Adam (and Eve) may initially have been oblivious to the truth that trust is essential to a relationship, the serpent was not; he knew that his primary target had to be the core element of man's relationship to God—i.e., trust. The serpent's argument was not even necessarily unreasonable; it simply contradicted Adam's faith. Where rationality and trust cannot be reconciled, one will eventually dominate. The root of Adam's disobedience, therefore, was his failure to subject reason to faith.

Although it would be inconceivable to conclude that God was in any way responsible for Adam's violation, the fact remains that the latter's disobedience did afford God the opportunity to further reveal himself as one who is faithful to his own covenantal obligations. For the Evangelical to declare—as a bold statement of faith without qualification—that "God can do all things," is not strictly accurate. (I say this as someone who is unashamedly evangelical by conviction.) In fact, God can do absolutely nothing that is inconsistent with his intrinsic sense of righteousness and justice. Nor can God behave in such a way that militates against his divine perfections. God is good; there is no trace of evil in him. Because our understanding of goodness is tarnished and temporally related to immediate well-being, we may not always fully appreciate how good

---

4. Hammond, *In Understanding be Men*, 82.

God's dealings with us are. Our limited understanding, however, in no way negates God's inherent goodness; in truth, he can be no other way.

The consequences of Adam's transgression were also fully in keeping with God's faithfulness. Overcome by shame (Gen 3:7), he and his wife Eve were so conscience-stricken that they impulsively sought to escape from the holy presence of their God (Gen 3:8). They were eventually banished from the paradise of Eden, and each was burdened with, respectively, toilsome labor (Gen 3:17–19) and painful childbirth (Gen 3:16). The seeds of life planted in the soil of rebellion had produced a harvest of decay. Yet God remained loyally disposed toward them, providing more suitable coverings for their nakedness than they had found; indeed, the animal skins were suggestive of another covenant element—the shedding of blood.

Here we must note a subtle—though nonetheless real—distinction between *relationship* and *fellowship*. Adam's relationship to God was that of a creature to its creator. Indeed, he was as a created "son" in relation to his creative "father." Prior to the fall, Adam experienced perfect *fellowship* with God. Subsequently, fellowship was tarnished forever—or so it seemed—for all of humanity. The *relationship* that existed between them, however, remained largely unaltered. If my wife and I have such a heated disagreement that strong words are exchanged or that one of us does something that the other finds offensive—even detestable—then, for a time, our fellowship will be strained. The duration of such antipathy will depend on a number of factors: how severe the argument and the circumstances surrounding it, how uncompromising each of us may be about our position, how quickly one of us realizes that we are cutting our nose off to spite our face, etc. However long this situation—i.e., the breach in our fellowship—lasts, we nevertheless remain husband and wife until a mutually satisfactory resolution is found: indeed, we remain man and wife throughout the dispute, and afterward. Fellowship may well have been temporarily suspended; relationship, however, continues.

Relating to Others

Although the most obvious pattern of lateral relationships, i.e., relationships between peers, to be seen here is that of husband and wife, the expression of covenant between Adam and Eve serves as an archetype of *all* interpersonal relationships. The level of intimacy possible between them was certainly far higher than they could have found with any of the rest of creation. Having experienced the blessings of divine covenant in comparative isolation prior to Eve's creation, Adam was ideally placed to initiate a reflection of that first relationship, with the woman who joined him. It is perhaps significant, in the context of their sexual freedom before the fall, that intrinsic to their covenant mandate was the command to reproduce. As has already been noted, the work ethic was instituted prior to Adam's disobedience; it is not the product of a postlapsarian curse. By the same token, faithful heterosexual companionship was the hallmark of their relationship before the fall; sexual deviance—in all its forms—can only legitimately be traced to the time after the covenant was broken.

Although it would be incorrect to suggest that this one relationship exhibited all the features common to lateral covenants, the extension of the family through children certainly forms the ideal biblical framework for all interpersonal relationships. In the Old Testament, the Hebrew word most frequently translated "family" (*mishpaha*) is used in a variety of settings, and it is difficult to suggest a single, narrow, definitive meaning for it. The Septuagint usually translates *mishpaha* by the Greek *patria*, a word used to describe people who are related in a wider sense than we might normally understand by the word family. This rendering is partly called for given the Hebrew culture of extended families, but it is also in no small measure a consequence of the lack of a direct equivalent for *mishpaha* in the Greek tongue.

Adam's relationship with Eve was one of partnership, procreation, and relief from loneliness. It is difficult to imagine that Eve was an afterthought of the creative mind behind God's economy. It has been suggested that Adam was initially created alone so that he would have first-hand experience of solitude and would therefore come to appreciate all the more the gift God had in store for him. Those who defend their independence on the pseudo-spiritual grounds that they lack nothing and no one, as long as they have God in their lives, have failed to acknowledge that they are incomplete without a life partner. Is it irreligious or blasphemous to concede that they are incomplete if they do not? No, it is merely accepting a divine creational ordinance: we are this way because God made us so.

David Lyon defines society as ". . . an abstract concept referring to the system of interrelationships connecting individuals who share a common culture."[5] Given that definition, it does not seem far-fetched to suggest that the seeds of society arrived with Eve. Of course, the potential was always there with Adam, but a society could only be realized once

---

5. Lyon, "Society," *Dictionary of Christian Ethics*, 801.

Adam was no longer alone and had more to focus on than just himself as an individual. Although society may be analyzed and defined as a collection of individuals, each responding to their mutual obligations, in Scripture, society is much more about the social implications of human interaction. In other words, how we *relate* to one another is a far more important feature of society than merely how we manage to *coexist*.

Relating to their Surroundings

Adam's covenant responsibilities toward the created order, mandated by God, comprised subduing the earth and ruling its non-human inhabitants (see Gen 1:27–28). The Hebrew verbs translated "to subdue" and "to rule" are *kabash* and *radah*. Although these verbs are more commonly translated "to conquer" (*kabash*) and "to trample" (*radah*), the context of this passage suggests a different rendering, as the overall context identifies man as created in God's image and, therefore, as bearing a responsibility to reflect something of the (communicable) divine attributes, albeit in facsimile form.

Some suggest that there is really no distinction between *dominion* and *domination*. Their similarity, however, exists only in English, for the Hebrew *radah* (dominion) is more closely associated with stewardship than is *shalat* (domination), which implies exploitation (see, e.g., Eccl 8:9). When considered in this biblical context, the dominion of man over creation effectively enables that creation to maximize its own potential and thereby glorify the Creator. This end is to be achieved through diligent endeavor on man's part and, as this mandate is conferred before the fall, the argument that the work ethic is part of the postlapsarian curse must fail. Rather, it is auxiliary evidence of God's image being reflected in man.

Stewardship requires commitment; it also calls for obedience to a command. In this sense, it is compulsory and not voluntary: mankind is governed by the divine command. However, in the primary context of relating to God as a loving Father, and then to others as family, it is possible for us to engage with our environmental responsibilities—and for those responsibilities to be a matter of law—without their becoming legalistic. God has invested creation with integrity and beauty. He has invited those he has created in his image to maintain creation's splendor and to develop its resources with his authority and a measure of his care. We are creatures, but we are first and foremost sons and daughters of the creator God. Indeed, it might be said that the foundations of godly stewardship are image and intimacy, i.e., that mankind was made in God's image and was invited to live in intimate relationship with him. Given that these are gifts from God, in the sense that God was under no obligation to make image and intimacy accessible to man, it becomes clear that the concepts of stewardship and grace are also strongly connected. So much so, in fact, that it is possible to speak of both the grace of stewardship and the stewardship of grace, though it is the former that we have in mind here.

Although, in principle, stewardship is itself a grace of God, in practice it is also the administration of God's grace on his behalf. In terms of the apostolic responsibility to present the gospel to the Gentiles, we see this is so from Paul's reminder to those at Ephesus (see Eph 3:2–3). In a similar vein, Peter jogs the memory of his intended readership regarding their new covenant obligations toward each other as co-ministers of God's grace (1 Pet 4:10). And so it is in relation to the Adamic creational directive. When we see that work, *per se*, is not a product of the fall, but that it formed part of God's original covenantal ordinance given to Adam, then perhaps we will also come to acknowledge that it is both unnecessary and unhelpful to speak of activities as either religious *or* secular. In the mindset of many, work is nothing but a synonym for structured employment or a regular job with remunerative benefits. My question is this: what was work before it became engulfed by the capitalist ethical paradigm? Moreover, if work is a product of the fall, as some maintain, then how did Adam fulfill his mandate in relation to the created order before he fell?

Summary

Adam ruled over creation not as sovereign, but in his capacity as viceregent. He was appointed steward over God's property on earth, a caretaker with both privileges and responsibilities. It is of the essence of covenant that there are penalties for abusing its privileges and neglecting the responsibilities it entails. Interestingly, William Dumbrell even goes so far as to say this:

> The world and man are part of one total divine construct, and we cannot entertain the salvation of man in isolation from the world [that] he has affected. The refusal to submit in Eden meant a disordered universe and thus the restoration of all things will put God, man and the world at harmony again.[6]

---

6. Dumbrell, *Covenant and Creation*, 41.

THE NOAHIC COVENANT—A COVENANT OF FAVOR

Such is the clarity of expression in the story of God's covenant with Noah that John Murray[7] is convinced that this one—more than any other—shows us the essence of covenant relationship. Moreover, nowhere is the author, initiator, promissory signatory, and dispenser of blessing and penalty alike more overtly revealed to be God himself than here. We also find ourselves confronted here, for the first time in Scripture, with the word *berith*, though everything the word signifies was also present in God's dealings with Adam, a fact Murray seems hesitant to concede.

A New Beginning

Although the Noahic covenant was of the "royal grant" type, insofar as it was based on an unconditional promise, it might reasonably be argued that the precondition for the initiation of a covenant agreement between God and Noah had already been met, in that Noah's righteousness was the determining factor in his being chosen by God. Of course, it might also be argued that God's sovereign grace extended to keeping Noah from becoming unrighteous. However, to speak of a prediluvian and a postdiluvian covenant with Noah might imply two separate covenant agreements (cf. Gen 6:17–22; 9:1–7), where the commitment on God's part to preserve Noah is central to both. It is not unusual for the details of a single covenant to be discussed across a broad timescale, giving the impression that they refer to separate covenants, whereas they are more accurately understood as component features of one covenant where "preliminary dealings precede formal inauguration procedures."[8] In real terms, of course, what is identified as the prediluvian covenant was not one at all; rather it was the promise God made to Noah that he, God, would establish a covenant with Noah at some time in the future.

There were eight human survivors of the flood: Noah, his wife, their three sons (Shem, Ham, and Japheth), and their sons' wives. It is perhaps noteworthy that, in biblical numerology, the number eight is considered by many to represent a new beginning,[9] principally because it is the number that immediately follows seven, whether in relation to days in the week or musical notes in an octave. God's judgment upon

---

7. Murray, *Covenant of Grace*, 12.
8. Robertson, *Christ of the Covenants*, 110.
9. See Davis, *Biblical Numerology*; cf. Bullinger, *Number in Scripture*.

the face of the earth by means of the flood certainly brought about a new beginning for mankind through Noah and his family.

In many ways, Noah came to represent humanity in much the same manner as Adam had done in Eden. It should come as no surprise, therefore, to find some of the key elements of the Adamic covenant reiterated here: both the commission to be fruitful in filling the earth and the authority to exercise dominion over creation (see Gen 1:28; 9:1–3). There were, however, important differences to note between the human envoys of these two covenants. God's original treaty had been with the unfallen Adam; this new initiative was with righteous, though sin-tainted, Noah. Moreover, Adam had represented the whole of his race from the beginning onward, i.e., he was the federal representative of all of humanity; Noah was primarily the ambassador of his own distinct family, albeit the only one through whom the human race could thereafter increase and prosper.

The covenant with Noah was, therefore, a redemptive covenant of grace as opposed to a creational covenant of works. God had chosen Noah from among his generation, revealing himself through this act of redemption to be a gracious God, for "Noah found favor in the eyes of the Lord" (Gen 6:8). Concerning God's covenant with Noah, Arthur Pink writes:

> [Here] we see man reinstituted over the lost inheritance, not on the basis of creature responsibility and human merits, but on the basis of divine grace . . . on the foundation of the excellency of that sacrifice which satisfied the heart of God. Consequently, it was as the children of faith that Noah and his seed became heirs of the new world.[10]

Although the Sabbath principle, which typified Adam's covenant obligations, is notably explicitly absent from the Noahic directive, the fact that Noah's name actually means "rest" (Hebrew—*nwh*) implies its centrality to the covenant agreement here. Whether by accident or intention, naming his son Noah was certainly a prophetic act on the part of his father, Lamech. It is also perhaps significant that, though the principal features (that is, multiply and subdue) of the Adamic covenant are reiterated here, the parameters of man's salvation are extended, lest he consider his deliverance to be exclusively spiritual. God's mandate to Noah makes it quite clear that his social and cultural responsibilities are

---

10. Pink, *Divine Covenants*, 74–75.

not to be neglected; every living creature is the recipient of his assurance (See Gen 9:10; cf. Rom 8:22; 2 Pet 3:3–10).

Autocracy Instituted?

Much has been written regarding the so-called institution of man's God-given right to govern himself, based on the alleged introduction of capital punishment in Genesis 9: "Whoever sheds the blood of man, by man shall his blood be shed; for in the image of God has God made man" (Gen 9:6). Theological opinion seems to be divided over what precisely is meant by this text. Perhaps its being linked to man's creation in the image of God provides a clue. In making this connection, is God simply reminding Noah of his covenant responsibilities to act on God's behalf in such matters, under the terms and conditions of his previous arrangement with Adam? Or is God inaugurating something completely new here? Is the government of man implied at all, or is it simply suggested by way of an unsatisfactory translation? After all, the context also speaks of similar demands being made of animals that cause the death of others (Gen 9:5). As Palmer Robertson points out: "It would be rather difficult to imagine a wild beast serving as instrument of God's judgment in the same sense in which a man would function in this regard."[11]

Robertson goes on to suggest that a better understanding might simply be that God would personally exact justice upon the perpetrator of a malicious death, irrespective of whether the one responsible is human or animal. This would certainly seem to be a satisfying translation. I am not entirely convinced, however, that it would be innocent of the charge of sacrificing the Bible's true meaning on the altar of twentieth (and twenty-first) century human sensitivities. To be fair to Robertson, he too seems to dismiss the notion almost as soon as he posits it, in favor of the idea that the original structure of the verse does rather suggest the *lex talionis*, that is, the proportional distribution of retributive/punitive justice, such as is inherent in the principle of an eye for an eye, a tooth for a tooth (Exod 21:24).[12]

This leaves us pretty much where we began, and the question remains unanswered: Is God now entrusting Noah with judicial responsibility for dealing with those guilty of murder? Gerhard von Rad is in

---

11. Robertson, *Christ of the Covenants*, 117.
12. Ibid., 118.

no doubt of it, attesting that such a divinely appointed task expresses a "strong legal tone" accompanying "the gracious Noahic dispensation."[13] Martin Luther agreed with John Calvin on this matter, believing not only that these verses (i.e., Gen 9:5–6) established temporal government, but also that the instrument of justice is through them placed at man's disposal.

There are, of course, those—some notable Christian thinkers among them—who deny altogether that this is the meaning of the passage. They usually do so by citing two episodes in the Hebrew Scriptures that seem to be at odds with God's command to Noah, given here. The first is in the treatment of Cain after he killed his brother, Abel. The divine sentence passed upon Cain for this act of fratricide was not execution but exile. Indeed, God pronounced judgment on any who would exact vengeance upon Cain (see Gen 4:1–16). The other alleged evidence cited is an interpretation of the sixth commandment of the Decalogue: "You shall not murder" (Exod 20:13). To kill a murderer, they argue, is itself murder and thus makes the executioner no better than the original offender. Both are fine-sounding arguments. So fine, in fact, that I would dearly like to be one of those swayed by them. However, the evidence of Scripture—or, at least, my present understanding of it—will not allow me to be so moved. Instead, what my mind finds pleasant must finally and fully submit to that by which my spirit finds itself convicted.

A Token of Blessing

Though no doubt thankful to be the one through whom the earth would thenceforth be blessed, Noah must have been concerned that God might at some future time repeat his act of judgment, should the condition of man deteriorate once more. In order to quell this natural foreboding, God instituted the covenant of preservation with and through Noah, promising never again to universally destroy life through flooding (Gen 9:11). God's limitless promise is not only explicitly stated, it is also emphatically sealed by a sign—the rainbow—that will accompany any subsequent gathering storm clouds. Translated from the Hebrew *qeshet* (meaning "archer's bow"), this symbol of God's judgment is to be a sign that his sense of justice has been appeased and that only mercy remains. James Jordan notes its particular significance thus:

---

13. Rad, *Genesis*, 129.

> God gave a special sign for the new Noahic covenant: he placed his warbow in the sky as the rainbow. The warbow, God's weapon, is parallel to the flaming sword of the cherubim (Gen 3:24), this being the special sign of the Adamic covenant under judgment . . . the unsheathed sword of God's wrath and his unstrung warbow of peace.[14]

Because it includes God's promise never to inflict such widespread catastrophe again, the divine agreement with Noah is often referred to as the covenant of preservation or of "common grace," its provisions entirely dependent upon God's volitional loving-kindness. The Hebrew word for this concept is *chesed*, which underpins the whole idea of the covenant (when spoken, it also sounds remarkably similar to the Hebrew for warbow/rainbow, *qeshet*). Although its origin is uncertain, Norman Snaith is probably closest to the mark by defining *chesed* as "covenant faithfulness" or "steadfastness."[15] Moreover, this preservation is but the mechanism that effects the purpose of God, which is redemption. In other words, man is kept that he might be saved, not vice versa.

According to Talmudic tradition, the seven colors of the rainbow correspond to seven "laws" allegedly given to Noah by God, adherence to which by non-Jews (that is, "righteous" Gentiles) brings with it the assurance of a place in heaven. The seven socalled "Noahide laws," purportedly reaffirmed by Moses on Mount Sinai in what is regarded as oral Torah, are the following:

- Do not deny God;
- Do not blaspheme God;
- Do not murder;
- Do not indulge in illicit sexual relations (e.g., incest, adultery, bestiality, or homosexuality of any kind);
- Do not steal;
- Do not eat flesh torn from a living animal; and
- Establish a justice system to deal effectively with those who contravene the other six laws.

---

14. Jordan, *Through New Eyes*, 174.
15. Snaith, *Distinctive Ideas*, 94–130.

Not much there for a Christian to find offensive, you might think, until you realize that those who follow Jesus would have been considered to be idolaters and, therefore, in breach of the first law (both of the Noahide set and of Moses' Decalogue). The actual colors in the rainbow, which many of us remember from childhood mnemonics, have also found themselves the subject of colorological speculation. Emmanuel Swedenborg (also known as Svedberg, 1688–1772), for example, draws the following, purportedly significant, conclusions about the meaning of the rainbow's colors in his *Arcana Caelestia* ("Heavenly Secrets"):

Color	Meaning	Description
Red	Outward good	The good life; full-blooded and vital
Orange	Mercy	Compassionate concern for others
Yellow	Grace	The bright positive thought of the gracious and humble mind
Green	Life	The evergreen life growing in usefulness
Blue	Truth	Insight revealed through the experience of goodness
Indigo	Wisdom expressed in mutual care	Inspiration active through wholeness and as harmony
Violet	Peace, innocence, and love	The inflowing of peace creating an outflowing of love

What Swedenborg perceives as a syllabus of inner peace is not so far removed from the Chakra stages of yoga. His outline really seems to be more of a syncretistic attempt to infer Eastern mystic allusions from isolated passages of Scripture than to conduct any legitimate exegetical analysis.

Summary

If we are to acknowledge the historicity of the flood—and nothing in the biblical evidence suggests that we are at liberty to do otherwise—then the rite of passage through judgment for Noah and his family (and the living creatures with them) was not only symbolic; it was objectively real. The same waters that wrought universal destruction elsewhere were effectively their waters of baptism. Moreover, as a type of the new covenant, they were kept safe in the ark of God's design and purpose. Of God's covenant with Noah, Palmer Robertson writes:

> [It] provides the historical framework in which the Immanuel principle may receive its full realization. God has come in judgment; but he also has provided a context of preservation in which the grace of redemption may operate. From the covenant with Noah it becomes quite obvious that God's being "with us" involves not only an outpouring of his grace on his people; it involves also an outpouring of his wrath on the seed of Satan.[16]

THE ABRAHAMIC COVENANT—A COVENANT OF PROMISE

Archaeological evidence suggests that Abraham lived around the nineteenth or twentieth century BC.[17] It also lends credence to the idea that Abraham's original background was highly sophisticated, much to the consternation of those who prefer to perceive the history of the Hebrews as one of determined progression from primitives to pastoralists. The argument that the reference to "Ur of the Chaldees" (Gen 1:28) must be anachronistic because "the Chaldeans did not penetrate southern Mesopotamia until toward the end of the second millennium BC"[18] is not without warrant. Even if true, however, it does not necessarily negate the truth of the text. The reference merely serves to proleptically identify the original location to a later readership.

The Gospel According to Abraham

In 1534, Swiss theologian Johann Heinrich Bullinger became the first to write a doctrinally structured thesis, in which he posited that Scripture in its entirety must be interpreted in the light of the covenant

---

16. Robertson, *Christ of the Covenants*, 125.
17. Albright, *Archaeology and Religion*, 1, 2.
18. Johnson, *History of the Jews*, 10.

with Abraham, by which God graciously offers himself to man and commands that man walk before him, blameless. As recorded in Genesis 12 (cf. Gal 3:6–9), God promised Abram that he would

- Make Abram into a great nation;
- Bless Abram;
- Make Abram's name great;
- Make Abram a blessing;
- Bless those who bless Abram;
- Curse those who curse Abram; and
- Bless all peoples on earth through Abram.

This act was clearly one of divine self-commitment (see also Heb 6:13), for in this initial phase of the covenant, no explicit obligations were placed on Abram. The covenant might, therefore, be seen as effectively unconditional; however, it might also be argued that the condition that evoked such favor—i.e., his faith—had already been met by Abram.

God's covenant promise to Abraham was essentially two-fold: the *seed* (Gen 12:2; 15:18) and the *land* (12:7; 15:7). Indeed, the assurance of territory was dependent upon a dynasty to inherit it. This promise was to form the basis for the tangible hope of Israel throughout the Old Testament. As Paul Johnson observes: "The election of Abraham and his descendants for a special role in God's providence, and the donation of the land, are inseparable in the biblical presentation of history."[19] According to William Hendriksen, the promise of seed relates to an "abundant prosperity," while the promise of the land bespeaks a "fertile country."[20]

Covenant Blessings

The two episodes in Abraham's life relating to the covenant established with him by God can be distinguished as follows:

| Genesis 15 | Inauguration | Divine oath |
| Genesis 17 | Institutional seal | Human oath |

---

19. Ibid., 19.
20. Hendriksen, *Survey of the Bible*, 212.

Accordingly, John Calvin differentiates between the two parts of the Abrahamic covenant in the following manner: "The first was a declaration of gratuitous love, to which was annexed the promise of a happy life. But the other was an exhortation to the sincere endeavor to cultivate uprightness."[21]

Having received the promise of covenant blessings with gratitude, Abraham's concern thereafter was how such a "reward" (Hebrew—*sakar*, basic to which is the idea of wages paid and received in return for service rendered) would be conveyed following his death (Gen 15:1–3). It was not uncommon for the chief male servant to legally assume the rights of an adopted son in such circumstances. It was also customary on such occasions for the master to formalize the matter by arranging for the adoption to be legally recognized. But God's promise was according to his purpose for Abraham's natural line.

It is perhaps significant that, even in the natural world, the promise was not given to all of Abraham's descendants, but only to those who would issue through Isaac, the child of promise and the product of faith. Ishmael, as a son of unbelief and human endeavor, was thereby left out (cf. Gen 21:12; Rom 9:8; Gal 4:28). However, just as Abraham's "fleshly initiative" did not exclude him from the earlier promises made to him, neither was any blame apportioned to Ishmael; he was merely the product of his father's impatience. Indeed, God promised to be favorably disposed toward Hagar's son. It might even be said that Ishmael prospered under the previous Noahic covenant, although he was not a principal beneficiary of the Abrahamic one.

The extent (or limits) of covenant benefits is an issue that will be dealt with in more detail in the discussion of Christ's fulfillment of the covenant agreements. It is a question upon which scholars disagree, even when they are of the same doctrinal persuasion in other matters. Of course, Scripture provides the answer; it is to Abraham and his *seed*. The difficulty, however, lies in the interpretation of that word: seed. To my mind, the apostle Paul resolves the difficulty by clearly identifying the principal character—and character principle—of Abraham's progeny: faith. Abraham's seed, therefore, includes all who demonstrate a similar believing disposition in and through Christ Jesus. It is difficult to imagine how much more explicit Paul could have been in this regard: "The promises were spoken to Abraham and to his seed. Scripture

21. Calvin, *Genesis*, 444.

does not say 'and to seeds,' meaning many people, but 'and to your seed,' meaning one person, who is Christ . . . If you belong to Christ, then you are Abraham's seed, and heirs according to the promise" (Gal 3:16, 29; cf. Rom 4:11–13).

God's covenant with Abraham and, especially (though not exclusively), the blessings for obedience to its obligations, included both temporal benefits and spiritual advantages. As Louis Berkhof points out, however, "[i]t should be borne in mind that the former were not coordinate with, but subordinate to, the latter." As such, "[t]he temporal blessings did not constitute an end in themselves, but served to symbolize and typify spiritual and heavenly things. The spiritual promises were not realized in the natural descendants of Abraham as such, but only in those who followed in the footsteps of Abraham."[22]

Covenant Ritual (Genesis 15:9–20)

When Abraham asked how he should know whether he would, indeed, inherit the land as promised, he may not necessarily have been giving voice to doubts over God's veracity, but rather to doubts concerning his own interpretive skills. Was the promise to be understood literally or metaphorically? Would the inheritance pass to an as yet unknown son or to the chief servant, who had effectively been adopted, as was the custom in such circumstances? God assured Abraham that he had understood correctly, and that the inheritance would, in the first instance, be received by members of his own "natural" line.

The Hebrew phrase *karat berith* literally means to "cut a covenant," implying the concept of an agreement sealed by blood. Because blood represents life itself, the shedding of blood as part of the establishing of a covenant signifies a sacrificial commitment, foreshadows forgiveness under the new covenant, speaks to family loyalty, and exemplifies the penalty for breaking its conditions. First introduced in this context, *karat berith* retains its association with covenant-making throughout the Old Testament.

The symbolic rite was effectively an oath of life. There is extra-biblical evidence to suggest that the ceremonial slaughtering of animals in this way was quite common during the ratification of such treaties. The parties involved were effectively invoking a curse upon themselves

---

22. Berkhof, *Systematic Theology*, 296.

should they become guilty of disregarding their contractual obligations. Note the wording of God's judgment upon those in Judah, in the words of the prophet Jeremiah: "The men who have violated my covenant and have not fulfilled the terms of the covenant they made before me, I will treat like the calf they cut in two and then walked between its pieces. The leaders of Judah and Jerusalem, the court officials, the priests and all the people of the land who walked between the pieces of the calf, I will hand over to their enemies who seek their lives. Their dead bodies will become food for the birds of the air and the beasts of the earth" (Jer 34:18–20).

It is not without significance that God took the initiative to endorse the pledge by personally passing between the halved animals, but only after Abraham had driven away the scavenging birds of prey. As Peter Golding notes:

> A self-maledictory oath is the most likely explanation of the incident recorded in Genesis 15 where, at God's instigation, Abraham takes a heifer, a she-goat and a ram and divides them in the midst, laying each piece one against another. The lamp of fire which passed between the pieces belongs to the same order as the burning bush (Exod 13:21) and the pillar of fire (13:21). It is a symbol of the presence of God, represented here as "cutting a covenant" with Abraham—in other words, God invoking upon himself the covenant curses if his promises should fail.[23]

Covenant Sealed (Genesis 17)

Divine promises	vv. 4–8, 15–21
Human responsibilities	vv. 9–14, 22–27

It is at this point that God revealed himself to Abraham as *El Shaddai* (Gen 17:1). Elsewhere, *El Shaddai* is usually translated "Almighty God" (see Exod 6:3; Ps 89:8; Amos 5:14–15). The word *shadday* probably means "mountain" and is used to symbolize Yahweh's immutability and enduring power, in stark contrast to man's complete helplessness and utter dependence. It may also be derived from the Hebrew word *shad*, meaning "breast" (i.e., a mother's breast), thus signifying God's all-sufficient provision. Taken together, we can clearly see the idea of great

---

23. Golding, *Covenant Theology*, 72.

power combined with blessing and comfort. It is also here that the original promise to Abram is expanded to take account of the name change that identifies him now as the father of many nations (Gen 17:5). Notice also: Abr(ah)am—Sar(ah)—ah! ah! Laughter is added to the names of the primary human players in the covenant of promise. ("Isaac" also means "he laughs.")

It must be noted that God's promise to Abraham was not based upon the latter's acceptance of the former's invitation, but as a consequence of Abraham's obedience to a given command. Moreover, the seal of circumcision in the Abrahamic covenant seems to highlight the irreversible nature of the covenant agreement with which it is identified. Perhaps it was because Ishmael was the product of Abraham's confidence in the flesh that the surplus flesh in the male reproductive organ was to be ritually removed as a token of covenant trust in the divine promises (see Phil 3:2–3). In the words of Meredith Kline:

> The practice of circumcision found earlier among other peoples was adopted to serve as a sign of incorporation into the Abrahamic covenant. Its continuing significance is learned from the function it performed at its institution. Covenants were ratified by oaths, the oath-curses being dramatized in symbolic rites. A characteristic curse was that of cutting off the vassal to destruction and cutting off his name and seal. Accompanying this was . . . the knife rite by which the Abrahamic covenant was cut.[24]

The permanence and irrevocable nature of circumcision is typical of God's (unconditional) promises. The same can be said of the Holy Spirit's seal on a believer's life. As a gift (that is, not something merited or a wage), it is neither impermanent nor subject to the benefactor's changeable disposition, nor to the recipient's worthiness. Note also that the covenant does not exist independently of the seal. In other words, circumcision is not an optional extra. Robertson may have gone too far by insisting that "the seal *is* the covenant,"[25] but I most certainly agree with the premise of his argument. As a sign (Gen 17:11), it must point to something bigger than itself. That is precisely what a sign is: an indicator of something other and greater. Even in the age of satellite navigation, if I am travelling to a previously unknown destination, road signs direct me so that I may arrive at the right place and in good time. And that is

24. M. Kline, "Genesis," *New Bible Commentary*, 96.
25. Robertson, *Christ of the Covenants*, 96.

their *raison d'être*: to aid me in my overall purpose. They are means to an end, not the end itself. Without them, however, the object would remain "unsignified." As if to reinforce the point, the lot of anyone who chooses to reject this covenantal sign is excommunication (v. 14).

Summary

Consistent with the dual (or even multiple) applications of much biblical prophecy, the promises given to Abraham have already been fulfilled naturally. By the time of David's son and heir, Solomon, God's assurances regarding both the people and the land had been realized. Abraham's descendants were, indeed, as numerous as the dust of the earth (see Gen 3:16; cf. 2 Chr 1:9), the stars in the sky (Gen 22:17; 1 Chr 27:23), and the sand on the seashore (Gen 22:17; 1 Kgs 4:20–21). Moreover, the land possessed by his natural descendants, through Jacob, extended to include all territory from the Nile to the Euphrates, as God had promised (see Exod 23:31).

In the words of Arthur Pink: "The Abrahamic covenant . . . [was] a striking advance in the development of God's gracious purpose toward man."[26] That "striking advance" consisted primarily in the apparent change of covenantal emphasis from the whole human race, *per se*, to a distinct ethnic group. This, in turn, marked the beginning of the church in its etymological sense—a people called out and set apart by God—the redeemed community (or elect). The purpose of that call, however, was not that they might thereby become exclusive and bask in their unique status, but rather that they might become a channel of blessing to those outside the community's limits, with the express purpose of seeking to draw them in. It is appropriate, therefore, to speak of the Abrahamic covenant as arguably one of the most precious heirlooms that the church enjoys.

THE MOSAIC COVENANT—A COVENANT OF THE LAW

The premise of this book is that covenant as a concept is a vital hermeneutic by which to interpret Scripture. More specifically here, the argument is that a proper understanding of the Mosaic covenant is indispensable to coming to terms with much of the history of Israel, the worship of Israel, and the prophetic voice heard within Israel during the period covered by the Old Testament. If the principle of development

---

26. Pink, *Divine Covenants*, 113.

that has been asserted regarding the divine covenants is a valid one, then it must follow that the Mosaic covenant marks a stage of progress from the Abrahamic in the outworking of God's redemptive purpose. This is not to say that the difficulties the covenant people seemed to have in observing covenant regulations were thereby reduced. On the contrary, the trials faced on any advance toward maturity are as likely to be compounded as minimized. Similarly, the apparent advantage of a comparatively trouble-free infancy is not necessarily a predictor of our later preference for fulfilling or disregarding our covenant obligations: what seems to be the easy option now may become more fraught with difficulty in the long term than the alternative choice. Moreover, just as the Mosaic covenant represented a development in the revelation of God's covenant plan for humanity when compared to covenants that preceded it, by the same token it did not reveal as much as did those that were to follow.

A Chosen People

Although commonly referred to as the Mosaic covenant, God's treaty was essentially directed toward the nation of Israel *through* Moses. Often also spoken of as the "Sinaitic covenant," it is a further development of its predecessors, bringing a clearer revelation of the God of the covenants. Abraham had been promised seed and land, though without having received the fruit of such a pledge, except by faith for a future generation. Now, Moses was being used by God to prepare Abraham's descendants for possession of their inheritance. He was shown, specifically, how they were expected to conduct themselves in worship, at work, and in life in community, all instructions revolving around the essence of covenant—relationship. The book of Exodus details Israel's rite of passage into being God's covenant people in two distinct parts. Chapters 1–19 outline the people's sanctification as those called out of Egypt; chapters 20–40 speak of their consecration under the terms of the Sinaitic covenant.

The Mosaic covenant introduces an important theme in the unfolding revelation of God, a theme encapsulated by the Hebrew word *chesed*. It is used elsewhere of God's relationship toward individuals like Abraham, Jacob, and Joseph. Here, however, it is in the context of God's dealings with corporate Israel that the word is more extensively employed in relation to covenant. In addition to the meanings suggested above, the semantic range of *chesed* can extend to include "kindness," "goodness," or "loving-kindness." Moses uses it in the sense of unfailing love (Exod 15:3). Whether divine covenant (that is, *berith*) is the basis of God's loving-kindness (*chesed*)—or vice versa—has been the subject of much theological debate, although Scripture appears to validate both points of view. Perhaps it would be more appropriate to say that the biblical position is one of loving-kindness being the pervading influence on and character of covenant from design to execution. *Chesed*, then, provides both the framework for, and the substance of, covenant—i.e., God's steadfast, unceasing love.

In some ways, the Sinaitic covenant appears to be the exception to the rule seen in previous covenants, as there seems to be a condition attached to it (see Exod 19:5). It must be acknowledged, however, that it is the promised blessing—not the establishing of that covenant— that is conditional upon obedience within the framework of an already existent covenant.[27] It might be better described, therefore, as an unconditional covenant with conditional blessings. Charles Hodge articulates it well: ". . . the Mosaic covenant was a national covenant with the Hebrew people. In this view the parties were God and the people of Israel; the promise was national security and land prosperity; the condition was the obedience of the people as a nation to the Mosaic law; and the mediator was Moses. In this aspect it was a legal covenant. It said, 'Do this and live.'"[28]

The promise of blessing for adhering to covenant obligations, as far as Israel was concerned, meant that the people would be regarded by God as his "treasured possession" (Exod 19:5–6). The Hebrew word used here, *segullah*, usually refers to something that is a private possession and of specific functional value. Out of all the nations of the earth, Israel was especially chosen as a "kingdom of priests" and to be "a holy nation." Neither implies selection according to merit; election was on the basis of divine favor, and Israel was to be a channel of testimony to the rest of creation. The whole law—in its spiritual, social, and moral enactments— stemmed from the dictates of the Ten Commandments (20:1–7), which were concerned with how people should relate first of all to God and then to their fellow men.

27. See Murray, *Covenant of Grace*, 21–22.
28. Hodge, *Systematic Theology*, 117–122.

The Moral Law and Social Justice

If covenant is the basis of the relationship that God entered into with Israel, then the law was the chosen mode of administration of that covenant. As a covenant of law, therefore, it must be distinguished from the earlier covenant of works. The covenant of works with Adam was in his prefallen condition (note again that the work ethic is thus not a consequence of our forefather's lapse). The covenant of law, however, is made with a chosen race, tarnished by the sin of Adam. Note also that the law came after Israel's redemption and could not, therefore, be regarded as the condition upon which it was effected. Neither did the covenant of law negate, suspend, or replace the covenant of promise with Abraham. Faith was always—and still is—the key to righteousness, which expresses itself through obedience to the divine covenants.

The Mosaic law can be identified under three distinct categories:

- The moral law (encapsulated in the Decalogue);
- The civil law (concerning social justice); and
- The ceremonial law (relating to Israel's religious responsibilities).

To translate the Decalogue as "the Ten Commandments" (with accompanying definite article) is potentially misleading. They are perhaps more accurately described as "ten utterances" that form the core of the Mosaic code. As Paul Johnson reminds us: ". . . the Decalogue is merely the heart of an elaborate system of divine laws set out in the books of Exodus, Deuteronomy, and Numbers. In late antiquity, Judaic scholars organized the laws into 613 commandments, consisting of 248 mandatory commandments and 365 prohibitions."[29]

The Ten Commandments may be divided into two groups:

(1) The first four refer to how man should relate to the sovereign God.
- Do not serve any other God (Exod 20:3);
- Do not regard any creature above its Creator (vv. 4–6);
- Do not dishonor the name of God (v. 7); and
- Do not deny him his due (vv. 811).

---

29. Johnson, *History of the Jews*, 35.

(2) The remaining six deal with how man is to relate to those created in God's image.
- Acknowledge all God-given authority (v.12);
- Honor all human life (v.13);
- Revere the marriage covenant (v.14);
- Show respect for the possessions of others (v.15);
- Do not bring the name of your fellow man into wrongful disrepute (v.16); and
- Be in control of ungodly desires (v.17).

The broader aspects of the covenant responsibilities are expounded over several chapters in Exodus (20:22–23:33). Here we see how Israel was expected to behave in such crucial matters as slavery (having themselves been delivered from bondage), violent conduct (having themselves been until recently violently oppressed), wise stewardship of property as divinely appointed tenants, marital fidelity as reflective of the divine covenantal relationship, bearing accurate testimony without partiality, and with reference to worship and work, celebration and creativity.

On hearing the finer details of the Lord's contractual agreement with them, the people of Israel immediately declared their commitment to its terms. Offerings were sacrificed as a token of their decision, vows were freely expressed, and Moses set out to receive further instruction regarding the building of the tabernacle. Amazingly, however, within weeks of entering into the covenant, in Moses' absence the Israelites, *en masse*, broke its primary conditions. Moses refused God's offer to wipe out Israel and make him, like Noah, the new leader of a great nation. Then, upon Moses' return, the covenant was renewed in accordance with the Lord's covenant faithfulness.

The principle identified by Palmer Robertson, that " covenant is a bond in blood,"[30] is surely nowhere better attested in the Old Testament than in connection with the Sinaitic covenant: "Then [Moses] took the Book of the Covenant and read it to the people. They responded, "We will do everything the Lord has said; we will obey." Moses then took the blood, sprinkled it on the people and said, "This is the blood of the covenant that the Lord has made with you in accordance with all these words" (Exod 24:7–8).

---

30. Robertson, *Christ of the Covenants*, 14.

A Timely Reminder

Although the title of the concluding part of the Pentateuch suggests the giving of the law for a second time, it is essentially the recording of a farewell address by Moses to Israel on the eve of the people's entry into Canaan, an address in which he reminds them of their covenant obligations. Of the book of Deuteronomy, Charles Slemming writes: "It is not just a mere recapitulation of the law, nor a verbatim report . . . It is a repetition to a new generation with no amendments so far as the moral law was concerned, but with certain adjustments to the civil law and ceremonial law by [virtue of] the changing conditions as these people moved from a nomad life in the desert to a more settled and established life in the land."[31]

The book of Deuteronomy essentially comprises three distinct sermons or addresses given by Moses:

(1) A description of the historical background to the covenant with Israel (chapters 1–4);

(2) A reminder of the people Israel's covenant responsibilities toward God and each other, along with the associated privileges and penalties for obedience and non-compliance respectively (chapters 5–28); and

(3) An appeal to the new generation to surpass the covenant (dis)loyalty of their predecessors (chapter 29).

By the time we arrive at the concluding chapters, there really is little more that Moses can do other than recite the words of a prophetic song (chapter 32), bless the tribes of Israel (chapter 33), and die peacefully (chapter 34). His departure from this world was not a commonplace death, for Moses was no ordinary man. The glory surrounding his death, however, not to mention the mystery regarding his burial, should not hide the fact that he died with certain regrets. This is particularly brought into focus given the poignancy of his surroundings when life escaped him—he was on the very threshold of the land he could not enter. God showed him the land he had promised, not as a taunt, but rather to treat Moses to something he could hardly have hoped for, given his past—a glimpse of the future in his very last present moment.

---

31. Slemming, *Bible Digest*, 84.

The Grace of God's Law

The connection between the Abrahamic and the Mosaic covenants should not be overlooked. It is not without significance that Yahweh introduced himself to Moses as "the God of Abraham" (Exod 3:6), which name Moses would probably have understood in covenantal terms. Indeed, Edward Young goes so far as to imply that the covenant made at Sinai was, in fact, but the "administration" of a covenant already in existence.[32] It is of equal import that whenever Israel sinned and subsequently repented, God promised to remember his covenant—not with Moses—but with Abraham. Any apparent distinction between the two, on the grounds that one is a covenant of grace and the other of the law, can be maintained only by viewing law and grace as mutually exclusive features. Even under the terms of the new covenant, it is clear that legal requirements are not automatically suspended: It is the relationship between law and grace that we must grasp. We will consider this matter in more detail in a subsequent chapter. Suffice it to say for the moment that I concur with these words of Leon Morris:

> The [Mosaic] covenant is of the free grace of God, but nevertheless, having chosen the people, God imposed upon them ethical demands, and these can be spoken of as the people's part in the covenant without derogating from the freeness of God's grace.[33]

In other words, although law and grace might be considered opposing principles, they are not thus wholly incompatible. The law is essentially the statement of the holy requirements of a holy God for his holy people. As such, it necessarily emanates from God's holiness. But to consider God's law as somehow a feature to be seen in contradistinction to his grace is to misunderstand the inherent consistency of the nature of God. His grace is no more absent from the Sinaitic covenant than it is from any other divine covenant agreement. The choice of Israel for redemption testifies to divine grace; the revelation of Yahweh as the self-guarantor of his covenant promises is a gracious unveiling; and the provision of the sacrificial system as the shadow of the full extent of God's grace to come was itself not without grace.

The whole of the Old Testament testifies to God's grace. The Sinaitic covenant of Moses is no exception. Indeed, the very acts of choosing Israel to be his covenant people, giving them a land to enjoy, ordering

---

32. Young, *Study of Old Testament Theology*, 64.
33. Morris, *Apostolic Preaching of the Cross*, 81.

their lives in accordance with divinely instituted principles, even chastising them when they breached their covenantal responsibilities, all found their origin in God's gracious disposition. Simply put, God was under absolutely no obligation to perform any of these deeds. Equally, we may say that God's law is a law of grace for no other reason than that it emanates from a God who is essentially gracious.

Summary

A significant trend may be observed in these first four Old Testament divine covenant agreements. God led each of the covenant parties out of one experience into something significantly better:

- Adam was created outside of the garden and then presented with his new inheritance (Gen 2:15);
- Noah was saved from the perils of his prediluvian experience in order to become the head of a new population (Gen 9:1);
- Abraham was called out of Ur of the Chaldees and glimpsed, albeit briefly, the land of his promise (Gen 11:31–12:7); and
- Israel, under Moses, was brought out of Egyptian bondage in order to possess the land (Exod 19:4–6).

It is important to reiterate, however, that God's purpose in electing Israel was that the people might be a channel of blessing to all of humanity (cf. Exod 19:5; Rom 2:11).

THE PHINEHATIC COVENANT—A COVENANT OF THE PRIESTHOOD

I have been amazed at the distinct lack of due recognition given to the covenant undertaken by God with Phinehas. Indeed, of the great names associated within Reformed theology, only Archibald Hodge seems to make any mention of it and only then by way of summary as "[t]he covenant with Aaron of an everlasting priesthood."[34] Notwithstanding Palmer Robertson's view that the covenant established by God with Phinehas is not of the same significance as the others discussed here,[35] I include it because it specifically foreshadows Christ's priestly fulfillment in the same way that the Davidic covenant points toward his kingly role. Surely that alone means it merits attention.

34. Hodge, *Outlines of Theology*, 368.
35. Robertson, *Christ of the Covenants*, 27.

Priestly Zeal in the Face of National Apostasy

Eryl Davies expertly draws our attention to the subtle dissimilarity between the Levitical temple responsibilities, which were of a general nature, and the Aaronic priesthood, the duties of which were more specific:

> Within the priestly hierarchy . . . the Levites were to occupy a subordinate position to the "sons of Aaron," and this basic distinction between the priests and Levites is a theme which recurs several times in Numbers. The primacy of the priesthood is evident, first of all, from the position which the priests occupied in camp, for the most favoured location, on the eastern side facing the entrance of the tent of meeting, was reserved for Moses and the "sons of Aaron" (3:38). The inferior status of the Levites is also apparent from the service which they rendered in connection with the tabernacle. Their duties included the burdensome task of dismantling the structure of the tabernacle whenever the tribes were about to move camp, and reassembling it whenever they arrived at a new site (1:51ff). In performing this work, however, they were forbidden to touch (4:15), or even to look upon (4:20), any of the sacred objects of the tabernacle, lest they die; consequently, the task of dismantling and covering these had to be entrusted to the priests (4:5ff). The Levites were also responsible for transporting the tabernacle furniture during the march through the wilderness (1:50), but even this duty was to be performed under priestly supervision (4:16, 28, 33). The priests, on the other hand, were in sole charge of all the rituals in connection with the sanctuary and the altar (18:5); the Levites were permitted to assist them, but only in such a way that they did not come into contact with the sacred objects (18:3). It is clear, therefore, that with regard to the tabernacle, the Levites functioned merely as auxiliary personnel; their task was to serve the priests, and all the duties which they performed were under priestly control.[36]

In stark contrast to the moral and religious laxity of his uncles (see Lev 10:1–3), Phinehas demonstrated his zeal for the honor of his God (Num 25:1–13). The root of the problem was Baal worship, coupled with Israel's marital relationships with Moabite women; in regard to each, Phinehas showed himself to be spiritually attuned and morally virtuous. Although commentators are correct to avoid any speculative assertions that the level of Phinehas' anger was intensified by the illicit sexual act

---

36. Davies, *Numbers*, lxi.

between the Israelite and his Midianite woman, the fact that he was able to impale them both with one spear blow does suggest that they were killed *in flagrante delicto* (see vv. 7–9). Moreover, although it must be acknowledged that Phinehas' intervention was strictly in defiance of the priestly code in relation to ritual cleanliness, which prohibited an Aaronite from such a bloody deed, on this occasion of genuine and godly zeal, his action obviously met with divine approval.

It must be observed that the divine blessing that followed was not for Phinehas' obedience to a specific command, for Scripture gives no record of any such decree having been issued. He was simply rewarded for having a legitimate understanding of Israel's covenantal responsibilities and for taking appropriate action when confronted with their being so blatantly and unashamedly violated. It is somewhat ironic that the context of God establishing a specific covenant with Phinehas was the Israelites' unfaithfulness to the more general Mosaic covenant. Not only were Phinehas' actions mediatorial, it might even be said that he provided an atonement of sorts for the people.

Martin Noth may well be right to conclude that "[t]his chapter contains elements of tradition, of varied content and varied age, in a juxtaposition which is difficult to disentangle, and in a presentation which is remarkably inconsequential and fragmentary." However, he is forced to admit that "[t]he point of departure is formed by the narrative of the Israelite apostasy to the cult of their Moabite neighbors and the punishment of that apostasy."[37] Whatever linguistic difficulties or hermeneutical discrepancies there may seem to be between verses 1 through 5 and what follows, they are nowhere as overwhelming as those that would be created by verses 6 and onward, if they had stood alone. It has even been suggested that the "weeping" of verse 6 is a cultic lament in response to what preceded it, though the evidence is far from convincing.

The essence of God's undertaking with Phinehas was not—as has erroneously been posited—the conferring of priestly office, but a commitment to maintaining that office for his descendants, in perpetuity. It must also be noted that Phinehas and his descendants were not to be the only beneficiaries of this *berith kehunnat olam*, i.e., "covenant of an everlasting priesthood." If all who followed in that line were to take their mediatorial obligations as seriously as had Phinehas, then all Israel, too, would be blessed by its fruit.

37. Noth, *Numbers*, 195.

Characterized by "life and peace" (Mal 2:5), the intention of God's heart for the Aaronic succession under the priestly covenant was to build upon the level of righteous integrity that Phinehas had displayed at its foundation—that his successors should be jealous, with the Lord's jealousy, in reverence for their covenantal responsibilities. This reverence would be expressed in their instructing Israel in the fear of the Lord, so that the corporate priesthood of the whole nation might pass on this wisdom to the surrounding peoples. Sadly, far from being an example to the ungodly, the Israelites—the house of Aaron included—soon showed themselves to be more vulnerable to the influence of others' idolatry, partiality, and corruption.

Parallels of Rebellion

Although the centre of our attention in this incident is Phinehas—and rightly so in the context of covenant—Mary Douglas[38] draws an interesting parallel between the episode of Miriam's challenge of Moses' authority and that of Cozbi's cultic defiance:

Miriam	Cozbi
Moses' and Aaron's sister (Num 26:59)	Daughter of Zur, head of a chief town in Midian (Num 25:15)
Wanted a share in Moses' prophetic role (12:2)	Seduced a man of Israel near the tent of meeting (25:6)
Miriam punished with leprosy (12:10)	Cozbi punished with death (25:8)
Miriam's living shame (12:10–16)	Cozbi shamed in death (25:16–18)
The Lord angry, as if her father had spat in her face (12:14a)	The Lord's anger almost consumes the people (25:8)
Miriam's punishment remitted to seven days outside the camp (12:14b–16)	Phinehas' deed stayed the plague (25:11)
Moses commended; spiritual leadership confirmed (12:6–9)	Phinehas commended; confirmed in priesthood (25:13).

---

38. Douglas, *In the Wilderness*, 200.

Their respective names are also not without significance, for Miriam means "rebellion" and Cozbi means "deceitful." The biblical narratives about them suggest a certain overlapping. Miriam's best known act of rebellion against Moses (albeit one done in conjunction with her brother, Aaron) deceitfully cloaked her intense jealousy of Moses (Num 12:1–3). Indeed, a stone inscription at Sinai translates as follows:

> Miriam, prophetess of lying lips and deceitful tongue.
> She causes the tribes to conspire against the pillar and prince of the people.
> Convoked for tumult, perverted, full of strife, the people revile the meek and generous man.
> They lead with reproaches the blessed one of God.

Similarly, Cozbi's deceitful seduction of Zimri provoked him to openly rebel against his position as "the leader of a Simeonite family" (Num 25:14). Her name, too, is now indelibly inscribed in Scripture as an example of the cost of compromise on the part of one of God's covenant people. The political implications of a potentially successful union between Zimri and Cozbi cannot be underestimated. The fact that Zimri was of the tribe of Simeon, entrusted with guarding the south-eastern flank of the Israelite camp bordered by Midian, brings the danger in which he placed the tribes' security into stark relief. Left unchallenged, the consequences of his relationship could have been far more hazardous than simply damage to one man's moral standing. Moreover, Zimri's open defiance calls into question his attitude toward the leadership of Israel. It was, in fact, a challenge to Moses' authority and could have endangered Israel's unity.

A Lasting Legacy

The incident described in Numbers 25:1–13 is but the first in a series of episodes recorded in Scripture that identify Phinehas as *Fidei Defensor*. The second such occurrence appears six chapters later in the battle against Midian at Peor (Num 31). This was a particularly bloody war, in which only the young virgins were ultimately spared (vv. 17–18). Among those killed was Balaam, son of Beor (v. 8), whom many commentators regard as the chief protagonist in the Moabite seduction of the Israelite men to worship Baal (25:1–3).

Later still, under Joshua's leadership, it was Phinehas who most vociferously opposed the Transjordanian tribes' erecting of an alternative altar on the other side of the river at Geliloth (possibly Gilgal). Upon being accused of treachery, the leaders of the Reubenites, Gadites, and the half tribe of Manasseh protested that the altar served only as a reminder of the one true sanctuary of sacrifice at Shiloh. Satisfied by their explanation, the representatives of the Cisjordanian tribes returned to Canaan and reported their findings. Unnecessary bloodshed was thereby averted (see Josh 22). Whether intentional or not, the altar erected by the Transjordanian tribes also served as a witness to their rightful claim to Israelite heritage (v. 34).

As guardian of Israel's covenant responsibilities, Phinehas again stood before God's covenant ark when the rest of Israel sought to take revenge against the tribe of Benjamin for atrocities committed against a Levite's concubine (Judg 19–20). Once more, the emphasis is upon Phinehas' defense of Israel's covenant terms against those who sought to violate them. The phrase "the zeal of Phinehas" (and variants) thereafter became almost proverbial in Jewish tradition (cf. Ps 106:30; 1 Macc 2:24; 4 Macc 18:12).

Although some of Phinehas' actions at first appear shocking and spontaneous, especially given his priestly background, he was not the only priest to express militaristic fervor (cf. Exod 32:25–29). Moreover, prior to the establishment of the monarchy, priests were representatives of God to the people, and representatives of the people before God. Such was the esteem in which Phinehas was held that Jewish folklore honors him only slightly less highly than Moses and Aaron: "Phinehas son of Eleazar ranks third in renown for being zealous in his reverence for the Lord, and for standing firm with noble courage, when the people were in revolt; by so doing, he made atonement for Israel (Sir 45:23–24).

Summary

As a more clearly and emphatically defined extension of God's covenant with Israel, the specific treaty with Aaron's grandson is significant in its own right. At a time of national apostasy, which resulted in God's judgment by way of plague, Phinehas showed himself to be zealous for the honor of the Lord's commitment toward his people. With the killing of an Israelite leader who had behaved in flagrant disregard of his covenant obligations, the curse of the Lord was halted. Moreover, the promise of a "lasting priesthood," established in peace, was made explicitly with Phinehas. According to G.P. Hugenberger:

> From the biblical record, supplemented with the extrabiblical evidence, it appears that Phinehas' progeny did enjoy a lasting priestly ministry and that, in particular, they also provided the succession of high priests from his own day down to the time of Eli [which] resumed with Zadok in the days of David . . . and it continued down through Ezra at least until 171 BC.[39]

Disclaimer

The author wishes to make it clear that any reference to the Phinehatic priesthood contained in this work—or any other by the same author, for that matter—should not be understood to mean, signify, or stand in favorable relation to what is known today as the Phineas [*sic!*] "hoods" or "priests," which appears to be a loose organization of self-appointed modern day vigilantes who claim biblical authority for racist, anti-Semitic, and/or anti-homosexual homicide. The everlasting nature of the covenant with Phinehas—as with all Old Testament covenants of divine origin—is perpetuated today only in and through Christ Jesus. There can be no biblical grounds to suggest that he would endorse acts that are so obviously and heinously un-Christlike.

THE DAVIDIC COVENANT—A COVENANT OF THE KINGDOM

As alarming as it was to discover few scholars who considered the covenant with Phinehas to be of sufficient import that they would include it in their writings, I was recently equally amazed to read a book entitled *The Story of King David*, published by the *Journal for the Study of the Old Testament*, from which mention of this covenant is entirely absent.

F.C. Fensham observes that, in part, the Davidic covenant became necessary because the temporal elements of the earlier covenants' promises had been largely fulfilled.[40] While this is undoubtedly true, the real significance surely lies in a different phase of Israel's history, a phase which was to foreshadow an aspect of the coming new covenant that had not been previously revealed (i.e., the kingdom concept). The establish-

---

39. G.P. Hugenberger, "Phinehas," *ISBE*, 852.
40. F.C. Fensham, "Covenant, Alliance," *New Bible Dictionary*, 242.

ment of this new covenant also introduced a new role into the kingdom idea. Hitherto, the only mediator between the people and their God had been the priest. Indeed, King Saul was severely reprimanded by Samuel for assuming priestly authority in offering sacrifices (see 1 Sam 13:1–13), an act that was to ultimately cost him not only the kingship, but also his dynastic place in the kingdom (v. 14). Hereafter, however, God was pleased to allow his regal representatives to mediate on his behalf:

People → Priest (Phinehas) → God
God → King (David) → People

Thus, the covenants undertaken with Phinehas (priest) and David (king) subsume both aspects of covenantal mediation. The significance of the two elements represented by these particular covenants will become even more apparent in the chapter that follows.

Covenant Development

At a time of increasing spiritual decline, the people Israel sought a military figure to lead them, as had Israel's enemies, and this despite repeated warnings from prominent jurists, who prevailed upon Israel to respect its covenant obligations. Saul was appointed king and, in no time at all, proved himself to be unworthy of the mantle, and so God instructed Samuel to anoint David as Saul's successor.

All we really know about David is gleaned from the pages of Scripture. David probably lived from about 1040 to 970 BC, i.e., some three thousand years ago. Yet his actions would not have seemed out of place in our time. If this proves anything at all, it is surely that nothing changes as slowly as human nature. Many words could be used to describe David, some of them incongruous with others: singer/songwriter, son, father, shepherd boy, king, victor, victim, impulsive, patient, reckless, responsible, manipulative, adulterer, loyal, and many more besides. The prophet Samuel's testimony as to God's appraisal of David (after God rejected Saul as king) is surely also worthy of our attention: "The Lord has sought out a man after his own heart and appointed him leader of his people" (1 Sam 13:14; cf. Acts 13:22).

Contrast that description with Scripture's evaluation of Saul: "Saul was the most handsome man in Israel—head and shoulders taller than anyone else in the land" (1 Sam 9:2 (New Living Translation)). Saul was naturally good looking, naturally intelligent, and naturally strong. Spiritually, however, he proved to be unappealing, indecisive, and weak. God chose David not just for his potential in relation to the temporal world, but also as the one through whom God's eternal purpose might eventually be realized. Fearing a Philistine attack, Saul disregarded Samuel's instructions and impatiently offered unauthorized sacrifices—that act cost him the kingship. Some time later, David enquired of the Lord whether he should engage in battle and, following instructions, he obediently defeated the same Philistine hordes, restoring the ark of God to Jerusalem in the process. This act elicited a divine promise of an enduring kingdom (2 Sam 7:1–17). The internal evidence of Scripture clearly identifies the prophetic promise uttered by Nathan to David as covenantal:

> You said, "I have made a covenant with my chosen one, I have sworn to David my servant, 'I will establish your line forever and make your throne firm through all generations.'" (Ps 89:3–4)

As John Murray has succinctly put it: "No example of covenant in the Old Testament more clearly supports the thesis that covenant is a sovereign promise, solemnized by the sanctity of an oath, immutable in its security and divinely confirmed as respects the certainty of its fulfilment."[41] However, the promise to David was not only covenantal; it was also constitutional, insofar as it would thereafter be the basis upon which Israel defined itself and was described by others as a nation.

Just as the covenant promise to Abraham centered on the two-fold promise of seed and land, so too the Davidic covenant can be said to be two-fold: to promise dynasty and locality—David's line and Jerusalem's throne.[42] Indeed, when Solomon's unfaithfulness seemed to threaten the covenant promise, God remembered his own covenant obligations: "for the sake of my servant David and for the sake of Jerusalem" (1 Kgs 11:32). As we have seen, God's covenant promise to David was that he would establish David's dynastic line, ensuring his throne through all generations (Ps 89:3–4).

---

41. Murray, *Covenant of Grace*, 23.
42. See Robertson, *Christ of the Covenants*, 232.

A Radical New Departure

The focus of God's covenant with David was essentially the coming of the kingdom in tangible ways, and the establishment of his dynastic line. Although David had been acknowledged by many as Israel's legitimate king for some time, the kingdom itself awaited the following developments:

- The taking of Jerusalem as the more central (than Ziklag and Hebron) and permanent locality from which to extend his rule (2 Sam 5);
- The recapturing of the ark of the covenant, thus publicly identifying David's rule as a theocratic expression (2 Sam 6); and
- The establishing of a sustained period of relative peace and national security (2 Sam 7:1).

The significance of the timing of this covenant cannot be allowed to escape our attention. Arguably the single-most coincident of Nathan's prophetic words had been the fairly recent capture of Jerusalem from the Jebusites. The ancient city of Urushalim had remained the capital city of Jebus for centuries, even after much of the rest of Canaan had been allocated to the tribes of Israel. It was, in effect, the last bastion of God's promised land. The Benjamites had made several unsuccessful attempts to capture the city, but its lofty location made it seemingly impregnable. The only apparent weakness in its natural defense was a tunnel from the center of the city to an external water supply. Few knew of its existence, but that tunnel proved to be the route of David's surprise attack. The city of Jebus thence became the City of David, the site of his royal palace.

As an expression of God's heavenly kingdom on the earth, the human monarchy was also dependent upon the divine sanctuary being accorded its rightful place. The ark of the covenant contained the two covenantal tablets inscribed at Sinai and was covered by a lid on which were formed two winged cherubim, denoting God's enthronement. There is surely a vital lesson to be learned here, for God is especially present where his word is enduringly expressed.

The joy that attended the return of the ark was not shared by all. Uzzah's death, a consequence of touching the ark as the oxen stumbled (2 Sam 6:6–7) may initially seem too harsh a judgment, until one is reminded that the ark was being carried on a cart in direct contravention of the law, which clearly stipulated that it must be transported on poles carried by the Levites (see Exod 25:14; Deut 10:8). Also, as David celebrated the ark's return, Michal (David's wife and Saul's daughter) expressed her displeasure (vv. 20–23), possibly in part because she resented her own father's failure. The pronouncement that her womb was barren effectively terminated Saul's dynastic line and might even be regarded as a just reward for Saul's earlier attempt to put an end to Israel's spiritual heritage (see 1 Sam 22:11–18).

The promise to David comprised the following elements:

Renown	2 Sam 7:9	A great name
Settlement	v. 10	A place for Israel
Security	vv. 9–11	A sustained period of rest
Intimacy	v. 14	A father/son relationship with descendant kings
Offspring	vv. 12–16	A permanent dynasty

While divine election may prayerfully be deemed a privilege, the biblical emphasis seems always to be on responsibility. This is especially true of the covenants we have considered and is no less so with David. Perhaps significantly, the play on words is not restricted to God's use of "house" as contrasted with David's. David had been chosen for demonstrating his pastoral care over the flock entrusted to him—he had proved himself to be a faithful "shepherd" (Hebrew—*neged*). Now he was being asked to translate that same concern as a "prince" (Hebrew—*nagid*) over God's people. In other words, David was called essentially to serve (Ps 89:3–4)—to be the archetypal Servant King.

To the child of the new covenant in Christ, some episodes in David's life seem, at best, alien, and, at worst, diabolical, not least of which are his illicit relationship with Bathsheba and his manipulation of the circumstances leading to her husband's death. These are not glossed over in Scripture, however; the word of God is essentially and vitally the word of truth, and Scripture records that "David . . . served God's purpose in his own generation" (Acts 13:26). Ask any orthodox Jew, "Who was responsible for establishing the historic kingdom of Israel?" Very few will answer, "Saul," though the name of David might well be on the lips of the vast majority.

Passing on the Baton

It seems clear from David's death-bed charge to his son and successor, Solomon, that he did not consider the covenant made with him to have negated the promises of the Mosaic covenant (see 2 Kgs 2:1–4). It must also be noted that the stability enjoyed by Solomon was not due to his own moral superiority over his father David, but more to the legacy of national strength that he inherited. Indeed, Ellison makes the potentially valid—though at the same time highly speculative—point that "[h]ad Israel been faithful in the conquest of the land, they would not have experienced the dark period of the judges, and David would have ruled over a people too strong to be lightly attacked, as was Solomon's fortunate position."[43]

David's legacy to his son was safety and affluence, but David recognized their source and wanted Solomon to be in no doubt about it, either:

> And you, my son Solomon, acknowledge the God of your father, and serve him with wholehearted devotion and with a willing mind, for the Lord searches every heart and understands every motive behind the thoughts. If you seek him, he will be found by you; but if you forsake him, he will reject you for ever. Consider now, for the Lord has chosen you to build a temple as a sanctuary. Be strong and do the work . . . Be strong and courageous, and do the work. Do not be discouraged, for the Lord God, my God, is with you. (1 Chr 28:9–10, 20)

Tragically, security and prosperity are often also harbingers of complacency. Solomon's fleshly appetites proved too ravenous to find satisfaction within legitimate parameters. Consequently, it was not long before his sexual promiscuity paved the way for spiritual adultery. Covenant relationship was still maintained, as that was dependent upon the faithfulness of one more honorable than Solomon, but the pleasures of covenant fellowship with Israel's covenant God were temporarily suspended.

Kingdom is an indispensible concept in terms of Jehovistic worship, for its substance is the rule of God. David and his successors, as representatives of the kingdom covenant, were meant, as ambassadors of covenant responsibilities, to exemplify God's authority. That they

---

43. H.L. Ellison, "1 Chronicles," *New Bible Commentary*, 380.

largely failed, due in no small measure to Solomon's syncretistic policy of seeking to integrate pure worship with the idolatrous worship of his wives, did not result in God's violation of his own covenant loyalty. That would have been contrary to his nature. Indeed, the primary revelation of God's character, common to all the divine covenants we have considered in Old Testament history, is his unwavering faithfulness in the face of human fickleness, his dedication all the more evident in contrast to mankind's disloyalty. The basis of God's covenant with David regarding the monarchy was the restoration of the ark of the covenant to the sanctuary of God. And giving foremost attention to his relationship with God was the key to David's success as the divine representative among his people.

It is noteworthy that covenant unfaithfulness by one party (in this case, Solomon) does not absolve the other party (here, God) of his covenant obligations. Or, in the words of Palmer Robertson: "God's chastening activity in the rending of Solomon's kingdom does not terminate the covenant commitment made on behalf of David and Jerusalem."[44] God's unique faithfulness to David's line—even in temporal terms—can only properly be appreciated in the context of other dynasties. Over four hundred years elapsed between David's accession to the throne and the fall of Jerusalem. No dynasty of the northern kingdom endured for even a quarter of that length of time. The last of David's direct descendants to rule over an independent kingdom of God's chosen people was in power when Judah fell to the Babylonians in 586 BC. As Peter Craigie points out, however:

> The everlasting nature of the covenant with David was brought out . . . not in the pages of ancient history, but in the expectation of a Messiah who would be born of David's descendants.[45]

Summary

The actual word "covenant" is entirely absent from the records of God's dealings with both Adam and David. Nevertheless, all the elements and features of a covenant are found in them, and the undertaking is unmistakably described as such by David in later years (see Ps 89). Moreover, his son and successor, Solomon, understood his obligations

---

44. Robertson, *Christ of the Covenants*, 237.
45. P. Craigie, "Covenant," *Encyclopedia of the Bible*, 535.

and responsibilities in terms that were clearly covenantal (see 1 Kgs 8:23; 2 Chr 6:14). It is arguably the Davidic covenant—more than any other in the Old Testament—that shaped Jewish messianic expectation. The "kingdom of heaven" was now tangibly expressed as the "kingdom of God" on earth through a regal representative, such that, by the time of the New Testament era, the two phrases were used interchangeably and synonymously. Indeed, the whole purpose of the Davidic covenant may be described as a foreshadowing of the coming of the King of the covenant, who would appear from his house and lineage (see Gen 49:10; Isa 11:1; Jer 33:14–25). It is in this context primarily that we must view the progressive revelation of the covenants. Each, in turn, unveiled a little more of the coming Messiah:

Adam	He would be born of a woman
Noah	He would usher in a new beginning for humanity
Abraham	He would be of the seed of faith and be accessible only by faith
Moses	He alone would fulfill all the requirements of the law
Phinehas	He would exercise a unique priestly ministry
David	He would be born a king of the tribe of Judah.

2

The New Covenant

Ern Baxter once said: "To Adam we relate racially, to Abraham we relate redemptively, and to David we relate regally, Jesus Christ being the fulfillment of all three." I would add to this that we relate restoratively to Noah, forensically to Moses, and mediatorially to Phinehas, Christ Jesus fulfilling the terms and conditions of each of the covenant phases of which these six Old Testament saints are representatives.

The premise of this chapter is not so much that Christ *did* fulfill all the requirements of each successive covenant described in the previous chapter, but that it was *necessary* for him to do so. It might even be argued that the accessibility of the new covenant of mercy is contingent upon the conditions of the covenant of works having been fully met. Similarly, the new covenant of grace could only be made available when the forensic requirements of the covenant of law had been legitimately satisfied.

FULFILLING THE ADAMIC COVENANT

It is beyond the scope of this work to discuss the possible relationship between a divinely exclusive covenant of redemption (i.e., *pactum salutis*) and the new covenant of grace or, indeed, to discuss whether both components are actually but modes or expressions of the one covenant of mercy. Suffice to say, however, that Scripture makes it clear: Within the mysteries of eternity—and allowing for our finite understanding of it—God always intended for a redemptive plan to unfold in a manner that can only truly be described as covenantal (cf. John 6:38–40; Eph 1:4; Jas 2:5). In the words of Irving Jensen:

> Associated with the old covenant were outward ordinances and objects, which were not intended to save, but rather to teach the sinfulness of sin and the lost condition of men and to [prefigure] Christ as Savior.[1]

Relating to God, to Others, and to the Created Order

In the previous chapter's discussion of the salient features of the Adamic covenant, it was observed that Adam was called to obedience in order to honor his relational commitments on three distinct levels:

- Toward his God;
- Toward his wife (and other people); and
- Toward the created order.

It must be noted that Christ's fulfilling of the Adamic covenant's obligations essentially saw him victoriously succeed in all three areas where Adam had so miserably failed. As the purity of Adam's relationship with other humans and the rest of the created order was dependent upon his first establishing and then maintaining an uncompromising relationship with his Creator, so too it is with Christ and the Father. The product of this latter relationship, for those who belong to this new covenant by faith, is identified by the apostle Paul in these words: "If, by the trespass of the one man, death reigned through that one man, how much more will those who receive God's abundant provision of grace and of the gift of righteousness reign in life through the one man, Christ Jesus" (Rom 5:17). Grant Osborne points out the universality of sin when he comments on this passage, writing that "[t]he aorist sense of 'reigned' is global, incorporating the age of Adam into a single sweeping whole."[2]

Scripture is generally silent regarding the mechanics of the transmission of sin through Adam to his race. Strictly speaking, the same might be said of the imputation of Christ's righteousness to believers. One may only presume that it is unnecessary—or impossible—for us to understand anything beyond the facts as they are presented, and to believe them by faith. And those who deny the historicity of Adam are left with no alternative but to deny that the work of Christ reversed the effects of Adam's disobedience.

---

1. Jensen, *Jeremiah and Lamentations*, 89–90.
2. Osborne, *Romans*, 143.

As part of the new creation, believers also find this component of the Adamic mandate—i.e., right relationship with God—vital to all that follows. Our ability to deal with problems, relate to others, and rule our circumstances is governed by our continuing to walk with God as adopted "sons." We do so by being—and remaining—united with Christ (1 Cor 6:17). Significantly, the word used to describe that unity is also used to express our being joined in common purpose with others who are also "in Christ" (cf. Acts 5:13; 9:26). It is the Greek *kollaō*, which also means "to glue or cement together." Its more intense form, *proskollaō*, means "to hold fast" or "to be bound firmly to."[3] Ultimately, the Church, the Bride of Christ, will be presented to him as a thing of beauty who has made herself ready through her present and continuous union with him, and not as some grotesque caricature.

Although it cannot be denied that the welfare of our planet is the responsibility of all, God's covenant people—more than any other corporate body—should be acutely aware of that obligation. God gave Adam a stewardship mandate that has not been rescinded. Because of Adam's sin, however, man's ability to rule righteously as God's vice-regent has been hampered by his greed, abuse, and willful subjection to the sin principle. But if Christ has fulfilled the federal responsibilities associated with the Adamic covenant, then we can expect the blessings annexed to it to be restored as well. Is it too far a stretch, then, to imagine that the new earth will be as the old earth would have become had it not been for the intrusion of sin? Perhaps the image in John's apocalypse provides a clue, when the potential identified in Genesis is seen to be fully developed in Revelation (cf. Gen 1; Rev 21, 22).

The Second Man/Last Adam

The relation in which Christ stands to Adam is fundamentally one of federal headship: each is the primary representative of a covenant. As Louis Berkhof points out: "According to Paul, the essential element in justification consists in this: that the righteousness of Christ is imputed to us, without any personal work on our part to merit it. And he regards this as a perfect parallel to the manner in which the guilt of Adam is imputed to us. This naturally leads to the conclusion that Adam also stood in covenant relationship to his descendants."[4]

---

3. Vine, *Expository Dictionary*, 606.
4. Berkhof, *Systematic Theology*, 214.

Those who deny that Adam is a type of Christ (or, indeed, that Paul presents him as such) often do so on the grounds that the two are beyond comparative resemblance. However, the typological parallel that Paul employs is not comparison, but contrast. In this way, Adam is indeed a type of Christ, for he foreshadows him in the sense that each imparted something of his own nature to those to whom they stand in covenant relationship (see Rom 5:15–17). Adam's sin wrought judgment, condemnation, and death; Christ's obedience brought justification, righteousness, and life. And Christ's efficacy for good prevails over Adam's efficiency for evil.

It must also be noted that to speak of the distinction between the old (Adamic) covenant and the new covenant (in Christ) as that between covenants of works and grace is to do so from an entirely anthropocentric position. As far as Christ's personal involvement in the covenant of grace—both as its head and its surety—was concerned, it was a covenant of works, and conditional in the sense that its success depended upon his meeting certain requirements:

- That he assume human nature, remain sinless and, thus, make atonement for sin (Gal 4:4–5; Heb 2:10–15);
- That he become subject to the law and its demands (Ps 40:8; Phil 2:6–8); and
- That, having attained the forgiveness of sins and the resultant eternal life for fallen humanity, the benefits of his saving actions would be made accessible to those who would acknowledge him as their Savior (John 17:12–22; Heb 7:25).

Death came by Adam's disobedience. Laterally implicit in this statement is the suggestion that his obedience might have been rewarded with life, i.e., had he met the conditions imposed upon him. That they were finally and fully met by Christ as the second man/last Adam (1 Cor 15:45–47) renders Christ the federal head of a new created order—the redeemed. For the believer, therefore, postlapsarian death has been swallowed up by the victory—and promise–of (post-)resurrection life. Christ is both second (that is, there is none between Adam and him) and last (there is none after him).

Adam had the opportunity to bring life—in its fullest sense—to all who were to follow him, but his personal disobedience prevented his receiving the reward that obedience would have permitted. Whatever other details we might consider, the principal examination was one of obedience: Adam failed that test; Jesus passed it, *summa cum laude*. The contrasts between the two can be outlined as follows:

First Adam	**Last Adam**
Was created (Gen 1:27)	Is the Creator (Col 1:15–17)
A man who wanted to become like God (Gen 3:4–6)	God who chose to become man for the sake of humanity (Gal 4:4–5)
Believed the father of lies (John 8:44)	Is the truth (John 14:6)
Disobeyed God (Gen 3:17)	Obeyed his Father's will, even unto death (John 6:38)
Was banished from God's presence (Gen 3:22–24)	Was welcomed into God's presence (Mark 16:19)
Wrought death for all who would live (Rom 5:12)	Brought life to all by his death (Rom 6:4–10)

What this Means for Believers

As we have seen, the sin principle that pervades the entire human race is grounded in the corporate solidarity of federal headship (Rom 5:12). The same principle of imputation applies to salvation, but only in terms of attainability. In other words, one can only speak of the universality of atonement in terms of its availability to all who will receive (Greek—*lambanō*; literally, to "take possession of") its benefits, although some well-respected Christian teachers do not accept the limited application of Christ's atonement. Among those who support the so-called doctrine of ultimate reconciliation (or *apokatastasis*) are Thomas Talbott, Carlton Pearson, and Cormac Murphy O'Connor. Each offers biblical texts as evidence for his claims, though often disregarding either the immediate context of these texts or else basic principles of hermeneutics.

It must also be observed that, although the new covenant fulfills the old and differs from it in its mode of administration, the divine requirements remain constant: God requires a covenant-keeping people (Matt 5:17–20). This will be dealt with in more detail in the next chapter. Suffice it to emphasize here, however, that meeting such requirements is now made possible by the inner working of the Holy Spirit as opposed to an external command. Palmer Robertson identifies the new covenant in Christ as "the covenant of consummation," primarily on the basis that "[t]he heart of this consummative realization consists of a single person. As fulfiller of all the messianic promises, he achieves in himself the essence of the covenant principle: 'I shall be your God and you shall be my people.' He therefore may be seen as the Christ who consummates the covenant."[5] All of the primary features of the Adamic covenant were fulfilled in Christ for our benefit, as outlined below:

Feature of Adamic Covenant	Fulfillment of Feature in Christ
Sabbath principle	True rest is to be found only in Christ
Marriage institution	Christ and the church are in perfect union
Godly stewardship	Honoring God's creational handiwork
Obedience	Perfect obedience met by Christ on man's behalf
Labor	Godly endeavor

We must clearly understand, however, that the work of Christ did not merely wipe out the effects of Adam's sin in the sense that redeemed humanity now finds itself back in the position of pre-fallen Adam, a consequence significant enough on its own to arouse wonder. If Christ's work had only done this, then the new covenant in Christ would have the same potential for despoilment as had the Adamic covenant. The assurance of the gospel is that it is built on an immeasurably more sure foundation, one that is, in fact, indestructible. The thread of Paul's comparison between the two covenants suggests elements of constancy when he writes "just as . . . so also" (Rom 5:12, 18, 19, 21), but he also declares that the new covenant extends beyond the old when he writes "if . . . how much more" (vv. 15, 17). If there were no difference or extension, the new covenant would really be little more than a fresh start under the terms and conditions of the old, a new page in the covenant of works. In a tone reminiscent of that of the writer to the Hebrews, Wayne Grudem posits:

> In this new covenant, there are far greater blessings, for Jesus the Messiah has come; he has lived, died and risen amongst us, atoning once for all for our sins; he has revealed God most fully to us; he has poured out the Holy Spirit on all his people in new

---

5. Robertson, *Christ of the Covenants*, 272–273.

covenant power; he has written his laws on our hearts. This new covenant is the "eternal covenant" in Christ, through which we shall forever have fellowship with God, and he shall be our God, and we shall be his people.[6]

Summary

That we recognize a need does not necessarily mean that we will take advantage of the tools placed at our disposal to meet that need. The entire human race falls into one of two categories. Although corporate solidarity is maintained within these parameters, the determinant factor of each one's ultimate destiny is individual choice, even if the choice is made out of ignorance. We are all either "in Adam" or "in Christ." Because we are all born in sin and, therefore, "in Adam," we must choose to become "in Christ" (cue the Calvinist uproar). Thus, every person's eternal destiny—leaving aside for the moment the mysteries associated with divine election—is governed by the decision each person makes about God's Christ. This is quite literally—and in its ultimate sense—a matter of life or death, as I trust the following diagram amply demonstrates:

Adam	Christ
Divine command	Divine command
Test	Test
Disobedience	Obedience
Selfishness	Sacrifice
Condemnation	Justification
All sinned	All made alive
Death	Eternal life

Humanity

FULFILLING THE NOAHIC COVENANT

In the previous chapter, I identified the Noahic covenant as essentially one of favor. Some speak of it as a covenant of grace. Given, however, its especially temporal effects—i.e., that Noah and others escaped the flood—it would perhaps be more appropriate to label it as a covenant of common grace. It was also duly noted that this covenant

---

6. Grudem, *Systematic Theology*, 522.

was fundamentally one of preservation through judgment, with those left alive being the beneficiaries of God's grace. It was further observed that the two primary features of the Noahic covenant were that it was to be a completely new beginning for those preserved, and that God would issue a token of his blessing—the rainbow—a deposit, if you will, guaranteeing what was to come. The vehicle of their conservation, of course, was the ark, especially built according to God's own design. Thus, preservation was a necessary prelude to redemption.

There's Nothing Common about Grace

It is the universal nature of the Noahic covenant (i.e., a covenant not only with man, but also with the whole of the created order) that lends a certain credibility to the argument for unlimited atonement in the new covenant. The promise of perpetuity might seem to advance the argument further (see Gen 9:12). The interpretation of Scripture is, however, necessarily subject to clearly established principles of hermeneutics, one of which is that the obscure must be governed by the obvious, not vice versa. The weight of less ambiguous evidence than is offered in this single passage suggests that those who hope in a universal salvation for mankind do so in vain. As Peter Golding reminds us: "[T]he Noahic covenant was concerned primarily with the natural rather than the spiritual."[7] Thus, it perhaps finds more affinity with the prelapsarian Adamic covenant than with any other.

So far as the new covenant in Christ specifically fulfills the conditions of the Noahic covenant, we can expect it to be no different from its predecessor covenant. As the Noahic covenant prepared its beneficiaries (by preservation) for the redemptive and regal elements of later Old Testament covenant agreements, so too Christ's fulfillment of the Noahic is preparatory to his fulfilling those covenants that followed it. It is for this reason that the Noahic covenant is also referred to as the covenant of common grace, Louis Berkhof identifying it as "a necessary appendage" to the covenant of grace. He clarifies this point further thus: "The revelation of the covenant of grace in Gen 3:16–19 already pointed to earthly and temporal blessings. These were absolutely necessary for the realization of the covenant of grace. In the covenant with Noah, the

---

7. Golding, *Covenant Theology*, 151.

general character of these blessings is clearly brought out, and their continuance is confirmed."[8]

It is to this non-salvific context that Christ's fulfillment of the Noahic covenant must be applied, unbelievers most assuredly—though unwittingly—benefitting from certain of its features, though of an exclusively temporal nature. Jesus himself hinted at this when conveying the principles of God's kingdom rule in parabolic form: "Though [the mustard seed] is the smallest of all your seeds, yet when it grows, it is the largest of garden plants and becomes a tree, so that the birds of the air come and perch in its branches" (Matt 13:32).

Wayne Grudem defines common grace this way:

> Common grace is the grace of God by which he gives people innumerable blessings that are not part of salvation. The word *common* here means something that is common to all people and is not restricted to believers or to the elect only . . . [It] is different from saving grace in its *results* (it does not bring about salvation), in its *recipients* (it is given to believers and unbelievers alike), and in its *source* (it does not directly flow from Christ's atoning work, since Christ's death did not earn any measure of forgiveness for unbelievers, and therefore did not merit the blessings of common grace for them either).[9]

While I find myself in agreement with many of Grudem's conclusions, including this one, I also feel that further clarification is required here. Although Christ's specifically atoning work does not directly affect unbelievers positively, indirectly surely they benefit from the subsequent good influence of believers upon society. They also attract some advantage from this very aspect of Christ's fulfillment of the Noahic covenant within the period of the new covenant's expression (that is, the church age). The promise of God never again to destroy the earth by flood is one such example. Not only is common grace to be distinguished from saving grace, however. Neither can the deeds of unbelievers resulting from their state of common grace summon eternal rewards, simply because they are not the fruit of faith (Rom 14:23). Ultimately, "good" works that are not grounded in genuine God-consciousness are incapable of meeting with divine approval (see Matt 23:37).

---

8. Berkhof, *Systematic Theology*, 295.
9. Grudem, *Systematic Theology*, 657–658.

Berkhof has rightly identified the new covenant as one of grace by identifying three of its gracious characteristics, gifts from the triune God:

(1) God the Father allows a surety to meet our covenant obligations;

(2) He himself provides that surety in the person of his Son, Jesus Christ, the one true Mediator; and

(3) The operation of the Holy Spirit within empowers us to live up to our covenant responsibilities.

Berkhof concludes that "the covenant originates in the grace of God, is executed in virtue of the grace of God, and is realized in the lives of sinners by the grace of God. It is grace from the beginning to the end for the sinner."[10]

Both the Noahic covenant and the new covenant were initiated and accomplished by God. While all flesh has benefited from the common grace of God as promised in the Noahic covenant, only those who are "in Christ" benefit from the blessings of the new covenant. Similarly, the beneficiaries under both covenants share the distinction of not needing to fear the consequences of divine wrath. Whereas the promise associated with the Noahic covenant guaranteed that God would never again destroy all life by a flood, the assurance of the new covenant is that its beneficiaries will not face the outpouring of divine wrath through fire (2 Pet 3:10).

The gospel of Christ, too, stands in the grace of Christ. In the words of David Matthew: "His sovereign grace, which had reached out to lost humanity in the old covenant, found even more lavish expression in the new one. By an act of grace in the person of his Son, God made it possible for men to be freed from the downward pull of a sinful nature."[11] It is by this covenant of grace, therefore, that we have access to "... everything we need for life and godliness through our knowledge of him who called us by his own glory and goodness. Through these he has given us his very great and precious promises, so that through them [we] may participate in the divine nature and escape the corruption in the world caused by its evil desires" (2 Pet 1:3–4). Indeed, it might reasonably be argued that Jesus lived according to the covenant of works on our account and died in accordance with the penalty of the law so that we may live in conformity to the gospel of the covenant of grace.

10. Berkhof, *Systematic Theology*, 278.
11. Matthew, *Covenant Meal*, 34.

Preserved in the Midst of Judgment

Just as Christ is the mediator of the new covenant, as well as its federal head, so too was Noah the mediator of the covenant over which he assumed responsibility. Moreover, the Noahic covenant was not ratified merely by a promissory oath, but by typological salvation in the midst of real judgment. So, too, the new covenant. It must also be noted that Christ's fulfillment of the Noahic covenant not only assures the godly of their eternal destiny, as those in the ark during the deluge were assured of theirs; the unjust are assigned a fate similar to that of those who mocked Noah.[12] Palmer Robertson's erudite comment deserves repetition here:

> [T]he covenant with Noah provides the historical framework in which the Immanuel principle may receive its full realization. God has come in judgment; but he also has provided a context of preservation in which the grace of redemption may operate. From the covenant with Noah it becomes quite obvious that God being "with us" involves not only an outpouring of his grace on his people; it involves also an outpouring of his wrath on the seed of Satan.[13]

Notably, having left the ark, Noah's first act was to voluntarily offer a sacrifice to his Savior, God, who responded by affirming the removal of the curse (Gen 8:20–21). Christ's whole life was one of sacrifice to his Father, thus effecting the removal of the law's curse (see Gal 3:13). Perhaps clearer still is Jesus' own idiomatic comparison of the coming Day of Judgment with the time of Noah: "Just as it was in the days of Noah, so also will it be in the days of the Son of Man. People were eating, drinking, marrying and being given in marriage up to the day Noah entered the ark. Then the flood came and destroyed them all" (Luke 17:26–27). Of course, "them all" refers only to those who had not availed themselves of the opportunity to take refuge in the ark of God's provision. Thus, preservation in the midst of judgment is a feature common to both type and antitype, the Noahic covenant and its fulfillment in the new covenant in Christ.

---

12. See Lloyd-Jones, *2 Peter*, 164–165.
13. Robertson, *Christ of the Covenants*, 125.

A New Beginning

When referring to the example set by Noah, the apostle Peter twice highlights the fact that only eight souls were found to be righteous at that time (1 Pet 3:20; 2 Pet 2:5). We have seen that biblical numerology treats the number eight as suggestive of a new beginning. It is perhaps not without significance, therefore, that the New Testament Greek word translated "regeneration" is *palingenesia*, which literally means "new beginning" or "new birth."[14] Furthermore, the New Testament associates this rebirth with having been washed clean, as in baptism (Eph 5:26; Titus 3:5), though the cleansing spoken of via the Scriptures is admittedly more forcibly implied. In this respect, Helmut Burkhardt is correct to identify the following emphases in the biblical presentation of regeneration:

- It is not the result of human endeavor, but a creative act of God's Spirit;
- It is a once-for-all event, in which God substantially intervenes in a person's life; and
- It involves being added to the family of God: the regenerated person becomes a child of God and is also incorporated into the fellowship of the children of God.[15]

I would also add, on the basis of Jesus' use of the imperative to the enquiring Nicodemus (John 3:3–7), that new birth is not an optional extra. It is absolutely vital to the induction process of the Christian walk. (It is principally for this reason that I often refuse to identify myself as a "born-again" Christian. It is not that I fail to regard myself in such terms; rather, I cannot conceive of any kind of Christian, based on my understanding of the biblical evidence, who is *not* born again. I, therefore, find it redundant.)

In his first epistle, Peter clearly associates such regeneration with the act of baptism, although it would not for that reason alone be legitimate to conclude that baptism is thus the *means* of such new birth; baptism is simply the vehicle through which the new birth is expressed. However, we must be clear in our understanding that, although baptism is symbolic of our identification with Christ's death, burial, and

---

14. See Vine, *Expository Dictionary*, 939.
15. Burkhardt, "Regeneration," *New Dictionary of Theology*, 574.

resurrection, it is not customary to bury someone (in this case, the "old nature") in order to kill the person, but because death has presumably already taken place.

Summary

T.C. Mitchell identifies three salient features of the Noahic covenant:

- Its universality;
- Its unconditional character; and
- Its everlasting nature (within the confines of the time/space continuum).[16]

It must be noted, however, that the new covenant differs from the Noahic in the following respects:

- It is not universally applicable, though it is universally attainable;
- It is conditional upon the repentance of each individual, though no further works on our part can add to, or, indeed, detract from, its effects; and
- It is everlasting in an eternal sense, though its provision(s) will not always be accessible.

In considering Christ's fulfillment of the Noahic covenant, it has been right and proper to focus exclusively on the features of the latter that were enhanced or developed to their fullest potential by the former. One aspect of Noah's postdiluvian existence was forfeit, however, but it has been restored in Christ, i.e., the garden of Eden, which existed in Adam's world. After the fall, Adam and Eve were banished from the garden (in the Septuagint, the word is *paradeisos*, meaning "enclosed park"), but the imagery of it being guarded from access suggests that it remained *in loco*. After the flood, there is no mention of it, from which we may reasonably infer that this sanctuary of God was thence lost to mankind. In Christ, however, the paradise of God has been wonderfully regained.

---

16. T.C. Mitchell, "Noah," *New Bible Dictionary*, 838.

FULFILLING THE ABRAHAMIC COVENANT

As we saw in the previous chapter, God's promise to Abraham was essentially twofold: the seed (Gen 12:2; 15:18) and the land (12:7; 15:7). In purely natural terms, both of these commitments were fulfilled long ago (see 1 Kgs 4:20–21; 1 Chr 27:23; Neh 9:23). Paul, however, argues that this was only a shadow of Gentile conversion—they who are justified by faith, as was Abraham (Gal 3:7–8)—with the whole earth becoming their inheritance (Rom 4:13). Such promises were redefined when the Father said to his Son, "Ask of me and I will make the nations your inheritance, the ends of the earth your possession" (Ps 2:8).

A Mistake Rectified

Abraham's folly was his attempt (through Sarah) to legalize the liberty with which he had been endowed to produce an heir in accordance with divinely appointed means. Faith was tainted with reason, and the fact of Sarah's physical condition, due to her advancing years, caused the couple to "arrange" for God's promise to be fulfilled through another channel. The ensuing conflict between Ishmael and Isaac and their respective descendants continues to this day, illustrating that good ideas not rooted in God's provision will inexorably, and inevitably, produce results that may appear to have achieved their desired objectives but can never, however, fully attain the potential of divine blessing. Abraham's attempt to solve his dilemma is an example of this kind of problem-solving, and of its results.

Strictly speaking, however, the word "dilemma" is not a synonym for "problem." Rather, it refers to a specific type of problem, i.e., one for which there are two known solutions, neither of which is entirely satisfactory. When Abraham committed himself to producing Ishmael, God did not abandon his plan to introduce Isaac and resort to an inferior—and imposed—plan B. Isaac was born, as promised. Abraham's dilemma lay in how to resolve the inevitable conflict between the child of promise and the one born according to his natural tendencies. Perhaps ironically, it was Sarah who provided the prophetic word to her husband: "Get rid of that slave woman and her son" (Gen 21:8–10).

Under the terms and conditions of the new covenant in Christ, true believers (that is, those who are genuinely of the seed of Abraham by faith) can ill afford to be any less radical. Legalism, that appeal to the letter of the law—along with its associated man-made structures, designs, patterns of worship, agendas orchestrated by committee, and plans produced with little or no reference to the guiding influence of the Holy Spirit of God—can have no place in the hearts, minds, and lives of children of promise. In other words, where the Spirit of God is absent, men devise strategies.

Ray Stedman reminds us that "Abraham's faith, grown through years of waiting, led at last to the fulfillment of his hope that he would have a line of descendants through whom all nations would be blessed. That hope found its ultimate fulfillment in Jesus, who said of Abraham, 'Your father Abraham rejoiced at the thought of seeing my day; he saw it and was glad.'"[17] In what way might it be said that Abraham saw the day of Christ and rejoiced? Well, he undoubtedly rejoiced at the birth of his son, Isaac (as noted in the previous chapter, Isaac, perhaps significantly, means "he laughs"). This, of course, would have been a perfectly natural emotion for any father to express, even more so given Abraham's advancing years. That it was a birth attendant upon a divine promise would certainly have increased the level of exuberance. But the promise of a son was itself annexed to an even greater promise—that all nations would be blessed through Abraham's line. The realization of that promise, of course, required a line of descendants through whom God would bless those nations. As the writer to the Hebrews puts it: "All those people were still living by faith when they died. They did not [physically] receive the things promised; they only saw them [by faith] and welcomed them from a distance" (Heb 11:13). That Abraham lived to see the birth of his grandson, Jacob, who was to become the father of the twelve tribal leaders of natural Israel, would no doubt have been cause for yet further celebration.

The Galatian Misunderstanding

Paul illustrates the whole salvation process from Abraham's covenant history in Galatians 3, where he concludes:

- Those who believe are children of Abraham (v. 7);
- God . . . announced the gospel in advance to Abraham (v. 8);
- Those who have faith are blessed along with Abraham, the man of faith (v. 9);

---

17. Stedman, *Hebrews*, 77.

- By faith . . . we receive the promise of the Spirit (v. 14);
- The promises were spoken . . . to his seed . . . meaning one person, who is Christ (v. 16);
- What was promised, being given through faith in Christ Jesus, might be given to those who believe (v. 22); and
- If you belong to Christ, then you are Abraham's seed, and heirs according to the promise (v. 29).

Commenting on these verses, Jim Packer asserts that "[s]uch Scriptures require us to interpret Christ in terms of God's covenant, just as they require us to interpret God's covenant in terms of Christ, and this fact alerts thoughtful readers to the centrality of the covenant theme."[18] Paul's purpose in addressing the Galatian believers as he did seems to have been to counter the misguided influence of those who still associated covenant identity with the outward sign of circumcision. Even under old covenant stipulations, however, circumcision was just that: a sign. It was an outward, (very) physical representation of an inner reality— faith. Indeed, the righteousness reckoned to Abraham was based upon his trust in God (Gal 3:6). Trust was his initial and immediate response to God's promise; it should also be the primary and principal response of believers to the fulfillment of that promise in Christ Jesus, exclusive of any other imposed ethnic, social, cultural, or religious admission rites. Paul's conclusion, therefore, is that the Galatians—and every subsequent generation of "Gentile" believers—belong to the Abrahamic line simply because they share this one essential family characteristic—faith (v. 7), the authentic sign of covenant membership. Thus do the faithful share in their "father" Abraham's blessing (v. 9).

God had promised that "all nations of the earth" would be blessed through Abraham and his seed (Gen 12:1–3). In effect, this was the foundation of the gospel, made known to Abraham centuries before Christ—by faith (Gal 3:8–11). The apostle Paul identified the fulfillment of this promise with the conversion of the Gentiles (vv. 7–8). Thus, the line of Abraham's inheritance includes all those who are justified by faith, irrespective of gender, race, cultural proclivity, social status, or any other distinguishing feature. It had always been God's intention to bless the Gentiles: Corporate Israel was supposed to have been a nation of priests

---

18. Packer, *Saving Work of God*, 20.

who would witness to the surrounding peoples as to the goodness of God and God's accessibility by way of faith, the ultimate expression of God's blessing being the promise of the Holy Spirit (v. 14). God promised Abraham an inheritance through his seed, and that seed was Christ Jesus (v. 16). The law was neither the basis—nor the abolishment—of the promise, for it, too, was essentially a covenant of grace (vv. 17–18). We, as Christians, are sons and, therefore, recipients of God's promise as the "faith-seed" of Abraham in Christ Jesus (vv. 26–29).

In the final verse of Galatians 3, Paul asserts once again that only those who are organically united to Christ may expect to receive the blessings of the Abrahamic covenant. Earlier, Paul had stated that Abraham's seed was Christ (Gal 3:16); here, however, he says that all those who believe are this seed (Greek—*sperma*). Thus, when Paul speaks of believers as "heirs according to promise," he does so on the basis that all believers share in Christ's one inheritance. It surely follows as a corollary, therefore, that believers do not so much possess their own individual sonship; rather, they share in the one sonship of Christ. The most logical interpretation of this whole passage is that Christ alone has inherited all the promises made to Israel and all the blessings of keeping God's covenant. Christians partake of these blessings only by virtue of their organic union with Christ.

The essence of Paul's argument to the Galatians is to present, side-by-side, the pros and cons of their attitude toward the privileges associated with the gospel over against God's dealings with men. Ungodly infiltrators had convinced them that they could justify their deeds on the basis of fleshly descent; Paul's counsel was that God's justification emanates from a faith dynamic.[19]

Fulfilled, not Replaced

According to Kenneth Campbell, the Abrahamic covenant "constitutes the first truly clear revelation of the gospel of salvation and prepares the way for the covenant-nation and, thus, later the true seed of Abraham, the Messiah."[20] The exile of Israel from the land of promise in the latter stages of its Old Testament history was effectively a reversal of the covenant promise given to Abraham. It was identified at the very outset

---

19. See Ridderbos, *Paul to the Churches of Galatia*, 150.
20. Campbell, *God's Covenant*, 32.

of this study that the essence of God's covenant dealings with the people Israel was that he would be their God and they would be his people. Apostasy, rebellion, idolatry, and general disregard for the covenant ultimately caused God to declare to Israel that they were no longer to be considered his people. The significant feature of Jeremiah's prophecy regarding the coming new covenant in this respect was a full restoration of God's blessing on the land of promise (Jer 30:3; 31:38–40; 32:43; Ezek 37:12, 26). Moreover, the new covenant would not be subject to potential suspension or abandonment; it would be an everlasting covenant (see also Isa 55:1–5; 61:1–9; Ezek 16:60–63) guaranteed by the foundation upon which it was to be built, God himself meeting its demands in the person of his Son, Jesus Christ. Palmer Robertson puts it this way:

> When the parallel passages to Jeremiah 31 speak of this new covenant as being "eternal" in character, the concept best may be understood as referring to the "irrevocable" or "definitive" aspect of this covenant. No possibility exists for an annulment of the new covenant. It cannot fail to achieve its intended goal of heaping redemptive blessing and restoration on its participants.[21]

Thus, the scriptural position regarding natural Israel as participants in God's covenant with Abraham is quite clear. There is—and ever has been—only one "church" (Hebrew—*qahal*; Greek—*ekklesia*), comprising both Gentile believers and repentant Jews. The church of the New Testament has not replaced Israel; it is equally the redeemed community of God's people, i.e., the true sons of Abraham who have believed. Unbelieving Jews are no more God's chosen people than are nominal churchgoers; faith is the key. It is noteworthy, by the way, that although Israel had a historic tradition of "breaking" covenant through disobedience, mutiny, and insurgency, the people were allowed to retrieve the blessings of covenant upon repentance (2 Kgs 11:17; Ezra 10:3) and a renewal of their covenant vows (Deut 5:2–3; Josh 24:25–27).

Peter Golding is correct to allude to the origin of the church as being found in Abraham and his family, reminding us of the apostle Paul's illustration to the Roman Christians wherein he identifies Gentile believers as being "grafted in to stock already in existence, [that] of Abraham."[22] In the words of Samuel Mikolaski: "The true heirs of Abraham are not

---

21. Robertson, *Christ of the Covenants*, 285.
22. Golding, *Covenant Theology*, 154.

those who claim the suzerainty of the law, but those who know the freedom in Jesus Christ."[23]

Moreover, this messianic context is also to be found in Psalm 2, clearly suggesting that it is prophetic in relation to the ascension of God's Anointed One. The writer to the Hebrews certainly believed it to be so (see Heb 1:1–5). It would seem that the psalmist is here given access to the contents of an internal dialogue between the first and second persons of the Trinity, in which the ascended Christ is invited to merely ask of his Father and he will be given the nations for his inheritance and the ends of the earth for his possession. Thus, the original promise given to Abraham of "seed" and "land" has been magnificently extended to become "the nations" and "the ends of the earth" (see Ps 37:11; Matt 5:5). The promised heritage is no longer restricted to the geographic location of Canaan; it is now enlarged to encompass the entire world (cf. Gen 15:18; Rom 4:13). Contained within the two-fold promise of God to Abraham, we can see that "God's particularization . . . had a universalistic purpose"[24]—the one seed of Abraham would yield a harvest of sons of righteousness, by faith.

Summary

It is not all Abraham's natural descendants who are reckoned to be his children (Rom 9:6–7), for "a man is not a Jew if he is only one outwardly" (2:28–29). Only those whom the Son has set free to do the things Abraham did, who love Jesus, and hear what he says are truly children of Abraham (John 8:39–43). As for the others, even though they are descended from him they are regarded as illegitimate (v. 41). God's covenant promises to Abraham were always intended to have been the exclusive birthright of those who believe. The continuing hope for Israel, i.e., being regrafted in, is conditional upon the people not persisting in unbelief (Rom 11:23), for as yet their hearts are veiled. But "whenever anyone turns to the Lord, the veil is taken away" (2 Cor 3:15–16).

---

23. S. Mikolaski, "Galatians," *New Bible Commentary*, 1101.
24. Hendriksen, *Galatians*, 120.

FULFILLING THE MOSAIC COVENANT

It is perhaps significant, as Wayne Grudem[25] points out, that the only covenant referred to as "old" in the New Testament is the one made under Moses' leadership at Sinai (see Exod 19–24; 2 Cor 3:14; Heb 8:6, 13). It must also be acknowledged that the Mosaic law could not promise salvation to those who adhered to its requirements. Indeed, this was not its design. If anything, the whole purpose of the law was to convince men of its inherent weakness and, therefore, to direct those who recognized its failure to Christ. Moral rectitude does not convert a sinner to a saint, because it only deals with external acts of righteousness, leaving the inner sinful conditional unaltered. This is what Paul refers to when he reminds the Roman believers that the law was effectively powerless (Rom 8:3).

If we concede that the law was essentially given as a step in mankind's education leading to Christ, then surely we must also admit that its usefulness is now ended: This is clearly not the case, however, as we shall see. This is not to say, of course, that the law did not function pedagogically, but rather that such is not its essence. The law retains a purpose even though that particular task has now been fulfilled.

The Pauline Position

In his second epistle to the believers at Corinth, the apostle Paul contrasts the inaugural glory of the Mosaic and the new covenants. The covenant of law was accompanied by God's glory as it radiated from Moses' face after their meeting on Mount Sinai. The greater glory of the new covenant, however, consists in "the light of the knowledge of the glory of God in the face of Christ" (2 Cor 4:6). Whereas the former gradually diminished, the latter perpetually increases (3:18).

It is perhaps worthy of our attention that when Paul expounds the superiority of the gospel over the old covenant, he employs the Greek word *kainos*, which means "new" in qualitative terms (temporal newness, as in "more recent," would have been *neos*).[26] Whereas the old written code set out a standard impossible of achievement—i.e., that sinful man should live sinlessly, the new code's standard is attainable, by the Spirit of God in Christ. Norman Hillyer identifies three specific

---

25. Grudem, *Systematic Theology*, 521.
26. See Vine, *Expository Dictionary*, 781, 782.

contrasts between the covenants, drawn out by the apostle Paul in his second letter to the Corinthians:[27]

Mosaic	**New**	
Letter	Spirit	2 Cor 3:7–8
Condemnation	Justification	v. 9
Passing	Permanent	v. 11

Although the terms and conditions of the Mosaic covenant were educational, they only really instructed man as to his moral ineptitude. There was a certain splendor in this covenant by virtue of its divine origin; however, it was as the moon in the darkest of skies. Now that the sun of righteousness has appeared to herald God's "new day," any previous insufficiency is swallowed up by the potency of God's provision (2 Cor 3:10–13). Now we are free not from the law's demands, but from the fear of our own incapacity to meet them (v. 17).

In his letter to the churches at Galatia, Paul contrasts the Mosaic covenant and the new covenant, referring to the differing circumstances of Abraham's wife and his concubine. The covenant conferred at Sinai resembles the Egyptian maidservant, Hagar (a Semitic name, perhaps meaning "flight"), who produced a child according to her master's fleshly restructuring of God's promise (Ishmael, meaning "God hears"). The new covenant, however, is represented by Sarah (the Hebrew word *sarah* means "princess"), who was always destined to produce the child of promise with great joy (Isaac, meaning "he laughs").

The phrases "under law" and "under grace" have often been presented in purely antithetical terms, as if law and grace are diametrically opposed concepts. The biblical perspective, however, is that the law remains valid to those of whom it may be said the grace of God has been appropriated. The difference now is our relation to it. "The law is good," says Paul, "if used lawfully" (1 Tim 1:8), which implies that it is possible to employ the law in an unlawful fashion. Similarly here, Paul's polarization of the sons of Abraham as an allegory of two distinct approaches—one resulting from the children of the slave woman; the other the product of the free woman (Gal 4:31)—provides the key to understanding the whole of Paul's teaching in this regard. Paul never prescribes freedom in Christ as a justifiable reason for the wholesale abandonment of covenant

---

27. N. Hillyer, "2 Corinthians," *New Bible Commentary*, 1078.

responsibilities, but he does advocate resisting those who would seek to impose the law's requirements as a burden that has historically proven to be unbearable. As Walter Hansen points out: "Identity is the basis of behaviour: a clear understanding of who we are in Christ guides our conduct in the Spirit."[28] In other words, the realization of who we are should dictate that we do not abuse the freedom that is ours, but that we use it in a way that will bring honor to the author of such freedom. Liberty is not synonymous with licentiousness, as the Galatians were later reminded (Gal 5:13).

Because the gospel of grace discharges us from the law's penal demands by putting us to death in Christ, if we subsequently seek to reapply ourselves as slaves to the law, we thereby actively annul the "implementation" of the gospel in us by what Paul describes as "falling away from grace" (Gal 5:4). Improved performance will not deal with guilt; only repentance can do that. Self-condemnation can never be addressed by a "must-do-better-next-time" approach; it requires a conviction that "there is now no condemnation for those who are in Christ Jesus" (Rom 8:1). This would be sufficient if we were to take it at face value. However, Paul goes on to remind us that the reason for such confidence is that "through Christ Jesus, the law of the Spirit of life set [us] free from the law of sin and death" (v. 2). We are not free to indulge in lawlessness; we are released from the curse of the law so that "the righteous requirements of the law might be fully met in us, who do not live according to the sinful nature, but according to the Spirit" (vv. 3–4).

It is futile—not to mention foolish—to acknowledge that outside of Christ's grace we cannot be reconciled to God, only to then live a life trying to prove ourselves worthy of such grace. Not only can we never find justification in the law, neither can we be sanctified by it. The legalistic piety of religious externalism is of no value whatsoever in dealing with mankind's carnal nature (Col 2:20–23). It merely serves to whitewash yet another grave. We do not reign in life by virtue of a more rigorous set of self-imposed rituals, but by receiving "God's abundant provision of grace and of the gift of righteousness . . . through the one man, Christ Jesus" (Rom 5:17).

So grace triumphs over the law in this respect: it produces a walk in accordance with the Spirit rather than one after the flesh. Paul's exhortation to "work out your own salvation" (Phil 2:12) is not an advisory sug-

---

28. Hansen, *Galatians*, 151.

gestion that we should attempt to earn reconciliation with God by good works. Outside of Christ, these are of no value. Even our best efforts are as soiled linen (Isa 64:6). It is rather a recommendation that we express our appreciation of God's gift to us by bearing fruit that will last, because it is the product of a Spirit-filled life (see Gal 5:22–23). Not only are we "dead to sin"; that would be a glorious truth in itself. We are also in the realm of the operation of the reign of grace.

Peter's Perspective

We know little of Peter's theology compared to that of Paul simply because of the relative dearth of extant manuscripts that may be correctly attributed to him. Much of what we do know is gleaned from his first epistle. Here, he constantly refers to believers in a corporate sense as "God's elect," thus implying that he considered the church to be the spiritual heir of natural Israel (see 1 Pet 1:1–2; 2:4–10). Howard Marshall adroitly reminds us that "[j]ust as the covenant between God and Israel was sealed by a ritual in which the people were sprinkled with the blood of a sacrifice (Exod 24:7–8), so Christians can be regarded as dedicated to God by being *sprinkled* with the blood of Jesus. Their acceptance by faith of his death as an atoning sacrifice for them means that they are bound to him and will express this fact by obeying his commands."[29]

Peter consistently alludes to parallels between the Christian experience and that of Old Testament saints under Moses' leadership:

- Ancient Israel, having emerged from the trials of the Red Sea, wandered in the desert for forty years before the people finally availed themselves of their promised inheritance;

- New Testament believers have been delivered beyond their own baptismal Red Sea "through the resurrection of Jesus Christ from the dead" (1 Pet 1:3), so that they may triumph in the midst of adversity as they pursue their inheritance (vv. 4–12).

Peter also draws extensively from Old Testament history in general to present his New Testament message. Of course, this is equally true of other New Testament writings, but Peter does so in such a way as to imply the divine union of the two. Indeed, the dictum often attributed to Augustine could well have been Peter's epithet: "The new is in the old concealed; the old is in the new revealed." A major concern in my early

29. Marshall, *1 Peter*, 31–32.

days as a Christian was the emphasis on the personal to the detriment of the corporate. Personal salvation, individual holiness, and taking time to be alone with the Lord were all encouraged. These were all meaningful and worthy goals—in their place. However, I cannot remember such focus being directed to teaching about the church as a divine network or community of believers in Christ, although the doctrine of the church as a covenant people is given foremost attention by Peter:

- When believers respond to Christ, they are thence added to the church (1 Pet 2:4, 5, 10);

- The New Testament church of God correlates to the Old Testament temple of God and must, therefore be a living expression of its functionality (v. 9);

- In essence, the church (Greek—*ekklesia*), in its truest sense, has existed since long before Christ's earthly epiphany and is currently required to stand in continuity with its purpose—though not always attained—across all previous generations (vv. 11–12).

Peter goes on to promote covenant faithfulness (1 Pet 2:17), covenant responsibility (3:1–7), and mutual covenant service (4:7–11).

In many ways, the understanding of Christ's person and work within a covenantal framework could only be fully recognized after his death, resurrection, and ascension. Nevertheless, as Peter Golding observes: "The Apostolic proclamation of the gospel was greatly facilitated by the fact that such concepts as sacrifice, atonement, holiness, and priesthood were so clearly prefigured in the Law."[30]

An Anonymous Apology

It is beyond the scope of this work to discuss at length the question of authorship of the New Testament book of Hebrews. Despite years of scholarly conjecture and detailed textual criticism, all that can yet be said with any degree of precision is that its author's identity remains uncertain. In the context of this study, however, the writer to the Hebrews, whose familiarity with the old covenant barely requires explanation, insists that the new covenant—of which Jesus himself is personal guarantor (Heb 7:22)—is superior in a number of ways, including the following:

---

30. Golding, *Covenant Theology*, 169.

- Its penal demands have been permanently met, not temporally hidden from view (9:11–14);
- Its stipulations are not externally threatening, but are internally inspiring (10:19–39); and
- Its mediator is eternally present in order to execute its benefits (13:8).

Earlier in the epistle, the writer to the Hebrews had compared Jesus to Israel's revered leader thus: "Moses was faithful as a servant in all God's house . . . but Christ is faithful as a son over God's house" (Heb 3:5–6). Jesus himself had made the link between his own initiation of the new covenant and that by Moses of the old covenant (cf. Matt 26:27–28; Exod 24:8). In chapter 8, the writer to the Hebrews spells out the advantages of the latter over the former: "If there had been nothing wrong with that first covenant, no place would have been sought for another" (Heb 8:7). So, what was wrong with the old covenant? Well, first of all, its conditions had never been fully met, because it required sinful man to live sinlessly. Secondly, it remained incapable of motivating perfect obedience, because it was an external code dependent upon an essentially and willfully disobedient agent—the human heart. Palmer Robertson is correct to posit that "[t]he obedience to God's law, which did not materialize under the Mosaic covenant, shall find consummate fulfillment under the provisions of the new covenant (Jer 31:33)."[31]

Indeed, it is this covenantal law, grounded as it is in the eternal righteousness of God, which provides the continuing basis of his loving expression under both the old and the new covenants. In this regard, Carl Friedrich Keil draws our attention to the fact that ". . . the difference between the two consists merely in this: that the will of God as expressed in the law under the old covenant was presented externally to the people, while under the new covenant it is to become an internal principle of life."[32]

Summary

The relationship between covenant law and covenant grace, and how it is applied to the new covenant community will be discussed in fur-

---

31. Robertson, *Christ of the Covenants*, 275.
32. Keil, *Prophecies of Jeremiah*, 38.

ther detail in the following chapter. Suffice to note for the time being, however, that the law of Moses is not invalid as an expression of God's grace amongst believers. In this regard, the comment I made in the Introduction is well worth repeating: How much more gracious can he be than to draw us into a covenant that can be summed up by Jesus as one that requires us to love him with all our heart, soul, and mind, and then to allow that grace to flow through us by loving our neighbor as ourselves (Matt 22:37–40)?

FULFILLING THE PHINEHATIC COVENANT

As we saw earlier, Palmer Robertson correctly identifies the Phinehatic covenant as ". . . an adjunct to the Mosaic covenant, developing one specific aspect of the priestly legislation given to Moses."[33] However, it is precisely this that arouses our interest in the present context. For just as Christ fulfilled the prophetic covenantal role typified by Moses, and the kingly responsibilities foreshadowed by David, so too he fulfilled the priestly commitments prefigured by Phinehas.

Divine Intervention

The episode in which Phinehas expressed his covenant loyalty in the midst of widespread covenant unfaithfulness was discussed earlier. Taking it upon himself to strike at the root of the community's sin, he effectively interceded on behalf of the entire nation, thus averting God's wrath. God's reward? An everlasting covenant. The typological significance of this episode is all too clear. The everlasting character of the new covenant in Christ, however, is not restricted by the boundaries of time; it is eschatologically eternal. It is, therefore, not only the new, but also the final covenant; there will be none to follow it.

Significantly, the psalmist's recollection of the same event (Ps 106:30) describes Phinehas' work as that of intervention (Hebrew—*palal*). Other legitimate translations of this word include "executed judgment" (KJV), "furnished justification," "interposed" (NASB), or "mediated." Interestingly, the Septuagint here translates the Hebrew by the Greek *exilasatō*, which means "to make atonement for" (see also NKJV). Although this particular word is entirely absent from the pages of the New Testament, others bearing the same meaning or conveying a

---

33. Robertson, *Christ of the Covenants*, 27.

similar concept are to be found in abundance: *katalassō* (reconcile), *hilasmos* (propitiation), and *mesites* (mediator). As Vine observes: "These [all] describe the means (in and through the Person and work of the Lord Jesus Christ, in his death on the cross by the shedding of his blood in his vicarious sacrifice for sin) by which God shows mercy to sinners."[34]

Integral to the concept of Christ's mediation is propitiation. This is not a fashionable word in current ecclesiastical circles, because it requires that we contemplate the wrath of God. Some have even translated the Greek texts in accordance with their particular sensitivities on this issue. However, Christ's atoning sacrifice did avert the wrath of God and must, therefore, be considered as an act of propitiation, thereby ensuring God's propitiousness toward man thereafter (see 1 John 2:2). That truth notwithstanding, however, the insistence that the word "propitiation" be employed does not in itself negate the reality of expiation, though those who prefer this word often do so because of their conscionable objections to the former. The propitiation of God's displeasure takes place precisely because the guilt of sin has been expiated by Christ's atoning sacrifice.

In the Old Testament, the act of mediation exists under two separate ministerial functions: The prophetic act of mediation was directed toward man by an essentially and divinely appointed representative, and the act was to express, declare, and convey the meaning of God's prescribed will to his covenant people. The priestly act of mediation, on the other hand, was directed Godward by intermediaries who besought his favor on behalf of those they represented—again, the covenant people of God. Both streams of mediation are consummated in Christ. Moreover, such fulfillment is complete and exclusive. Scripture provides no legitimate warrant for the practice of extra, derivative, or auxiliary mediation. We have access to the Father through Christ alone, and we have access to Jesus personally and directly.

It is, perhaps, no coincidence that both the doctrine of the mediatorial work of Christ and the place within the covenantal framework of God's agreement with Phinehas are almost absent from current evangelical theology. The terms "prophet," "priest," and "king" in relation to Christ are not merely figurative, for he is a prophet, a priest, and a king in the fullest and most real sense of each of the roles these words depict. Indeed, when compared with any other who has held any of these of-

---

34. Vine, *Expository Dictionary*, 78.

fices, it may be said that he is the *only* real priest (as, of course, he is the *only* real prophet and the *only* real king). Moreover, he carries the eternal divine endorsement: "You are a priest forever" (Ps 110:4; Heb 7:17).

The Sacrifice to End all Sacrifices?

It is true that only the writer to the Hebrews refers to Christ specifically as priest; indeed, the language employed might otherwise suggest metaphorical allusion. The priestly work of Christ is, however, not only described throughout the New Testament (see John 1:29; Rom 3:24–25; 5:6–8; Eph 5:2), it is also clearly prefigured in much of the Old Testament (e.g., Ps 110:4; Zech 6:13).

Old Testament sacrifices generally had one of two purposes:

- To effect temporal reconciliation; and/or
- To foreshadow the coming Redeemer.

For obvious reasons, the priest of the old covenant and the sacrifice he offered were separate entities. In the new covenant, however, they are one and the same: The priest, Christ, offers himself as the sacrifice.

Christ's atonement has potentially transformed the future of the entire human race. It also changed forever the nature of the priestly ministry. Not only was Jesus not of the direct line of Levi, as Phinehas was, Christ's priestly function is of the order of Melchizedek (Ps 110:1). The tribe of Levi had been set aside under Moses' overall leadership; this tribe of Israel would be exclusively and entirely responsible for the mediatorial requirements of the nation. Melchizedek, on the other hand, was both king and priest (Heb 7:1). Scripture affords little information about this mysterious figure: It reveals nothing of Melchizedek's lineage, a principal feature in determining Levitical succession. Toward the end of the prophetic record, Daniel foretold one who would end the need for sacrificial offerings (Dan 9:27), a key priestly function. In Christ, this practice is rendered unnecessary, thus releasing the true Israel of God to fulfill its calling as a holy nation, a royal priesthood (1 Pet 2:5, 9).

This is not to say, of course, that sacrifices, *per se*, are now to be despised. Peter invites believers to "offer spiritual sacrifices [that are] acceptable to God through Christ Jesus" (1 Pet 2:5), while the writer to the Hebrews identifies sacrifice as "praise to God, that is, the fruit of lips that acknowledge his name" (Heb 13:15), and identifies good deeds as such sacrifices (v. 16). The apostle Paul sums it up perfectly:

"I appeal to you . . . to present your bodies as living sacrifices, holy and acceptable to God, which is your spiritual worship" (Rom 12:1). But sacrificial acts of this nature, however laudable and characteristic of a true believer, hold no salvific merit; rather, they are the products of a redeemed soul.

Notice also that the full atonement was not completed by Christ's death alone, but by his being raised from death, for the benefits of his vicarious crucifixion could not have been made accessible to man had it not been for his victorious resurrection. Just as an acceptable penal substitution is dependent upon perfect submission, so too the priesthood of believers is governed by the whole mediatorial act of our priestly brother, Jesus Christ. In the words of Geerhardus Vos:

> Only when the believer understands how he has to receive and has received everything from the Mediator and how God in no way whatever deals with him except through Christ, only then does a picture of the glorious work that God wrought through Christ emerge in his consciousness and the magnificent idea of grace begin to dominate and form in his life.[35]

Uniquely Qualified

There are many differences between the type (that is, human priests) and the antitype (Christ as the Mediator). Arguably the most fundamental of these is that the mediatorial capacity of Phinehas and the members of his line was inherently diminished by the fact that they, too, were each in need of personal mediatorial representation, for they too shared in Adam's guilt. Not so Jesus. In the words of Emil Brunner: "The incarnation is the divine and merciful answer to our falling away from God. The Mediator in his Person, by his very "constitution," is the mediation between the Creator and the fallen creature, in a double connection—as the Mediator of revelation and the Mediator of reconciliation."[36]

I suspect Brunner means this: Christ's "constitution" is often referred to as "the hypostatic union," that is, the perfect unity of his divine and human natures in the one person. He is able to represent God to man as the perfect mediatorial prophet, by virtue of his deity; he is also able to represent man before God's throne as the perfect mediatorial

---

35. Vos, "Doctrine of the Covenant in Reformed Theology," *Redemptive History*, 248.
36. Brunner, *The Mediator*, 406.

priest, because of his sinless humanity. In the context of the former, he reveals God to man, as only he is equipped to do so. Similarly, within the framework of the latter, he reconciles man to God as no one else can. Our understanding of this representation is usually associated only with the work of Christ, but it is equally true of his person. This is not to say that the work of Christ is in any way unnecessary. However, in terms of his unveiling the Father, Christ is as much the actual revelation as he is the means to that revelation.

Neither should that revelation be perceived as entirely anthropocentric. God is not revealed primarily in order to meet man's psychological, physiological, spiritual, or emotional needs, but essentially that God's own glory might be made manifest. Such splendor is not increased by exposure nor diminished by remaining hidden. But God has decreed that his kingdom rule be established on the earth in increasing measure; he has also voluntarily engaged in covenant relationships with man, sealing them with promises that are guaranteed simply because they are effected by his words. As such, he is bound by his own nature to see them fulfilled and has chosen the way to do so—by revealing himself to us through the person of his Son. Christ as Mediator is, thus, the gift of God and the act of God, in accordance with the covenant purpose of God.

Christ's mediatory work of reconciliation was necessary, real, and beneficial.[37] The death of Jesus has often been portrayed in agonizingly human terms: the death of one who deserved better, a sinless benefactor, a scapegoat, he who took our place in some heroically noble act, the utmost expression of love. Of course, it was all of these things, but it was and is so much more. The death of Christ took place because it was necessary, even essential. Simply put, there was no other way. And it achieved something that had been previously, and otherwise, impossible.

The separation that existed between God and man because of the principle of sin in operation was no mere theory; it was objective reality. Similarly, the act of reconciliation was not effected by a simple accounting exercise of credit and debit, a mere forgetting of a debt owed. Sin's penalty was removed from our account because it had been fully endured by Christ in our stead. We are forgiven, not because the price of forgiveness is no longer required; rather because it has already been paid. Moreover, the only way we can possibly imagine the extent of the gulf that existed between ourselves and God is to consider what was required to bridge that gap.

37. See Woodall, *A Race in Need of Redemption*.

It must also be noted that the mediatorial work of Christ was no mere gesture. There is a tendency today for political figures and state dignitaries to be seen mingling with the workforce/troops/villagers of less economically developed countries in order to suggest empathy toward those less fortunate than themselves. It is quite often merely a tactic, a ploy designed to garner favorable press: the measures of privilege these individuals enjoy are almost always retained. The Christ-event, however, was not a marketing tool but a necessary act. Neither was Jesus' crucifixion simply an intense endurance test. It consisted of genuine suffering (physical, mental, and spiritual), culminating in a death more real than any other had ever experienced or will do so. When he cried out, "My God, my God, why have you forsaken me?" (Matt 27:46), he was not simply quoting the psalmist so that God the Father could tick off yet another box in the almanac of fulfilled prophecy; he really experienced a sense of abandonment on that scale.

The life of Jesus should never be separated from the death of Jesus, for the one is indispensable to the other. Indeed, it might even be said that his death—or, at least, his dying—was the pinnacle of his life and, therefore, as much a part of his life as his childhood. Furthermore, to distinguish between his "active obedience" and his "passive obedience" is to either ignore or obscure the connection between them. Without his active obedience, the evidence for which is clearly expressed in the pages of the New Testament gospel accounts, his passive obedience at the end of his life would have been rendered fruitless. Of course, such an observation is limited to the temporal dimension. In the eternal scheme of things, Christ's active obedience began (if such things may be permitted to be thought of as "commencing") in the council of the Godhead when he agreed/decided/chose to take up the role of Mediator. Theologians speak of this as the covenant of redemption, though its existence is based largely on assumptions rather than conclusive evidence.

Summary

The whole covenant principle is in reality an expression of the first commandment issued by God through Moses: "I will be your God and you will be my people" (see Lev 26:12; Jer 7:23–24); "I am the Lord your God . . . you shall have no other gods before me" (Exod 20:2–3; Deut 5:6–7). Both statements also underpin the entire concept of the gospel of Christ in the new covenant. Nowhere is this more fully expressed than in his mediatorial (that is, priestly) function. In general terms, Israel failed because it had a history of consistently flouting this one commandment, even when the people had a dedicated Phinehatic priesthood to guide them. According to the prophet Jeremiah, the guaranteed success of the new covenant would be due, at least in part, to the fact that its principles—or laws—would be inscribed on the flesh of human hearts by God's Spirit. Another reason for its guaranteed success is surely that the Mediator enables us to more fully comprehend the import and significance of the first commandment/covenant principle.

FULFILLING THE DAVIDIC COVENANT

In many ways, the promise made to David can only be regarded as having been fulfilled in Christ. David had received divine assurance that his monarchical line would endure forever (2 Sam 7:16). Yet, although its duration was beyond comparison with any other royal line in Israel (i.e., over four hundred years), it did come to an unceremonious end. Palmer Robertson resolves the problem thus: "The breaking off of Davidic throne-succession in Old Testament history may be evaluated in terms of the anticipative role of Israel's monarchy. David's line anticipated in shadow-form the eternal character of the reign of Jesus Christ."[38]

The Rebuilding of David's Fallen Tent

> "After this I will return and rebuild David's fallen tent. Its ruins I will rebuild, and I will restore it, that the remnant of men may seek the Lord, and all the Gentiles who bear my name," says the Lord who does these things that have been known for ages. (Acts 15:16–18; cf. Amos 9:11–12)

Although some have interpreted this prophetic word as originally given to anticipate the restoration of the nation of Israel to divine favor, its New Testament context suggests otherwise. James, as chief elder and possibly acting chairman of the council at Jerusalem, was responding to the testimony of God's work among the Gentiles and what—if any—impositions of Jewish law might be appropriate. The idea of salvation being made available for the Gentiles was not a new one. Indeed, it might reasonably be argued that God's choosing of Israel as a covenant people was for this very purpose. What was alien to the people of natural Israel was the thought that God's people could incorporate both Jew and Gentile on

---

38. Robertson, *Christ of the Covenants*, 249.

equal footing, without the latter needing to undergo a process of proselytization. And yet the prophets of old had foretold that this would be the case. As William Larkin observes:

> Here we have a reversal of roles for the promise and fulfilment. Usually it is the alleged fulfilment that must agree with the promise. Here the fulfilment becomes the hermeneutical key for understanding how the prophet Amos could prophesy that in the last days the "people of God" would include Gentiles who had not first become Jews.[39]

David's tent (or tabernacle) was the place in which the ark of God was housed during the latter part of his reign (see 2 Sam 6:17). It was the temporary symbolic residence of God's presence amongst his people. Then the prophet Nathan announced that, despite David's plans to build a permanent dwelling-place for God, the honor of doing so would go to his son, Solomon. Nevertheless, Nathan declared that God would establish David's house and his kingdom for ever (7:4–17). Given that this was the essence of the Davidic covenant—or, at least, the divine promises annexed to it—it seems initially mystifying that the later prophetic utterance concerning it does not link it with the rebuilding of David's house or kingdom, but rather with his fallen tent/tabernacle.

Let us consider the context of Amos' original words for a moment. He points to the glorious future under Messiah's rule, having personally witnessed the fall of the natural kingdom of Israel. Prior to speaking words of hope, the prophet had painted a dark picture indeed. Disaster and ruin had been his watchwords. But now he speaks of the fallen tabernacle/tent (literally "hut") of David being re-established one day. Although there are subtle hints that the dynasty to come would be a new one, there is not only a measure of continuity (note the words "rebuild" and "restore"), but also the suggestion that principles long neglected would be re-instituted: "build it as it used to be."

Speculation still abounds as to precisely what these principles might be. A detailed analysis of Israel's most productive years under David's reign, however, suggests the following:

- A kingdom undivided;
- A community committed to God and to one another; and
- A house in which true worship is the key to all its functions.

39. Larkin, *Acts*, 223.

Kingdom Unity

Jesus is uniquely *auto-basileia*—the personal representation of the kingdom. Thus, he could proclaim that the kingdom had, indeed, arrived (see Matt 12:28; Luke 11:20). In short, the kingdom of God in all its aspects (that is, present, immediate future, and distant future) is concentrated exclusively in the person of God's Son, Jesus Christ. Thus, it was in Christ alone, he of the house and lineage of David, that the monarchy in Israel found its absolute fulfillment. Indeed, it might even be said that the connection is not so much that Christ now sits on David's throne, as some dispensationalists have asserted;[40] rather, it was David and his line of succession who sat on God's throne, upon which the ascended Christ now sits (see 1 Chr 29:22).

The kingdom of the covenant is, therefore, a united one. The New Testament speaks of Christian unity in two distinct, though inseparable, dimensions: "unity of the Spirit" (Eph 4:3), which we are to endeavor to maintain; and "unity in the faith" (v. 13), toward which we are progressively working. The context in which Paul sets both dimensions provides clues as to how each is to be attained. Humility, gentleness, and loving forbearance are vital ingredients in our quest to preserve what Christ's reconciling death has produced (v. 2); keeping the unity of the Spirit is largely achievable by attitudes and actions. "Unity in the faith," on the other hand, is gradually and commensurately reached as our understanding of truth increases (vv. 13b–25). Walter Liefeld makes valid points regarding each. Of the former, he observes that "[s]ome notable divisions within the church might have been avoided by the exercise of these virtues. Not all doctrinal controversies have been purely objective; personal pride and stubbornness have made their contribution."[41] Of the latter, he comments that "[t]he definite article here refers to faith as a body of doctrine, not to faith as an act of trust. Christians are not called to maintain unity with those who do not hold to *the* faith, which is . . . linked with the person and work of Christ."[42]

Although at first glance these remarks may seem to be contradictory, their contexts suggest otherwise. Within the kingdom of God, there is ample room for us to hold and express a wide variety of opinions on

---

40. See, e.g., Walvoord, *The Millennial Kingdom*, 199–203.
41. Liefeld, *Ephesians*, 97.
42. Ibid., 108.

a range of subjects that ultimately do not affect our standing in Christ or alter the potential for fellowship with others who may beg to differ. There are, however, some topics about which there is not the same room for maneuvering. They are both crucially foundational and foundationally crucial. God grant us the wisdom to know the difference between the two.

Expressing Christ's Kingship

According to R.T. France, the kingdom of God, upon the throne of which Jesus sits, is essentially "the practical implementation of God's rule in human affairs."[43] When instructing his closest followers on how to pray more effectively, Jesus advised them to invite God's kingdom to come, his will to be carried out on earth as absolutely as it is in heaven (Matt 6:10). This is what the kingdom of God is capable of, in Christ through us. George Eldon Ladd put it this way: "The kingdom of God is his kingship, his rule, his authority, his sway, his reign in our lives."[44]

As we saw in the previous section, Christ's consummation of the covenant with Phinehas confers upon believers the privilege of priesthood (see 1 Pet 2:5). Are we, therefore, to assume that his fulfillment of the Davidic covenant also implies community kingship? Peter suggests we are, for he describes Christ's followers as "a chosen people, a *royal priesthood*" (v. 9). Paul also speaks of us as "reign(ing) in life through Christ" (see Rom 5:17; 2 Tim 2:11–13). Thus, not only are the promises made by God to David fulfilled in Christ, the blessings associated with those fulfilled promises are also conveyed through Christ to those who are found to be in him—the believing church. Herein lie the keys to Christian kingship: corporateness and identification. In other words, we reign while we remain in Christ; we rule only within a framework of communal relationship.

I have already remarked that Israel's most prosperous phase coincided with the reign of David as king. His rule is set apart from that of other monarchs because it was generally administered with both righteousness and justice. In Christ, we have the capacity to bring about God's covenantal kingdom rule to bear on society by expressing a righteousness that is by faith and justice that exercises the will of God in action.

---

43. R.T. France, "Life and Teaching of Jesus Christ," *New Bible Dictionary*, 581.
44. Ladd, *Gospel of the Kingdom*, 21.

The concept of God's kingdom cannot be divorced from that of Christ's kingship. Moreover, the promise of a Savior-King is inextricably linked to that of a saving kingdom. However, as important as evangelism is to the church's mission, it is not its primary concern, despite the current trend to present it as such. According to Scripture's revelation, worship should take precedence over evangelism for the following reasons:

- Evangelism is concerned with how we relate to our fellow man (that is, the unsaved); worship has to do with our relationship toward God, which should always come first;

- Although sharing the gospel message is commended to all believers, the "gift" of the evangelist is restricted to those so blessed by God; there is no such restriction stated or implied regarding the act of worship. In other words, not all Christians are necessarily called to be evangelists, but all are called to be worshippers; and

- The expression of evangelism is temporally restricted; worship will continue throughout eternity.

Worship as a Key of the Kingdom

In terms of the divine-human relationship, kingship and worship are inseparable: we worship because Jesus is King. However, Christ's kingship is not dependent upon or governed by our worship; nothing is added to the status of his kingship by our worship, and it suffers no diminishing by worship's absence. Interestingly, the words most commonly translated "worship" in English Bibles are *boda* (Hebrew) and *latreia* (Greek), both of which also convey the idea of service (that is, to serve). Moreover, encapsulated in these and other similarly employed nouns (e.g., Hebrew—*histahwa*; Greek—*proskyneō* and *leitourgia*) is the concept of the church as a *people* who worship, not as a *place* of or for worship.

Worship has been correctly defined as "the activity of glorifying God in his presence with our voices and hearts,"[45] though I would qualify that by saying that for the Christian it is to be a way of life rather than merely an excuse for singing religious songs. I have already noted that God's essence remains unaffected either by worship's practice or neglect. But it would be wrong to assume that it achieves nothing; neither are

---

45. Grudem, *Systematic Theology*, 1003.

its accomplishments entirely anthropocentric. Through worship, the following takes place:

- We achieve a measure of enjoyment that is otherwise unattainable (Ps 16:11; Luke 24:52–53);
- God responds favorably to our delight in him (Isa 62:3–5; Zeph 3:17);
- We draw near to God (Heb 10:19–22; 12:18–24);
- God draws near to us (Jas 4:8; 2 Chr 5:13–14; Ps 22:3);
- Divine blessing ensues (Exod 23:25; Heb 4:16);
- Enemies are dispersed (2 Chr 20:21–22; Jas 4:7); and
- Unbelievers become aware of God's presence amongst his people (Acts 2:11; 1 Cor 14:23–25).

Many local churches are identifiable by their particular approach to worship. While there are endless variants, they seem to fall roughly into one of two categories: formal and reverent or informal and exuberant. Some associate the type preferred with the average age of the believers. Thus, it is likely that churches that opt for the lavish expression of praise will generally attract a younger congregation, while a more structured approach will be favored by an older flock. In an attempt to be more inclusive, some churches offer both types of setting at different times in their weekly/monthly calendar. John Stott asserts that "[w]e need to experience each others' preferences,"[46] though he seems to do so with a sense of temporarily crossing over established and permanently polarized divisions.

There seem to have been no such divisions in the worship of the early church. There is no biblical record that they conducted meetings that were either formal or informal, and there is certainly no suggestion that alternatives were offered in order to accommodate personal preferences. Each gathering was an occasion for worship, which was both joyful without being disrespectful, and reverent without succumbing to the temptation to be funereal (see Acts 2:43–46).

First-century Athenians purported to "worship" an unknown god, whom the apostle Paul subsequently revealed to them. Of course, the evangelistically minded would seize on Paul's opportunism and remind us that we, too, need to be socially aware of such possibilities to preach the

---

46. Stott, *The Living Church*, 30.

gospel. Far be it from me to dissuade people from such efforts. However, to emphasize this one feature of this episode in the life of the apostle can veil an equally compelling truth: it is impossible to worship an unknown god, for true worship can only be validated by legitimate relationship. Indeed, worship without relationship is tantamount to idolatry. It is perhaps for this reason that John Stott correctly defines Christian worship as "a response to revelation."[47] This being so, would it not be more appropriate for our dedicated periods of worship to follow rather than precede the preaching/teaching of God's word (see Col 3:16)?

If Christian servanthood and the believer's worshipfulness are virtually interchangeable, then surely everything we do should be regarded as an act of worship. The assertion that there is only one prescribed way to worship God has often left the church befuddled, disjointed, and perturbed. Worship must first of all be pleasing to God, not to man. It should also be—according to the revelation of God's word—in spirit, from our rational consciences, and representative of a truth that is compatible with the way we conduct our lives (John 4:24). In other words, our worship should reflect integrity of being, which is entrenched in a lifestyle that conforms to the principles of the kingdom of God.

Summary

It is not without significance that Luke records the apostle Paul preaching to certain Jews in Pisidian Antioch about Christ's relationship to David. In the midst of his outline of Jewish history, and having reached the point of David's reign, Paul moves straight on to Jesus, whose resurrection from death is cited as fulfilling the divine proclamation: "I will give you the holy and sure blessings promised to David" (cf. Isa 53:3–5; Acts 13:34). The ascended Christ's reign at the side of the Father, where he will remain until all his enemies have become his footstool (1 Cor 15:25–26), is also a fulfillment of David's prophetic psalm (Ps 110:1–7). As Rolf Rendtorff reminds us:

> David was himself a fulfillment of God's promise of a king, and this promise is fulfilled also in Christ, David's son, and will ultimately be fulfilled again at Christ's return.[48]

---

47. Ibid., 37.
48. Rendtorff, *God's History*, 67.

3

Covenant Law, Covenant Grace

It is a common misconception to think of the old and new covenants as covenants of law and grace, respectively. The old covenant was indeed one of God's amazing grace: He was under no obligation at all to reach out toward sinful man, yet the substance of the covenant was the promise that he would be the God of his chosen people. Moreover, the new covenant, as prophesied by Jeremiah, was to be one epitomized by God's gracious decision to "put [his] law in [our] minds and write it on [our] hearts" (Jer 31:31–34). The distinctive feature of this new covenant was not that it would be grounded in grace instead of law, but that God would deal with the cause rather than the effects, laying the axe once and for all to the root of man's sinful nature.

Much of the perplexity about the character of the covenants is based on a misunderstanding of the New Testament writings of John, which often seem to depict law and grace in exclusively antithetical terms (see John 1:17; 1 John 1:5–10). Further confusion arises when Paul suggests that grace arrived on the scene only with Christ (Titus 2:11). The context of Paul's words, however, implies not that grace was previously non-existent, but that it had been partially veiled until Christ's full revelation of it in the incarnation event. Thus, the apostle does not contradict himself when he speaks elsewhere of the law and its precepts as "holy, righteous and good" (Rom 7:12), for therein are contained God's requirements for his chosen people. To believe that they are other than holy, righteous, and good is to regard God's demands as nothing more than arbitrary expressions of his authority to institute such laws, with little meaning other than that of satisfying some divine eccentricity. Neither does the institution of the new covenant render the whole of the old covenant law obsolete. Although keeping it was previously problematic, it is now gloriously possible; where Old Testament Israel considered it a burdensome duty, the New Testament church of God in Christ welcomes it as a blessed delight.

Nor should it be argued that God graciously gives us a second opportunity to earn salvation by keeping his commandments. If this were so, then the atonement did not place us in the risen Christ at all, but merely back in Adam's pre-fallen condition. If the history of Israel is to serve as any lesson at all, it is that the law's inherent holiness, righteousness, and goodness do not make it any less intrinsically powerless to effect forgiveness, justification, and eternal security.

So what precisely is the relationship between the new covenant people of God in Christ and the old covenant law of God as given through Moses? What was it originally intended to do, and is that use still meaningful? Can a proper understanding of the distinction between fulfillment and replacement aid us in our quest for truth? What lessons can we learn from the history of the nation of Israel as revealed to us in the pages of the Old Testament? What does freedom really mean? To these and similar questions we must now turn our attention.

THE LAW'S FUNCTION

In the Old Testament, a number of Hebrew words are translated by the English word "law." Each one reflects a different emphasis; however, their common thread is that they all seem to have their origin in the forensic decree of one in whom resides the authority to make such a pronouncement. While there are many similarities between the features of the law of ancient Israel and her contemporaneous near neighbors, there is sufficient evidence to claim a certain uniqueness. Albrecht Alt[1] distinguishes three types of law existing in Israel and among her neighbors at the time:

- Apodictic law (e.g., "you shall ... you shall not ...);
- Those involving participle clauses (that is, consequential penalties); and
- Casuistic law (if ... then ...).

---

1. Alt, *Old Testament History and Religion*, 101–171.

Old News can be Good News too . . .

It is a tragic fallacy to ascribe the law of God exclusively to his dealings with men under the Old Testament, and the gospel entirely to his new covenant revelation. The law and the gospel exist side-by-side under the terms and conditions of both covenant "dispensations." Louis Berkhof illuminates us further when he writes: "The law comprises everything in Scripture which is a revelation of God's will in the form of a command or prohibition, while the gospel embraces everything, whether it be in the Old Testament or the New, that pertains to the work of reconciliation and that proclaims the seeking and redeeming love of God in Christ Jesus. And each one of these two parts has its own proper function in the economy of grace."[2]

It might even be said that—in some measure, at least—the efficacy of the gospel is dependent upon the generative nature of the law. The gospel appears as early as Genesis, where the tragic consequences of the fall are tempered with the promise of a future redeemer (Gen 3:14–15). In theological terms, this is known as the protevangelium (not to be confused with the apocryphal document given the name the "Gospel of James" by Guillaume Postel in the mid-sixteenth century). Messianic prophecies throughout the Old Testament also herald a coming "good news," however distant (e.g., Isa 55:1–7; Ezek 36:25–28). The permanent validity of the law in the teaching of both Jesus and Paul surely negates, once and for all, the argument that it has no place in the new covenant (see Matt 5:17–19; Rom 13:9). Indeed, John equates sinful practices with lawlessness (1 John 3:1–3).

The intention of God in giving the law to Israel through Moses was not that it should thereby provoke frustration, inhibition, or embitterment. It was designed to be applied to Israel's *sitz im leben* and to release God's blessings, enabling the people to live life to the full extent of their potential as divinely appointed covenant people (Deut 30:19–20). It must, therefore, be seen that the giving of the law was not a deed of tyrannical oppression, but an act of loving mercy. Included among the finer details of the law's provision for Israel, recorded in the book of Deuteronomy, we see examples of abundant generosity (15:12–15), precautionary measures to prevent accidents (22:8), the protection of animal rights (v. 10), a sensible sanitation code (23:12–14), benevolent sanctuary for the oppressed (vv. 15–16), respect for the property of others (24:12–13), and guidance in matters of fair trade and honest dealings (25:13–15).

---

2. Berkhof, *Systematic Theology*, 612.

... Just not as Good as New News

At the very beginning of the Christian church, a correct understanding of the law was considered so vital that Paul dedicated a considerable proportion of one of his epistles to its treatment. Indeed, it has been argued that, had it not been for the apostle's teaching in his letter to the Roman believers, it is debatable whether the rest of what we know as the New Testament would have been collated and presented in the form that we now have it.[3]

There are several applications of the word "law" in the New Testament. It can refer to the whole, or part, of the Old Testament (see Matt 5:17; Luke 2:44; Rom 2:17–27), while at other times it may denote the Sinaitic dispensation given to Israel through Moses (Gal 5:17). Quite often, God's law is spoken of as synonymous with God's will (e.g., Rom 3:20; 13:8; 1 Cor 15:5–6; Jas 4:11), or as a governing principle (Rom 3:27; 8:2). Although these are its main uses, further nuances of each are to be found, depending on the particular context.[4]

Readers of the New Testament whose only language is English are not as handicapped in their quest to understand its use of the word "law" as they might think. Unlike other words which present significant translation difficulties, there are essentially only two Greek nouns commonly translated "law": *nomos* and *nomothesia*. The latter quite simply means "legislation" (literally, "the giving of the law" as in, e.g., Rom 9:4). *Nomos* was originally derived from the verb *nemō* (that is, "to distribute" or "assign") and was the name assigned to a mutually recognized system for the distribution of property based on a common understanding. Later, the word came to mean a collective agreement for the upholding of public order. While, in the context of this study, *nomos* is understood to mean essentially "law as prescribed by statute for the administration of justice," it has a variety of applications in the New Testament (approximately two-thirds of its occurrences are to be found in Paul's writings). In the New Testament, *nomos* means, *inter alia*:

- A general precept (e.g., Rom 2:12–13);
- An influence upon behavior (Rom 7:21–23);
- The law as conveyed through Moses at Sinai (Matt 5:18; Jas 4:11);

---

3. See Campenhausen, *The Formation of the Christian Bible*.
4. See Vine, *Expository Dictionary*, 643–647.

- The Hebrew Scriptures in general, wherein is contained the law of God (Luke 16:16; John 15:25; 1 Cor 14:21);
- The law of Christ (Gal 6:2);
- Specific principles. In these uses, the word is often preceded by the definite article, as for example in the following:
    - The law of faith (Rom 3:27);
    - The law of my mind (Rom 7:23);
    - The law of sin (Rom 7:23);
    - The law of liberty (Jas 1:25; 2:12);
    - The royal law (that is, the law of love; Gal 5:14; Jas 2:8);
    - The law of the Spirit of life (Rom 8:2);
    - The law of righteousness (Rom 9:31 (KJV)); and
    - The law of a carnal commandment (that is, Aaronic priesthood; Heb 7:16).

The difficulty of fixing on a meaning is compounded not only by the fact that different shades of meaning occur in uses of the word in close proximity to one another, but also by a certain overlapping between these variants. Confusion would likely be alleviated—if not completely avoided—by an appreciation of this diversity, especially where a transition occurs between one meaning and another in close clausal proximity. Paul's writings seem particularly prone to this, most notably where he seeks to differentiate between law and legalism; yet he employs the same Greek nouns to describe both. Although not entirely sufficient, thankfully the context is often helpful.

According to Paul, legalism is essentially active disobedience to previously revealed truth (Gal 5:7), in that it requires that we seek to live by human effort rather than by the Spirit (v. 16). It ignores faith as the foundation of righteous living and turns instead to weak and miserable principles, rules, and regulations—weak because they are powerless (Rom 8:3); miserable because they serve only to remind us of our own impotence outside of a life empowered by the Holy Spirit. It is not without warrant that Arthur Wallis described legalism as ". . . Satan's most effective means of infiltrating and undermining the work and witness of the Church."[5]

5. Wallis, *Radical Christian*, 155.

Law, Sin, and Righteousness

The law has long been acknowledged by Reformed theologians as a means of grace, though a minority has so vociferously contrasted the law and the gospel as to present them as wholly incompatible bedfellows. Scripture does not refer to the law as diametrically opposed to the gospel. It does, however, speak, of the law in a variety of different contexts. Louis Berkhof[6] distinguishes the three most common thus

(1) In attempting to restrain sin and promote righteousness;

(2) In conviction, by making man consciously aware of his ineptitude and inability to keep the law, thereby leading him to Christ; and

(3) In the rule of life for believers, the existence of which is denied by those of an antinomian persuasion.

The law is not—as some have argued—synonymous with sin, but it stands in relation to sin in terms of revelation, stimulation, and opposition. First of all, it shows sin for what it really is (Rom 7:7–8). Then, in response to the opportunity afforded by the commandment, sin rises up in direct rebellion to the law (vv. 9–13). Finally comes the conflict, when we either continue to sin, remorseless and unrepentant, or choose to acknowledge that the law is powerless to deal effectively with our sinful nature. The good news is that there is One who has overcome sin on our behalf, so that we need no longer be slaves to it but may become free and willing bondservants of righteousness unto God. What grace! What law!

However, it is upon the relation of law to sin that the focus of Scripture predominantly falls. In this regard, the following must be observed:

- The law incites us to sin (Rom 7:8–11);
- The law makes us consciously aware of sin (Rom 3:20; 9:13);
- The law condemns mankind on account of sin (Rom 3:19);
- The law demands that sin be punished (Deut 27:26; Gal 3:10); and
- The law is ineffective in dealing with the sin principle (Rom 8:3).

In spite of these characteristics, the apostle commends the law's commandments as "holy, righteous and good" (Rom 7:12). They are holy

---

6. Berkhof, *Systematic Theology*, 614–615.

because their origin is traceable to God; they are inherently righteous—even though they are incapable of overcoming sin in order to produce righteousness in us—because they are fair in their dispensation; they are good because they express the intention of God's heart toward his covenant people. The psalmist put it this way:

> The law of the Lord is perfect, reviving the soul. The statutes of the Lord are trustworthy, making wise the simple. The precepts of the Lord are right, giving joy to the heart. The commands of the Lord are radiant, giving light to the eyes. The fear of the Lord is pure, enduring forever. The ordinances of the Lord are sure and altogether righteous. They are more precious than gold, than much pure gold; they are sweeter than honey, than honey from the comb. By them is your servant warned; in keeping them, there is great reward. (Ps 19:7–11)

Notice also that righteousness and holiness are not synonymous terms. The former translates *dikaiosynē*, which is "the character or quality of being right or just,"[7] while the latter is the English equivalent of *hagiosmos*, which essentially signifies our separation unto God. Thus, we may say that it is perfectly possible to be righteous (in this sense) without necessarily being also holy; however, it would not seem possible to be truly holy under the terms and conditions of the new covenant without also being righteous. This is why we are instructed to seek first the rule of God (kingdom holiness) *and* his righteousness, whereupon we may anticipate the blessing of God to be meted out to us in other areas also (Matt 6:33).

Paul goes to great lengths to make it clear that the law was not intrinsically weak, but that its effects became weakened by "the flesh" (that is, sinful human nature; Rom 7:7—8:3). The design of the law could only produce its intended fruit once that "flesh" had been dealt with, and that could only take place "in Christ." But just in case any should thereby assume that the law could effect sanctification where it had failed to render justification, the apostle reminds us that this, too, is only possible—thank God—"through Jesus Christ, our Lord" (7:25a).

---

7. Vine, *Expository Dictionary*, 970.

Summary

The original purpose of the law was to order the lives of humanity in conformity with the intention of God's heart. The commandments themselves have been summed up by Jesus in the issuing of a new covenant based on what might reasonably be called "the Unilogue": "As I have loved you, so you must love one another" (John 13:34–35). This is the law of Christ. Believers are not lawless rebels but are rather those who have found, with Paul, that "love is the fulfilling of the law" (Rom 13:10). Whatever other commandments we may be required to keep are but expressions of that perfect love at work in us and through us, without which we are alien to God and our profession of Christianity is but vain deceit (1 John 2:4; 4:8). This law bears the image of the One who both gave it and kept it, for it is holy, righteous, and good (Rom 7:12). We, too, are to be imitators of God's character (Eph 5:1; Rom 8:29). Lord, hasten the day when we may echo the cry of the psalmist: "I desire to do your will, Lord; your law is in my heart" (Ps 40:8).

THE LAW'S REQUIREMENTS FULFILLED—BY GRACE

As we have seen, the new covenant is essentially one of grace, which is not merely passive, but is known by expressions actively emanating from its source. The grace of God is a supernaturally natural attribute of the divine Being, but we are only able to recognize it, and then only possibly, in the manifestation of gracious acts through which he chooses to reveal himself to us. The incarnation event was just such an act and may be regarded thus on many levels, none more so than in the exchanging of sin and righteousness between the sinless One and the transgressors. Here, the grace of God was fully demonstrated, for it truly was the bestowal of *God's Riches at Christ's Expense*.

Understanding Grace and Fulfillment

The word "grace" as employed in Scripture is a good example of a situation where English translations fail to do justice to the original. Today we speak of grace (and its cognate terms) as a virtuous quality, e.g., "he dealt graciously with that difficult situation" or "she moved gracefully among the dinner guests." However, the biblical words (Hebrew—*hen*; Greek—*charis*) signify an objective relationship of unmerited favor given by a superior to an inferior. In the context of divine grace toward humanity, grace is seldom—if ever—divorced from the accompanying idea of covenant. In relation to the law, we see the grace of God many times over. The fulfilling of the law by Christ was an act of grace; the resultant exchange of man's sin and Christ's righteousness cannot be regarded as anything but gracious; the giving of his Son in the first instance can only be perceived as a deed emanating from God's gracious disposition. The gracious acts of God are fully and perfectly consistent with his nature, for he is a God of grace. Indeed, the giving of the law itself must also be seen as an operation of immense grace. Arthur Wallis describes it thus: "The new covenant that came with Jesus was a covenant of grace, not a covenant of law. That is, it was more about promises than commands. It spoke more about what God had done for men than what men could do for God. It promised to put inside men the desire and ability to please him."[8]

Grace does not abound in a continual gratification of the sinful nature outside of the law. By reckoning ourselves dead to sin, we are thus alive to God through Christ (Rom 6:11). We have been transferred from the manifestation of the realm of sin into the operation of the sphere of grace. Nor are we merely placed back into some pre-fallen Adamic state with the potential to once more lose it all. We have a new covenant life under a new covenant head "in whom the tribes of Adam boast more blessings than their father lost."[9]

A distinction must be noted at this point between abolition and fulfillment. Whereas the former relates to an act whereby a practice, custom, or institution is ended or closed and, therefore, ceases to exist, the latter implies bringing consummation by way of satisfying a demand, performing a task, complying with prescribed conditions, and/or bringing a period or piece of work to its completion. This clarification of terms makes it evident that Jesus did not come to abolish the law, but to fulfill it (see Matt 5:17). He met its demands in life by virtue of his perfect obedience, and he satisfied its penal requirements on our behalf exclusively as the One for whom enduring them was otherwise unnecessary because of his personal sinlessness.

Fulfillment literally means "the filling out to full potential." This describes Christ's fulfilling of the law perfectly. The new covenant, the kingdom of God in Christ, and the law of Christ were not radically new

---

8. Wallis, *Living God's Way*, 89.
9. Isaac Watts (1674–1748).

in any sense other than that they brought to full fruition the seeds that had already been sown by God. Thomas Watson put it this way:

> Though a Christian cannot, in his own person, perform all God's commandments; yet Christ, as his surety and in his stead, has fulfilled the law for him: and God accepts of Christ's obedience, which is perfect, to satisfy for that which is imperfect.[10]

Not only did Christ fulfill the law's demands by virtue of his sinless life and unwarranted death, freely undertaken for the benefit of fallen humanity, but his very incarnation fulfilled its own function. We have already noted that a primary purpose of the law was essentially to lead us to Christ (see Gal 3:24). Thus, once Christ has come, would it not be reasonable to presume that the law has no further salvific usefulness? It would be a mistake to believe that we must now reign in life by meeting its demands personally, lest we fall once more under its condemnatory power. Yes, we reign by ruling, but the first step toward this state of control is receiving the gift of righteousness as the liberal provision of God's abundant grace (Rom 5:17).

If ever a man could have fulfilled the Pharisaical understanding of the law, it would surely have been Saul of Tarsus. But not even the apostle Paul could have rendered perfect obedience to Jesus' précis of the law's commandments: to love God with all his heart, with all his soul, with all his mind, and with all his strength and, in so doing, to love his neighbor as himself (Mark 12:30). However, such practices are not preached as effecting salvation, but as the fruit of having been saved. In other words, they are not preconditions, but products.

The law effectively formed the basis for the covenant of works. In this context, Martyn Lloyd-Jones is quite right to assert that the law is, in fact, God's moral law.[11] Because Christian believers are "in Christ" we are thus also "dead to the law." However, this does not mean, as some have supposed, that the Christian need not be concerned with the law's existence. God's moral requirements for his covenant people remain linked to his own nature, and their imitation of that nature, as those who bear the image of God in and through Christ Jesus. It is our relationship to that law that has been transformed: we are no longer under it, for it shall no longer have dominion over us. No longer does it say to us: "Do

---

10. Watson, *Body of Divinity*, 358.
11. Lloyd-Jones, *Sermon on the Mount*, 192–193.

this and you shall live" or "Do that and you will die," for it no longer has the authority to make such decisions.

Substitutionary Atonement

The requirements of the law were largely two-fold: preceptive and penal. Jesus met them both, though he was not personally obligated to meet the latter, having fully observed the former. Indeed, it was only because he lived his life in full, active obedience to the law's precepts that he was able to offer himself in passive obedience to the law's penalty on behalf of others. The grace of God "sent his Son . . . born under the law, to redeem those under the law" (Gal 4:4–5a). And the reason? ". . . that we might receive the full rights of sons" (v. 5b). The covenant itself was one of grace. The blessings it invoked were also those of grace, but they did not acquire that status by virtue of the fact that they emanated from a covenant that was gracious: The grace of both the covenant and its blessings was derived from their mutual source—the grace of God.

I am of the conviction that Christ's fulfillment of the law's demands was not only intrinsic to the whole salvific event, but that it was necessarily so. For justification to ensue, atonement had to be made. Christ's death was essentially substitutionary; it was also characteristically penal. It was an act of love on God's part because he was under no obligation, morally or otherwise, to perform it; it was an act of justice because, in meeting the forensic demands of his own nature, no moral standards were breached. Such a concept often attracts a critical response from within what might otherwise describe itself as evangelical quarters. Vincent Taylor responds in the following fashion: "The thought of substitution is one we have perhaps been more anxious to reject than to assess, yet the immeasurable sense of gratitude with which it is associated . . . is too great a thing to be wanting in a worthy theory of the Atonement."[12]

The argument in favor of regarding Christ's death as substitutionary is married to that of his sacrificial death as one of propitiation. While it is true that sin had to be removed from God's sight (that is, expiated), this element was included in Christ's propitiatory atonement (that is, the quenching of God's wrath against sinners). James Denney's summary is worth quoting in full:

---

12. Taylor, *The Atonement*, 301.

> It is Christ set forth in his blood who is a propitiation; that is, it is Christ who died. In dying, as St. Paul conceived it, he made our sin his own; he took it on himself as the reality which it is in God's sight and to God's law; he became sin, became a curse for us. It is this which gives his death a propitiatory character and power; in other words, which makes it possible for God to be at once righteous and a God who accepts as righteous those who believe in Jesus . . . I do not know any word which conveys the truth of this if "vicarious" or "substitutionary" does not, nor do I know any interpretation of Christ's death which enables us to regard it as a demonstration of love to sinners, if this vicarious or substitutionary death is denied.[13]

To those critics who accept that Christ's death was substitutionary, but deny the notion that it was necessitated by any judicial requirement, I would ask: "In what way, then, do you consider it to have been substitutionary?" The argument that the idea sullies the cross on the basis that it conjures an image of retribution is to misunderstand the active correlation of the divine attributes. God is love and God is just. His actions are always expressions of who he is in essence and what he is by nature. There is no biblical evidence to suggest that he at any time suspends one in deference to the other. Conjecture may yet abound concerning the mechanism by which the great exchange took place. How it might be possible that Christ could die for any abrogation of God's moral law (that is, sin) or that I could thereafter be clothed with his righteousness, and that God could find that acceptable, without circumventing God's intrinsic sense of moral justice is—and may forever remain—incomprehensible. The "whys" and "wherefores" continue to be a mystery. That it is so should be sufficient.

Jim Packer proposes the following as "ingredients in the evangelical model of penal substitution":[14]

(1) God . . . condones nothing, but judges all sin as it deserves: which Scripture affirms, and my conscience confirms, to be right.

(2) My sins merit ultimate penal suffering and rejection from God's presence (conscience also confirms this), and nothing I do can blot them out.

(3) The penalty due to me for my sins, whatever it was, was paid for me by Jesus Christ, the Son of God, in his death on the cross.

---

13. Denney, *Death of Christ*, 126.
14. Packer, *Saving Work of God*, 121.

(4) Because this is so, I through faith in him am made "the righteousness of God in him," i.e., I am justified; pardon, acceptance, and sonship become mine.

(5) Christ's death for me is my sole ground for hope before God. "If he fulfilled not justice, I must; if he underwent not wrath, I must to eternity."

(6) My faith in Christ is God's own gift to me, given in virtue of Christ's death for me: i.e., the cross procured it.

(7) Christ's death for me guarantees my preservation to glory.

(8) Christ's death for me is the measure and pledge of the love of the Father and the Son to me.

(9) Christ's death for me calls and constrains me to trust, to worship, to love, and to serve.

JUST as IF I'd diED

What precisely do we mean when we say that "Christ died for us," that "he gave his life for us," or that "Jesus gave himself as a ransom for us"? Much has been made of the preposition "for" in each of these and similar quotations. In some of the passages, "for" is the translation of the Greek word *hyper*, "on behalf of" (see Rom 5:8). In others, it is the translation of *anti*, "instead of" (see Mark 10:45). Some instances in the New Testament lend themselves more favorably to one word than to the other, but there are occasions where these translations are almost interchangeable (cf. 2 Cor 5:20–21; Gal 3:13). It seems clear to me that, in the context of the relationship between Christ's death and that of the sinner, both are equally valid: Christ died *on my behalf* and *in my stead*.

For the law to be fulfilled, Christ had to become what we are in order that we might, thereby, become what he is. Thus, justification allows sanctification to take place. This is why "good" deeds (or "righteous" acts) are ineffective as a means to salvation: because sanctification can never be a prelude to justification. The requirements of the law can only be met in us by the Spirit of God after our embracing of the sacrificial death of his Son has enabled our access to them.

Our English word "justification" translates the Latin *justificare*, which is a composite of *justus* and *facere*, meaning "to make righteous." This is the word by which the Vulgate translates the Greek *dikaioō*. In its biblical application, the verb form "to justify" has the sense of effecting a state of righteousness by means of a judicious decree. This may be executed in one of two ways:

- By acknowledging the right of the claimant to warrant such a decree (that is, the just deserve to be justified); or
- By crediting those who lack merit with the righteousness of another.

The consistent emphasis of the New Testament's use of the verb embraces the latter alternative. Although found also in non-Pauline writings, the apostle is responsible for approximately 75 percent of the New Testament's use of the verb *dikaioō* and its cognates. He uses it so extensively, in fact, that from among his works it is possible to formulate the following definition of justification:

> Justification is God's deed and decree to graciously forgive the sin of the convicted penitents and credit them to be righteous, and pronounce them as such, of his own volition and by his grace, according to a response in faith in Christ, not on the basis of works, but of the mediatorial keeping of the law and substitutionary death of the Lord Jesus Christ in their place.

In his observations of Paul's treatment on the subject, William Hendriksen[15] points out that justification is:

(a) God's gift (Rom 5:15–18);

(b) The product of his grace (3:24; 4:16; 5:15);

(c) Free (5:16);

(d) Not of works (3:20);

(e) The opposite of condemnation (8:1, 33, 34);

(f) That which deprives man of every reason for boasting (3:27);

(g) Appropriated by faith, even though that faith be God-given (Eph 2:8).

Paul's understanding of the doctrine of justification is not such a radical departure from the forensic view that prevailed within first-century Judaism. It may be seen as two-fold. First, the pronouncement as just of those who are justified releases them from any penal liability to

15. Hendriksen, *Romans*, 133.

which they would otherwise be subject had they instead been declared unjust. Second, and perhaps more positively expressed, is the implied feature that the recipients of justification are also entitled to all the privileges that would accrue through obedience to the law. This may be loosely designated as vindication. Thus, not only are those who are justified, in the theological sense of the word, reconciled to God, but they also become recipients of all that the imputed righteousness of Christ avails for them.

As a result, we are "heirs of God and co-heirs with Christ" (Rom 8:17). The Greek noun translated "co-heir" is *sunkleronomos*. It is used essentially of the sharing of an inheritance by virtue of relationship. The same word defines Isaac and Jacob's share in the promises of God attributed to Abraham (see Heb 11:9). Although some English translations offer "joint heir," there is a subtle but significant forensic difference between a joint heir and a co-heir. Whereas the former would, under normal circumstances, receive an equally distributed portion of the whole, the latter is entitled to the full benefits.

Imagine that a farmer has four sons. When the farmer dies, his will is read; he has made each of his sons a joint heir of the entire estate. This would usually mean that each son is to receive 25 percent of its proceeds. Had he made them co-heirs, however, each one would have had full ownership rights to the entire estate. That we are co-heirs with Christ does not mean that the blessings ensuing from his atoning sacrifice are divided equally among however many Christian believers there are at the end of the age. Everything that was attained by him is at the disposal of each and every one of us.

So fundamental was the doctrine of justification to Emil Brunner's Christology that he declared it to be

> . . . the most incomprehensible thing that exists. All other marvels are miracles on the circumference of being, but this is the miracle in the centre of being, in the personal centre. Justification means this miracle: that Christ takes our place and we take his. Here the objective vicarious offering has become a process of exchange. Apart from this transaction, forgiveness is not credible, for it contradicts the holiness of God. Justification cannot be separated from the "objective atonement," from the expiatory sacrifice of the Mediator. Indeed, justification simply means that this objective transaction becomes a "Word" to us, the Word of God.[16]

---

16. Brunner, *The Mediator*, 524.

Not only were the obedience of Christ and his fulfillment of the law complete, the effects rendered by them were as well. And not only is this the case, but it is my conviction that, equally, they all lie beyond the possibility of reversal. It must be acknowledged that there are specific instances of the change that takes place being instantaneous, while at other times it is more of a process; the change may appear at some times to stutter or advance more gradually than at others. Sanctification is, after all, a work-in-progress. But it is one that moves—little by little—toward a positive conclusion.

Neither can one be more of a Christian today than he or she was yesterday or will be tomorrow. We are either in Christ or we are outside of him; we are either alive or dead. Although it is possible to be or feel more or less Christ-like from moment to moment, this has absolutely nothing to do with our status in Christ. We have been and, therefore, are justified; we are becoming increasingly sanctified. One is a present, continuous state; the other is a progressively developing status. Justification, then, is not determined by the works of man; it is entirely dependent upon a judicial act of sovereign grace in Christ Jesus, faith being the hand that receives it as a gift.

Summary

By way of summary, the following points may be observed with reference to justification:

- Participation or otherwise is determined by covenant membership, irrespective of national identity, cultural background, ethnic distinction, social standing, or gender (Gal 3:26–29);

- The basis for the judicial decision is nothing more nor less than the substitutionary death and subsequent resurrection of Christ Jesus (Rom 3:24–26; 5:8–9);

- The blessings of justification in the present meticulously anticipate those of the divine decree at the end of the age (Rom 2:1–16);

- The corporate recipient of justification is the church, its individual members having undertaken a personal commitment to its head, Jesus Christ (see Gal 2:21; 5:4–6); and

- Justification is essentially and necessarily by grace through faith (Rom 3:22–26; Titus 3:7).

EXAMPLES FROM ISRAEL'S HISTORY

Israel's election in the Old Testament was a sovereign act of God's arbitrary will; it was not determined by any particular merit on the part of that nation. Indeed, as previously noted, according to Roy Kearsley both *charis* (Greek) and *hen* (Hebrew) convey ". . . an objective relation of undeserved favour by a superior to an inferior . . . [that] . . . is wholly unmerited, not evoked by the creature's disposition."[17]

Time and space do not allow for an in-depth historical analysis of the manifestations of God's grace to Israel during the period covered by the Old Testament. Rather, it seems appropriate to identify expressions of that grace at key moments in Israel's history. Given its almost constant turbulence, it will come as no surprise that its key moments were exclusively those of a change in fortunes from decadence and backsliding to one of obedience—albeit short-lived—and renewal. At such times, God often intervened by way of a solitary figure who had remained faithful against the tide of apathy and apostasy. Thus, we now turn our attention to consider Elijah, Jonah, and Nehemiah.

Elijah—Grace in the Midst of Rebellion

The division of the kingdom following Solomon's death was in many ways inevitable. Essentially, the nation rebelled against Rehoboam because he had revolted against the kingship of Yahweh. For the sake of God's covenant with David, however, a portion would remain faithful to the house of Judah. Jeroboam's return from exile in Egypt fuelled the north/south divide to such an extent that only Judah and—perhaps ironically—Benjamin remained loyal to the house of David in Jerusalem. Following his proclamation as "king of Israel" (that is, the northern kingdom) by its remaining ten tribes, Jeroboam quickly turned the hearts of the people to run after pagan deities and so called fertility gods. Despite their obvious historical differences, the one common feature of the two kingdoms was the depth of their degeneration, if not the rate at which it was achieved. The reason for their fall is oft repeated throughout the books of the Kings: they forsook the Lord their God, turning instead to pagan idolatry, in clear breach of their covenantal obligations. Alongside a continuing prophetic voice were the false prophets, who spoke only to please the occupant of the royal throne so that they might be rewarded for their lies. By stark contrast, the men of God were often severely punished for their unfaltering covenant obedience. Was this ever not the way?

---

17. R. Kearsley, "Grace," *New Dictionary of Theology*, 280.

The respective ministries of prophet, priest, and king were designed as those of anointed representatives of God before the people, and vice versa. While each retained a specific function within that framework, they were all entrusted with the responsibility for guiding the people Israel in their covenant faithfulness to the Lord and channeling his favor toward them. As God was under no obligation to furnish such conduits, their provision may be regarded as further tokens of divine grace.

After the division of the kingdom, the northern territories had known no faithful priests (1 Kgs 12:31), and all its kings had been united in singular unfaithfulness. By the time of Ahab, Baal and Asherah worship had become fully syncretized into the national religious consciousness. At this time, God's grace was extended still further by the provision of arguably the most expressive of all the Old Testament prophets—Elijah.

I would dearly like to be able to give a brief personal background to the character of Elijah. Unfortunately, I am unable to do so for the simple reason that he appears, unannounced, at the beginning of the seventeenth chapter of First Kings. His rather uncomplicated introduction is this: "Now Elijah the Tishbite, from Tishbe in Gilead, said . . ." (1 Kgs 17:1). All we know is his name and from where he came. The first and last words of this quotation may help us a little. He was a man for the moment ("Now . . ."), and he had something significant to say. His name is also not without some relevance, for it means "Yahweh is God"; the truth of which declaration Israel desperately needed to be reminded.

By almost any standard of the Christian era, Elijah was a formidable preacher. No marketing strategy, promises of prosperity, or cavalier displays of needless extravagance: he attracted the attention of large crowds solely through his singularity of purpose and his defiant challenge to apathy. Having seen the rainfall held back at his command (1 Kgs 17:1), those who gathered before him on Mount Carmel were perfectly primed for what God was about to do through his servant (18:16–39).

The imagery of Elijah's challenge to those gathered is somewhat lost in our English translation: "How long will you waver between two opinions?" (v. 21). The Hebrew is more accurately rendered thus: "How long will you hop from branch to branch?" The image is that of a small bird, undecided as to where it should perch. In modern sports parlance, such birds would be labeled "glory hunters"—i.e., those who support the team currently at the top of the league, until things begin to run anything but smoothly. At that point, the birds "hop" off that branch and head out to find the new team-of-the-moment.

Of course, the priests of Baal and the prophets of Asherah were nothing if not demonstrative in their efforts. They danced, they shouted, and they cut themselves frenetically (1 Kgs 18:26–29), no doubt attempting to conjure up an atmosphere of "other-worldliness." But no one came, no one answered; their offerings remained on the altar, but unaltered. By stark contrast, it required only a word of prayer from Elijah for the one true God to answer by fire, and for the sacrifice to be completely consumed (vv. 36–38). Suddenly, the crowd reaffirmed the supremacy of Yahweh (v. 39), and Elijah was a national hero (except in the royal court). The king had previously labeled him a "troubler of Israel" (v. 17). Those who are content to live their lives compromising rather than acknowledging their covenant responsibilities often regard others as rabble-rousers. Both Scripture and church history testify to this fact. But who was actually guilty of bringing trouble to Israel: Elijah or Ahab/Jezebel?

Elijah's moment of power was immediately followed by a period of depression. Because he had depended so entirely upon the grace of God in his hour of triumph, God stood by him in his moment of turmoil (1 Kgs 19:9–18). For much of the rest of his life, however, Elijah lived as a fugitive. He was unable to rid the people of their pagan curiosities, and the house of Omri remained largely intact, though it did eventually collapse in fulfillment of Elijah's prophetic words (cf. 1 Kgs 21:19; 22:29–38; 2 Kgs 9:25–26). In recognition of his covenant faithfulness in the midst of unimaginable hostility, God honored his prophet at the end of his life by allowing him to become one of only a few men not to taste natural death (2 Kgs 2:1–12).

The similarity between Elijah and Moses as men of God is fully recognized in Jewish Haggidic thought. Bruce Smith outlines why this may be so:

> Elijah's return to Horeb is obvious enough, but there is also the fact that Elijah is accompanied and succeeded by Elisha as Moses was by Joshua . . . Not only has the death of Moses an air of mystery about it (Deut 34:6), but his successor secured the allegiance of Israel by participating in the same spirit as Moses and demonstrated his fitness for office by a miraculous river crossing (Deut 34:9; Josh 4:14). The translation narrative (2 Kgs 2) reproduces this pattern precisely. The fact also that God answers Elijah by fire on two occasions (1 Kgs 18:38; 2 Kgs 1:10, 12) seems to look back to the exhibition of God's presence and judgment in fire in the exodus narratives (Exod 13:21; 19:18; 24:17; Num 11:1; 16:35).[18]

---

18. B. Smith, "Elijah," *New Bible Dictionary*, 321.

Just as Moses came to represent the Old Testament law, so Elijah is personally symbolic of the Old Testament prophets. It seems fitting, therefore, that they both appeared on the Mount of Transfiguration in the presence of the One who fulfilled them both (Luke 9:28–36). They had each appointed a "savior" figure to continue their respective ministries ("Elisha" is a variant of "Joshua," and both words mean "salvation from/of God"). God graciously allowed them a belated audience with the true Savior of those covenanted to God—Christ Jesus ("Jesus" is the Aramaic form of the Hebrew "Joshua").

No Old Testament prophet is referred to as often by the New Testament writers as is Elijah. Perhaps the most succinct—not to mention distinct—appraisal comes from the pen of Jesus' brother, James: "Elijah was a man just like us" (Jas 5:17). It might be easy to argue with such a sentiment, as some of Elijah's experiences were quite extraordinary. But he was a man like us in that he, too, was born in sin, he belonged to the people of the covenant, he had the potential to rejoice exceedingly in the good times and become incredibly dejected when circumstances deteriorated, and he was prone to seasons of great faith as well as periods of intense doubt. One thing remained constant, however: he never wavered in his love for his God.

What becomes abundantly clear from the narrative is that Elijah's experience of God's favor coincided with his obedience to God's will. At such times, his actions were never designed to justify his ministry. He did what he did because God told him what to do; he said what he said because God told him what to say. Elijah's authority did not derive from proving himself in the school of the prophets, or from always putting on a good show, or from having worked up from the bottom rung, as it were— i.e., from relatively unimportant prayers being miraculously answered, to the major event at Carmel—the "payoff" for all those years of practice. No. His authority came to him as one who represented the Lord, the God of Israel, before whom he frequently stood (see 1 Kgs 17:1).

Jonah—Grace Toward the Heathen

Jonah's hometown was Gath Hepher in Zebulun, about four miles north of what became Nazareth. He was, therefore, a Galilean. Thus, the Pharisees' taunt of Nicodemus that "no prophet is to rise from Galilee" (John 7:52) either displays ignorance of Jonah's personal background or demonstrates contempt for his claim to the prophetic office. Jesus both reminded them of Jonah's historicity and established his own (see Matt 12:41; Luke 11:31–32). Indeed, as D.W.B. Robinson, former Archbishop of Sydney, points out: "Jonah is the only Old Testament prophet with whom Jesus directly compared himself. Jesus obviously regarded Jonah's experience and mission of great significance."[19]

In fulfillment of Jonah's earlier prophetic word, the northern kingdom of Israel had restored its traditional borders in the area of Damascus, taking full advantage of Assyria's defeat of the Aramean capital (2 Kgs 14:26–27). However, despite the fact that Israel's good fortune was the direct result of godly favor, she soon became complacent in her newfound liberty. While Amos, speaking to the people of the covenant, and Jonah, speaking to Nineveh's Gentiles, both demanded repentance, the evidence suggests that a more genuine response—in the short term, at least—came from the inhabitants of the future captors of God's people. It might even be argued that God graciously chose Assyria from among the nations to receive such a message, as they would thereby become familiar with Israel's religious sensitivities when the time for captivity finally arrived.

A number of attempts have been made to offer possible interpretive paradigms, such as allegory, commentary, mythology, and parable, for the book of Jonah. While any potential allegorical value or mythological status is generally dismissed in current scholarly circles, it must be observed that any claim to a parabolic nature does not thereby exclude genuine historicity. Real events can teach valuable moral lessons. Given its length, however, it seems highly unlikely that the book of Jonah is simply a parable; at the same time, most attempts to refute its historicity are based upon a denial of the possibility of miracles.

Strictly speaking, a miracle can be defined as an act or deed beyond the capacity of merely natural means; consequently the act or deed must, therefore, be ascribed to supernatural agency. By this definition, Jonah being swallowed by a great fish was not a miracle, as some sperm whales and large sharks are capable of swallowing an adult whole. The miracle was in his preservation while being transported by the fish, and in his being discharged whole—frightened, but alive.

Perhaps unusually, the chapter divisions inserted into the book provide a neat framework within which to view it.

---

19. D.W.B. Robinson, "Jonah," *New Bible Commentary*, 747.

Chapter 1	Jonah's calling and disobedience	Running away from God	The great mistake
Chapter 2	Jonah's prayer and release	Running toward God	The great fish
Chapter 3	Jonah's preaching and Nineveh's response	Running with God	The great city
Chapter 4	Jonah's anger and Yahweh's love contrasted	Running ahead of God	The great God

Jonah's reasons for initially disobeying God's voice can only ever be the subject of speculation. The courage he eventually showed makes it unlikely that he feared the Ninevites. Perhaps his own words provide a clue: he was mindful of God's proclivity to forgive (see Jonah 4:2). Although it may have been, as Hendriksen suggests,[20] that he mistakenly believed that Yahweh would transfer his covenant sympathies from Israel to Assyria, it is more probable that he was aware of the danger Assyria posed to his own people and believed this to be an ideal opportunity for God to remove such a threat. As Sidlow Baxter points out, Jonah's choice seemed to be ". . . between suffering the divine vengeance upon himself for awful disobedience, and thus save Israel; or else he must go to Nineveh, and possibly cause [its] salvation . . . which would result in Israel's ruin."[21]

Jonah recognized that he was not merely a victim of circumstance, but was subject to divine displeasure (Jonah 2:3). To ignore God is to disobey God, but Jonah's plight was the product of rather more than passive disobedience: he actively pursued a course of action that took him in the opposite direction entirely to that which God had purposed for him. As a result, he felt banished from God's presence (v. 4). Of course, to be outside of God's presence is impossible this side of final judgment, as the psalmist knew only too well (Ps 139:7–8). But our response to that presence can range from a feeling of ecstasy to a feeling of expulsion.

When Jonah finally fulfilled his vow and spoke the word of the Lord in Assyria, the response was what a twenty-first-century evangelist can only dream about: repentance on a city-wide scale. This was no

20. Hendriksen, *Survey of the Bible*, 233.
21. Baxter, *Explore the Book*, 162.

mere recognition of wrongdoing accompanied by a vague promise to clean up their act or introduce a bit of religion into the proceedings. The Ninevites were genuinely turning away from their previous lifestyles of evil practices (Jonah 3:10). There should therefore be no need for a fourth chapter in this book. But once again, Jonah is dissatisfied (Jonah 4:1). His reaction to Nineveh's response was not elation, but enmity. He had not really changed inwardly at all; he was still encumbered by the same character traits as before: self-justification, self-importance, and self-pity. His catchphrases might well have included these: "I knew this would happen," "I have a reputation to preserve," and "I want to be left alone." "I . . . I . . . I . . ." There is perhaps little wonder that his "ministry" was at its most productive when his sentences began instead: "Thus says the Lord . . ."

God had graciously chosen Jonah for a unique task: to ultimately extend his message of grace to the heathen. Now Jonah needed to experience God's grace firsthand. Scripture teaches that justification is a critical act of God's grace appropriated by faith. Sanctification is also graciously made available to us, but it is a process finally attained by perseverance and diligence on our part, as we respond to the prompting of God's Spirit when he identifies those characteristics in us that are most in need of remediation or change. Thus, the fruit of sanctification is achieved by pruning, which is sometimes painful and often costly, but never without its due reward.

Although Jonah's appearance in Scripture is not limited to the Old Testament book that bears his name, it is somewhat surprising that these four chapters contain only eight words of actual prophecy. We are given only a glimpse of the Ninevites' response to him, and much of the rest of the book is concerned with Jonah's life and God's part in it. At times it seems that his aptitude was held back by his attitude, but God certainly saw the potential for character development. Once again, the grace of God extended beyond the gaze of men.

Nehemiah—Grace on the Threshold of Restoration

While the theme of restoration provides an organizing principle for the composition of the book of Nehemiah—i.e., chapters 1–7 deal with the rebuilding of Jerusalem's city walls and chapters 8–13 are concerned with the spiritual restoration of its people—Graham Scroggie sees Nehemiah's role more as one who is administering a return to social order: "Zerubbabel went to Jerusalem in 536 BC and effected religious reforms. Eighty years later Ezra went to Jerusalem and effected ethical reforms. Twelve years later, in 445 BC, Nehemiah went to Jerusalem and effected civil reforms."[22]

The content of chapter 1 sets the tone for the rest of the book of Nehemiah. The phrase "Hear me, O God" and variants of it are a constant theme. It is not so much that Nehemiah found prayer itself to be powerful, but that his prayerfulness proved to be the key to the power at work in him and through him. Moreover, he was a man of grace because he was a man who drew upon the grace of God in prayer. It is also not without significance that Nehemiah's plea was to the covenant relationship that existed between God and his people (Neh 1:8–10).

As cupbearer to the Persian king, Artaxerxes (Neh 1:11), Nehemiah was fortunately—or perhaps providentially—placed. Artaxerxes was Esther's stepson, and it is possible that the Jewish queen had some say in such appointments. Having boldly sought direction from God (v. 4), Nehemiah tentatively, yet faithfully, approached the royal throne, seeking permission to travel to Jerusalem in an attempt to ascertain whether its condition matched the distressing reports he had heard (v. 3). On his arrival there, Nehemiah immediately inspected the condition of the city walls (2:11–16). It did not take long for him to form a plan of action and make his intentions known (vv. 17–18).

Nehemiah's conviction was unequivocal: the walls of Jerusalem must be rebuilt. Sure in the knowledge of his divine appointment, his approach was bold, authoritative, and unapologetic. If Jerusalem was to return to purity of worship and moral uprightness, then independence was vital. Only by rebuilding the city walls could such liberty be achieved. Despite severe hostility, particularly from Sanballat and Tobiah, the mission was accomplished in the face of derision, attempted blackmail, and blatant intimidation. Similar threats assail us today. We have a common enemy, whose characteristics remain unaltered over time. If mockery fails to halt us in our common pursuit of godly directives, the enemy will seek to tarnish our reputations. If that proves equally unsuccessful, then the enemy will try to bully us into submission. The lesson of Nehemiah is that our ability to deal with such tactics lies in the grace of God and in our faith, which will allow us to appropriate such grace as his covenant people.

22. Scroggie, *Know Your Bible*, 98.

The corporate nature of the building process also provides a valuable insight into the function and role of the church. Priests, goldsmiths, perfume-makers, provincial rulers, and merchants all worked side-by-side in order to bring about the fulfillment of God's design. Such was the sense of urgency and unity that even Israel's enemies were forced to acknowledge the miraculous nature of their having completed the work in a little over seven weeks (Neh 6:15–16). When the people of God begin to draw upon the grace of God and relate to each other in the purpose of God, then the unchurched cannot help but be affected.

Having overseen the rebuilding of the temple and the restoration of the city walls, Ezra and Nehemiah then teamed up to renew the covenant among the people. The Feast of Tabernacles (also known as the Feast of Booths) was joyously celebrated for the first time since Joshua's day and, after hearing the Levites give a detailed account of Israel's backsliding, the people vowed never to neglect God's house again (Neh 10:39). Twelve years after his arrival in Jerusalem, Nehemiah returned to Persia, believing his task had been completed (see 2:11; 13:6). The measure of the success of a celebration, however, should not be taken in how electric the atmosphere of the closing night is or in how many triumphalistic "words" are proclaimed, but in the fruit it produces. Once again, the people's ways did not match their words. On a subsequent visit, Nehemiah was confronted with further neglect of God's house (13:10–11), the breaking of covenant obligations (vv. 15–21), and laxity in the taking of foreign wives (vv. 23–24).

In the following section, we shall be looking further at the relationship between law and grace, particularly at how the work of Christ has liberated believers so that they are now free to be governed. To many, this will seem like a contradiction in terms. Such a mindset is often the result of an erroneous understanding of the grace of God. God's grace not only allows us to gratefully receive the blessings that are ours in Christ and to look forward to even more of the same in eternity; it also "teaches us to say 'No' to ungodly and worldly passions, and to live self-controlled, upright, and godly lives in the present age" (Titus 2:11–12). The initial zeal of those who took on the responsibility for rebuilding Jerusalem's walls did not just naturally fade with time; it became peripheral to their sense of commitment as they permitted unrighteous thinking and ungodly conduct to take center stage. They had not allowed God's grace to teach them to say "No!" to legalism. However, in response to the sternest of rebukes from Nehemiah (Neh 13:25), the outlook appeared to be rather more promising. Civil government was re-established, the temple had been restored and was in full operation, the people were resettled in their homeland, and the covenant with Yahweh was renewed once more. Irving Jensen identifies the grace of God in his dealings with Israel at this time perfectly when he reminds us:

> There would have been no restoration for Israel were it not for the grace of God. The restoration was surely not deserved. And before there was even a captivity, the restoration was scheduled on a prophetic timetable by a gracious God who, in the forthcoming captivity period, would be calling out of the communities of Jewish exiles in Babylon a remnant of believers whom He could bring back to the promised land. With these He would perpetuate His covenanted blessings for the generations to come.[23]

Summary

The lessons of this study of Old Testament examples are rich and plentiful. Through the examples we have considered runs one persistent common thread: disobedience to the Lord inevitably brings about defeat and ultimately exile. The converse is, however, equally true: "If you remain in me and my words remain in you, ask whatever you wish, and it will be given to you" (John 15:7). The key to an effective spiritual walk now, as in the days of the kings and prophets of Israel, is to abide in him and to allow his grace to work in us and through us. Rebellion is always possible because of man's free will; restoration is always attainable because of God's grace. In the sagacious words of Bernard of Clairvaux (AD 1090–1153): "Remove free will and there will be nothing to be saved; remove grace and there is left no means of saving. The work of salvation cannot be accomplished without the co-operation of the two."[24]

FREE TO BE GOVERNED

Those who claim that an act only becomes unlawful *ipso facto* it being a whim of God's choosing, and that he might just as easily have made sedition an asset and integrity an offense, fail to see the correlation between the law of God and the moral nature of God. The outworking of God's volition cannot be divorced from that which prompts it: i.e., his moral

---

23. Jensen, *Survey of the Old Testament*, 219.
24. Bernard of Clairvaux, *De Gratia et Libero Arbitrio*.

perfection. It is for this reason that the law of God as a system of regulative principles must still be perceived as determining the conduct of God's covenant people: to conform to Christ-like behavior (Rom 12:2; 1 Cor 15:49) and to express the restored image of God in man (2 Cor 3:18).

The Law Originated with God

The law is essentially and necessarily the corpus of requirements provoked by God's moral nature, which is perfect. It follows then that the law is beyond being made perfect, in and of itself. Christ's fulfillment of the law changed the law's function and our relationship toward it. In the words of Robert Lewis Dabney, Christ also "freed [the] law from the corrupt glosses of tradition and . . . showed the true extent of its application."[25]

It is by the gospel that we are discharged from the law (Rom 7:6); we are now dead to that which held us captive (Gal 2:19). Does this mean that the gospel of God's grace in Christ Jesus, which is by faith, has put an end to the law? "By no means," argues Paul. "On the contrary, we uphold the law" (Rom 3:31). The law, being inherently good, had become agreeable to the inner man (7:16–25), because it was no longer a source of external accusation. Thomas McComiskey simplifies the situation thus: "The Old Testament law should be a delight to the Christian, for he has been freed from its condemning power. Its institutions contain promise of the greater institutions that have been realised in Christ. Its precepts continue to provide wisdom and strength."[26]

The English word we use to designate one who by conviction has no regard for the law in or upon a believer's life is "antinomian." Perhaps significantly, the corresponding Greek word employed in the New Testament is *anomos*, which is variously rendered in English Bibles as "lawless," "unlawful," "wicked," or "one without law." In each case, the context suggests not merely the commission of an unlawful act, but that one does so with a calculated disregard for the revealed will of God. Antinomian is a term first coined by Martin Luther, and the state to which it relates has subsequently been the subject of much theological debate and derision. Martyn Lloyd-Jones described it as "one of the most blinding curses that has ever afflicted the life of the Church."[27] The

---

25. Dabney, *Systematic Theology*, 357.
26. McComiskey, *Covenants of Promise*, 224.
27. Lloyd-Jones, *The Law*, 156.

essence of antinomianism is the contention that the believer's status is such that he is now under no lawful obligation. Not only is such an attitude anathema to Scripture in general, it is specifically at odds with the apostle Paul's counsel to the similarly minded Christians at Corinth, to whom he declares unequivocally: "I am not free from God's law, but am under Christ's law" (1 Cor 9:21).

It must be observed that behaving righteously has little to do with living according to a moral standard. There are many in our day who could never contemplate being knowingly involved in a criminal activity. Others would only consider committing an illegal act if, in their opinion, the law of the land that made it so was unjust. Even the moral compasses of some Christians are conditioned by the socio-cultural standards of their communities. But the criterion by which something may properly be regarded as righteous or otherwise is not the laws of man, nor even man's interpretation of God's law, but God's law *per se*.

The episodes in which Jesus allegedly countermanded the law of Moses are worthy of closer inspection, for they are critical to our understanding of the truth or falsity of these claims. There are five such incidents, relating specifically to divorce, the taking of oaths, acts of revenge, benevolence (Matt 5:21–48), and the eating of "unclean" meats (Mark 7:19). To my mind, the four that are contained within the Sermon on the Mount provide a key to our understanding of all five. In each case, Jesus introduces his exposition with the words: "You have heard it said . . . but I say unto you . . . " I do not believe that Jesus was dismissing the Mosaic law in its entirety, nor indeed these specific components of it, but rather the way in which they had been interpreted by the religious leaders of his day.

Spirit and law are not antithetical propositions, as some suggest. Indeed, it might even be said that, having fulfilled the law of God by the spirit of God, Jesus restored and revealed the spirit of the law of God. The argument that "the letter kills, but the spirit gives life" (2 Cor 3:6) might, therefore, be understood not as suggesting that there is a stark contrast between the Spirit and the law, but that the spirit of the law is opposed to the letter of the law. The letter of the law brings death because it is the harbinger of condemnation; the spirit of the law ushers in life because it heralds Jesus' mastery over the law's penal demands (Rom 8:1).

By the same reasoning, neither is it possible to do certain things in the Spirit and others in the flesh. A word of caution here, however, for

Covenant Law, Covenant Grace 107

I am not advocating the erroneous doctrine of sinless perfection: it is still possible—even likely—that we will continue to commit sinful acts. But to be "in the flesh" is synonymous (for the purposes of this context) with being "under the law" once more. While there are those who have tried to behave as if it were possible to do certain things in the Spirit and others in the flesh (e.g., the Galatian believers), they have rightly earned apostolic rebuke for their troubles, as to do so is at variance with our position "in Christ." Paul's use of past and present continuous tense when contrasting the two is particularly powerful: "This is what we were and what we did then. But now . . ." (see Rom 7:5–6). What we are and what we were are poles apart.

Because the gospel of grace effectively discharges us from the law's demands by putting us to death in Christ, if we subsequently seek to re-apply ourselves as slaves to the law we thereby annul the implementation of the gospel's full range of benefits to us, by falling away from grace (Gal 5:4). Improved performance will not deal with guilt; only repentance can do that. Self-condemnation can never be removed by a "must-do-better-next-time" mentality; it requires an acknowledgment that "there is now no condemnation for those who are in Christ Jesus" (Rom 8:1). This would be adequate if we were to take it at face value, but Paul goes on to remind us that "through Christ Jesus, the law of the Spirit of life set [us] free from the law of sin and death" (v. 2). We are not free to indulge in lawlessness; we are released from the curse of the law so that "the righteous requirements of the law might be fully met in us, who do not live according to the sinful nature but according to the Spirit" (vv. 3–4).

This is why grace is supreme over law: because it has the capacity to effect a lifestyle that is fully consistent with the prompting of the Holy Spirit, instead of one that craves the desires of the flesh. As mentioned earlier, Paul's counsel to the believers at Philippi—that they should "work out [their] own salvation" (Phil 2:12)—was not a recommendation that they should seek to attain a reunion with God on the basis of good works. In the soteriological context, good works are utterly worthless. Not even our most noble attempts are regarded any more highly than as grubby garments (Isa 64:6). Rather, Paul's proposal was that we convey our gratitude to God for his gift to us by producing fruit that will endure, because it is the result of a spirit-filled life (see Gal 5:22–23). We rejoice, therefore, that we are both "dead to sin" and, by the grace of God, alive to him.

Christ's public ministry was essentially one whereby he wrought liberty from the law, from sin, and from death. This he encapsulated in the personal declaration in the temple that his ministry had begun, immediately following the episode of temptation in the wilderness by Satan: "The Spirit of the Lord is on me because he has anointed me . . . to proclaim freedom for the prisoners . . . [and] to proclaim the year of the Lord's favor" (Luke 4:18; cf. Isa 61:1). It seems clear from the pages of the New Testament, however, that such emancipation is not to be equated with license or offered as an excuse for abrogation of responsibility. Or, as the apostle reminds us, although believers may "not [be] under law" as a means of salvation (Rom 6:14), that is not to say that we are without law toward God (1 Cor 9:21). The assertion of individual rights that impinge upon the sensitivities of others is at odds with the law of Christ (Gal 6:2), the law of liberty (Jas 1:25; 2:12), and the law of love (John 13:34).

Slaves to Righteousness

Despite Paul's warnings, the history of the Christian church has been punctuated by periods when the gospel was equated with the law. Medieval theologians were particularly susceptible to the idea that the keeping of the law was a means of accessing the benefits of the gospel. Both Lutherans and those within Reformed orthodoxy distinguished between the law and the gospel, although they did not always succeed in maintaining an adequate balance in the light of Scripture's revelation. Those who emphasized the liberating effect of the gospel tended toward antinomianism, while a more zealous pursuit of moral rectitude attracted the charge of legalism. The seventeenth-century Puritan preacher, Samuel Bolton, asserted that "[t]he law sends us to the gospel that we may be justified; and the gospel sends us to the law again to inquire what is our duty as those who are justified."[28] The couplet is so pithy that one almost hopes it is true for its own sake. And it is, as far as it goes, but it requires further qualification.

The apostle Paul also encountered this imbalance both in Corinth and Galatia. While the Corinthians had acknowledged their freedom from sin but refused to take upon themselves the yoke of righteousness, the Galatians had been captivated by sin for so long that they felt uncomfortable with the freedom that was rightfully theirs, and so they opted

---

28. Bolton, *True Bounds of Christian Freedom*, 71.

to become willingly enslaved to the law once more. Whereas Paul had to warn the latter not to allow themselves to become "burdened again by a yoke of slavery" (Gal 5:1), his counsel to the former was that liberty should not be confused with license. He cautioned them against abusing their freedom such that its expression was unbefitting God's covenant people, specifically in relation to sexual immorality (1 Cor 5; 6:12–20), self-indulgent insensitivity toward others (7:9–13), and gratuitous behavior in God's presence (11:17–22).

The apostle is not contradicting himself here. Any apparent tension is perfectly resolved by Paul's balanced declaration in his letter to the Romans: We have not been "set free from sin" and left to our own devices, but have become "slaves to righteousness" (Rom 6:18). In other words, having been released from the penal demands of the law, those who have embraced the new covenant are now free to be governed.

Paul goes on to declare that the law was not powerful; it was impotent in that it was inherently incapable of dealing satisfactorily with the sinful nature in man. Having initiated the task of rectifying the matter through his Son, God now expects that "the righteous requirements of the law be fully met in us, who do not live according to the sinful nature, but according to the Spirit" (Rom 8:3–4). We are free to be governed aright because sin is no longer our master. However, the standard by which we now live is still law; it is Christ's law (1 Cor 9:21), the keeping of which is both initiated and maintained by love. George Eldon Ladd puts it this way: "Christ has brought the law as a way of righteousness and as a ceremonial code to its end; but the law as the expression of the will of God is permanent; and the man indwelt by the Holy Spirit and thus energised by love is enabled to fulfil the law as men under the law never could."[29]

With respect to this issue, Martyn Lloyd-Jones makes a valid point about certain aspects of Paul's letter to the Romans. For example, when Paul affirms to the Roman believers that they had "been set free from sin . . . and become slaves to righteousness" (Rom 6:18), he was not encouraging them to behave in a certain way contrary to their status, but reminding them of the fact of their position in Christ.[30] Their freedom consisted in the fact that they had effectively transferred their allegiance from one master to another. In this context, liberty is not to be equated

---

29. Ladd, *Theology of the New Testament*, 510.
30. Lloyd-Jones, *The New Man*, 222.

with idleness, but with the opportunity to render obedience to a master for whom the rewards of obedience are not restricted by the impotent parameters of the old covenant. Moreover, the apostle's words were not addressed to the council at Jerusalem or to a first-century leaders' conference, but to ordinary believers. Thus, if his statement is true, then it is true for all Christians and in every age. And if we consider the logical implications of this declaration, then the converse is equally valid: if any individual can legitimately claim that he or she has not been freed from sin *and* become a slave to righteousness, then that person must seriously question whether he/she is a Christian according to the biblical presentation.

We have already established that it is by faith in Jesus Christ that unrighteous man receives God's righteousness in exchange for his sin. This imputed probity finds expression through intrinsically righteous acts, which conform to God's law as written on our hearts by the Holy Spirit. Although the basic meaning of sanctification is "being set apart for a specific task," we have in mind here the process by which the Spirit of God transforms the life of the believer to mirror the pattern set by Jesus. Indeed, it is the power of his risen life that is reproduced in the Christian as he or she grows in grace. Whereas justification is essentially a critical, once-for-all experience, sanctification is progressive, culminating in our final destiny that "we shall be like [Jesus], for we shall see him as he is" (1 John 3:2). The effects of such a radical change in the lives of ordinary people can have a positive influence even on a global scale.

Although Christians are not immune from the effects of social decadence, rebellion, and disarray, we are free from the slavery that such evil promotes. As the "salt of the earth" (Matt 5:13), the function of the church has always been essentially two-fold: to preserve the good and to purify the bad. While it must be acknowledged that we may anticipate only comparatively limited success, it becomes equally evident from Scripture that the world has yet to benefit from the full impact of a committed company of believers on the earth, whose influence in projects that foster godly standards—whether it be in the home, education, legal system, business enterprise, or political arena—can be quite substantial.

Observing the Law of Christ

The actual phrase "the law of Christ" occurs only twice in the New Testament (1 Cor 9:21 and Gal 6:2), though it is implied numerous times elsewhere (e.g., John 13:34; Jas 2:18). Although Scripture provides no definition of the phrase, it is employed in the context of love on both occasions. It does not, however, denote love as a merely abstract emotion. Rather, love finds expression through an individual's active caring for others. Paul was not slow to proclaim the freedom that he enjoyed in Christ and to encourage others to pursue and exercise that same freedom. Nor did he ever see fit to divorce the precept of Christ's command to love from the personal example Christ set in life. Indeed, Paul's perception of Christian freedom was not a freedom from obligation, but the freedom to serve others. The same idea is conveyed in the following paradoxical couplet, originally addressed in a letter to Pope Leo X in 1520:

> A Christian man is the most free lord of all, subject to none;
> A Christian man is the most dutiful servant of all, subject to everyone.[31]

Contrary to the apparent theology of some triumphalistic movements with which I am acquainted, Christianity is not a burden-free experience. Moreover, Scripture offers us no suggestion that we may expect it to be so. Far from it. Jesus actually went out of his way to dispel the prospect in no uncertain terms. "In the world," he told his disciples, "you will have trouble" (John 16:33a). Not "it's a distinct possibility and I want to prepare you, just in case." Difficulty and turbulence are certainties for believers and, if we are to avoid unnecessary heartache, we would do well to incorporate those words into our vocabulary at the earliest opportunity. If any Christian manages to avoid trouble, he or she is the exception that proves the rule. Either that or the expression of their faith is perhaps so flimsy that the enemy of their souls does not consider them to be real threats. But Jesus did not leave those early followers to wallow in despondency. "Take heart!" he went on; "I have overcome the world" (v. 33b). How did he overcome the world? Through love.

We, too, are called to overcome it in the same way. But we are also expected to enable others to overcome it by lovingly helping them to bear their burdens. Of course, first century burdens and those of the twenty-first century are likely to be very different. But the remedy is essentially the same. This may involve offering practical help in relieving financial complications, emotional distress, health problems, or spiritual deficiencies. The list is potentially endless; the treatment can be found in just one word—love. This is the law of Christ.

---

31. Martin Luther (1483–1546).

We have already identified Jesus' summary of the old covenant. When asked "Which is the greatest commandment?" he advised his disciples to "love the Lord your God with all your heart, and with all your soul, and with all your mind" and "love your neighbor as yourself" (Matt 22:37, 39). When he initiated the new covenant, it seems that he presumed the first part, as he knew intimately those he was addressing (although it is perhaps significant that he waited until Judas had left the room). It appears, however, that they required further clarification. It was not enough to tell them to love one another without giving them some point of reference. And he did: himself. "As I have loved you, so must you love one another" (John 13:34b).

How had Jesus loved them? Tenderly, affectionately, graciously, with discipline when required, and with increasingly measured responsibility where appropriate. But above all else, he had loved them with a servant disposition, which meant carrying their burdens. The law of Christ, then, is expressed in its only commandment, which is what Paul had in mind as he writes to the believers in Galatia (Gal 6:2). When the apostle speaks here of Christians carrying one another's burdens, the word he employs is *baros*, which literally means a weight or something that presses physically. When used metaphorically, it signifies something that places a demand on one's wherewithal.[32]

Moreover, it may be inferred, from the verse that follows, that we may all need to draw from the pool of such a resource at one time or another. Those who believe themselves to be exempt from the need for such mutual support are, according to the apostle, deceiving themselves (Gal 6:3). A similar sentiment is echoed elsewhere. Having identified several examples from Israel's illustrious history, when arrogance had preceded—if not precipitated—embarrassment, Paul warned the Corinthians: "So, if you think you are standing firm, be careful that you don't fall!" (1 Cor 10:12).

Furthermore, this expression of love is not to be restricted to fellow members of the new covenant. Toward the end of his Galatian epistle, Paul counsels his readers that "as we have opportunity, let us do good to all people, especially those who belong to the household of faith/family of believers" (Gal 6:10). The key word here is "especially"; it is not "exclusively." Brothers and sisters in Christ should remain a priority for the focus of our attention, but out of the overflow of grace that is chan-

---

32. See Vine, *Expository Dictionary*, 149.

neled through us, others too should become recipients of our service and blessing. Walter Hansen puts it into this perspective:

> The law of Christ is the love commandment fulfilled, confirmed and heightened in the life, death and resurrection of Christ. He loved sinners and gave himself for them; on the cross he bore the terrible burden of the law's curse against them; he set them free from the burden of the yoke of slavery under the law. Hence all who are united with Christ and are led by the Spirit will also fulfil the high standard of love established by the life, death and resurrection of Christ: like him, they will love sinners and carry their burdens. Serving one another in love in this way expresses Christ's love and so fulfils Christ's law.[33]

In many ways—and certainly in this context—the good of man and the glory of God are not so far removed from one another as we might otherwise imagine (see 1 Cor 10:23–33). Thus, because upholding the law of God can be regarded as a means of honoring its author, and because the law of Christ operates on the principle of love, then love and law cannot be mutually exclusive as some have presented them to be. In terms of kingdom rule, love may be perceived as the key that holds all other kingdom principles together. Generally, the law is fulfilled by love; more specifically, each of the law's commandments is upheld by an expression of love.

So, Paul's "law of love" (Gal 5:13) and "law of Christ" (6:2), and James' "law of liberty" (Jas 1:25; 2:12) are essentially and necessarily one and the same. The law is the governing principle of selfless and sacrificial concern for others, offered to the glory of God in Christ Jesus by the operation of the Holy Spirit. Jim Packer writes: "This life of love is the response of gratitude which the liberating gospel both requires and evokes. Christian liberty is precisely freedom for love and service to God and man, and it is therefore abused when it is made an excuse for unloving license or irresponsible inconsiderateness."[34]

We must be careful, however, that our understanding of the concept of love and its legitimate expression is governed by the Holy Spirit and not by the fleeting spirit of the age. For example, current secondary school curriculum for Religious Studies in the UK teaches that Christian morality is determined by the Bible, the church (that is, the opinions of church leaders), the individual's conscience, prayer, and situation eth-

---

33. Hansen, *Galatians*, 189.
34. J.I. Packer, "Liberty," *New Bible Dictionary*, 696.

ics. Although no particular order of pre-eminence is prescribed, there is an overwhelming emphasis in the material on Joseph Fletcher's premise that nothing is intrinsically evil if its application can produce the best possible outcome. For example, euthanasia is not necessarily murder if it can be shown to be the most loving thing to do in that particular situation. In such cases, the parameters of love are not the revealed will of God, but an anthropology anachronistically applied to what are essentially biblical matters.

Morality is not intuitive but spiritually discerned; quite simply, this is because the standards are not of our own making: they are God's. Each situation is unique, and not all are explicitly treated by the writers of Scripture. Moral decisions do require prayerful consideration and timely deliberation. What we can be absolutely sure of, however, is that God never suspends one spiritual principle of his kingdom in order to more highly elevate another.

It is perhaps unsurprising that situation ethics came to prominence in the early 1960s, at a time when certain, so-called Christian movements were particularly expressive in the area of "free" love. Situation ethics was effectively the governing maxim behind the "if it feels good, do it" mantra. What came of it was a perception of "human rights" that ultimately means I should be free to express myself as I choose, however that might impinge upon the "rights" of others.

Unlike the law of Moses, the law of Christ is not initiated, regulated, maintained, or upheld by observance of a written code. Its *modus operandi* is governed by the principle of action, not passivity. Where the legal code ensnared and enslaved, the love of God in Christ sets us gloriously free. We are liberated to love, and yet I have come across Christians who take even this to be an externally binding directive. "I don't like that person," they say, "but I love him or her because Scripture demands that I must." Love that does not emanate from the overflow of Christ's love for us, transmitted by the Spirit of God, is not the love of Christ and, therefore, is incapable of fulfilling the law of Christ. It is true that the New Testament records instructions, commands, exhortations, warnings, and examples that we should either follow or recoil from, but these are given as guidelines for the righteous expression of the love that is now placed within us. In other words, they are not methods of attracting God's grace; rather they teach us how to respond to it now that it has arrived.

By way of his atoning sacrifice on the cross, Christ has re-established the basic foundation of God's kingdom rule in society, to be administered through the church in every age of its history. Where believers live their lives in obedience to the principles of God's authority, they can—and should—be an influence for good. Godly structures in the family, community, government, and in artistic expression can again become areas where righteousness reigns as Christians begin to display a lifestyle that is regulated by Christ's rule—the law of love. The law enslaved because it produced in us a dilemma: It told us what we must do, but it also reminded us of our absolute impotence—it demanded the impossible. The law of Christ sets us free because it empowers us to meet its requirements.

SUMMARY

In this chapter, we have looked at the biblical concepts of law and grace and discovered that they are perhaps not mutually exclusive, as some would have us believe. While acknowledging that Scripture uses the word "law" in a variety of ways, particularly in the New Testament, it must also be conceded that in reference to God's law as a declaration of his will, which derives from his intrinsic nature, the transformation of its effect upon a believer is in his or her relation to it. The imposition of the law under the terms and conditions of the old covenant was by virtue of God's gracious disposition. Similarly, the grace that is now ours in Christ does not negate our responsibility to uphold the law of God in Christ. Rather, it better equips us to do so.

The relationship between the law of God and the nature of God can be neither overlooked nor underestimated. The law is an expression of God's will for those who are appointed to live in accordance with the fact that they were created in his image. The fulfillment of the old covenant(s) by the new covenant has not eroded that fact. In general terms, the law promotes civic righteousness for all mankind; more specifically, it directs Christians in holy living.

In one sense, the grace of God is not dependent upon anything or anyone outside of God for its existence. The reality of God's grace does not require our acceptance of it to become or remain valid. It is God's favor placed at the disposal of those who do not deserve it. If they did, it would not be grace. However, for that grace to become effective in producing the fruit that God intends, it must be applied through faith (see Rom 4:16). This has always been true of God's covenant people. The significant difference for those of us under the new covenant dispensation is that this grace is extended toward a people whose faith—itself a gift from God—has been appropriated, by faith, unto the forgiving of sin, release from the penal aspects of the law's demands, and the capacity to live by faith and in accordance with God's righteous requirements.

The law is an impotent husband; it has no power to produce life. What it does first of all is lead us to Christ by precipitating a crisis within us that requires a Savior—it makes us conscious of sin. Then, having been released from its penal demands by offering our bodies as living sacrifices to God and receiving his life-imparting Holy Spirit, the law provides a framework by which we voluntarily become slaves of righteousness. Once discharged from the law, it is no longer perceived as the basis for our relationship with God (not that it ever was, in reality). The very heart of the gospel of God's grace is that we "reign in life" (Rom 5:17). We achieve this not by doing anything, but quite simply by receiving the abundance of that grace and the free gift of righteousness. It truly is *God's Riches at Christ's Expense*.

4

The Covenant Meal

Of all the issues facing denominational Christendom, perhaps none is more in need of a biblical approach than that of the covenant meal. Even the varied terminology employed to advertise it on the ecclesiastical calendar suggests that in relation to arguably no other subject is the body of Christ's organic unity more threatened. However, whether we refer to it as "Eucharist," "holy communion," "the Lord's Supper," or simply "the breaking of bread," neither our traditions nor our democratically formulated constitutions should be relied upon as finally authoritative. As with all things, we must search the Scriptures for the basis of our conviction, which will in turn determine our rightful practice.

Some may consider that the covenant meal is relatively unimportant in the context of this study—that it does not warrant significant attention here. After all, they might argue, comparatively few verses of Scripture are devoted to the matter: is it really that important? In response, I would argue that the urgency is to be inferred not from the quantity of verses, but from their content and context. Certainly, in terms of its sacramental value, the covenant meal seems to conform to all of the commonly acknowledged criteria:

- It was appointed by Christ personally;
- It is symbolized by at least one visible sign or emblem; and
- It is directly associated with an inward grace.

If these are the criteria, then only two ordinances exist in Scripture: baptism and the Lord's Supper. Whereas the former marks initiation into the covenant body, the latter acknowledges identification with both the covenant head and other covenant members. Baptism is therefore a once-for-all rite, whereas partaking of the covenant meal is to be repeated often.

In this chapter, I propose to consider the roots of the covenant meal in Old Testament Jewish history, its sacramental origins and the words that accompanied that initiation, our duties as legitimate partakers of the meal, and the way that responsible involvement in the reality of what the meal symbolizes will release God's blessing to us and through us. It is my conviction that a biblically balanced understanding of the Lord's Supper is currently lacking in far too many ecclesiastical calendars and orders of service. These are solemn issues that will not be resolved with a frivolous approach, but neither are they matters that require an attitude so sober that they rob us of our enjoyment of them.

ROOTED IN THE PASSOVER

It is not without significance that the institution of the Lord's Supper took place within the context of a meal celebrating God's covenant recognition of his people Israel—i.e., the Passover. This was a memorial observance by the Jewish people of their deliverance from bondage in Egypt and, thus, a permanent reminder of their covenant membership. Similarly, the Lord's Supper is essentially for us a remembrance of our being beneficiaries of the new covenant, by virtue of our union with Christ in his sacrificial death. The other sacrament, baptism, is an identification with his burial and resurrection. Perhaps, then, it would be more appropriate for new believers to experience their first communion *prior* to being baptized.

The Occasion of the First Passover

The association between covenant and meals was common to the Hebrew culture of the period. Indeed, the centerpiece of many of Israel's religious festivals was the sharing of food and drink. To claim that they were both religious and social occasions, however, would be to miss part of the point. Old Testament Judaism did not perceive its commitment to ecclesiastical duties in anything other than a social framework. The converse is equally true. The sense of togetherness that bound the people Israel was in no small part due to their common covenant heritage.

The Jewish calendar was punctuated by a number of annual festivals, primary among them the Passover Feast, the Feast of Weeks, and the Feast of Tabernacles. Passover celebrated the deliverance of Israel from bondage in Egypt and, thus, the inauguration of nationhood. The Feast of Weeks was the opportunity for all Israel to express gratitude to God for his abundant provision. The Feast of Tabernacles served as a reminder of the people's desert wanderings prior to their assuming their inheritance in Canaan. At the time of Jesus' birth, these three festivals were still being held at Jerusalem, and all male Jews were required to make the thrice-annual pilgrimage there in order to honor their covenant obligations. For the Christian believer, these feasts and festivals are fulfilled—i.e., filled out to their fullest potential—by the Lord's Supper, Pentecost (that is, Spirit baptism), and water baptism respectively, though this order is not traditionally upheld.

The English word "passover" translates the Hebrew verb *pesach*, meaning "to spare in the midst of judgment." The Passover commemorates God's instructions to Israel in Egypt as to how the people Israel would be spared from the judgment of the final plague. The head of each household was to take a year-old lamb that was without defect, slay it according to the sacrificial rite, and smear its blood around the doorposts and lintels of the house. Thus, as God prepared to exercise judgment on Egypt, he assured his covenant people: "When I see the blood, I will pass over you" (Exod 12:13).

In terms of Israel's history, as recorded in the pages of the Old Testament, it would not be an overstatement to claim this night as its turning point. Indeed, it heralded the dawn of a new era for God's people, who were about to be miraculously delivered from the might of their oppressor by the almighty hand of their Redeemer (see Exod 6:6–7). Thereafter, the annual celebration served as a perpetual reminder of their experience (12:14). The significance of that first Passover is not, however, limited to the national history of natural Israel. As Irving Jensen observes, "[t]he Passover chapter is also a key chapter of the whole Bible. As you read it, look for what is taught about divine holiness, election and grace, and man's sin and salvation. Why did God institute blood sacrifice as an atonement ritual? In answering this, relate blood to life (cf. Heb 9:22)."[1]

It is also worth mentioning that, on the two instances during Judah's tumultuous history when the covenant was reaffirmed and the people's responsibilities were acknowledged once more, one of the first things to

---

1. Jensen, *Survey of the Old Testament*, 91.

be restored on each occasion was the celebration of the Passover, first under King Hezekiah (2 Chr 30) and later under King Josiah (2 Chr 35). In the context of a study like this, it is all too easy to isolate the first Passover from its original setting. It took place, of course, in the midst of the last of ten plagues visited upon Egypt for its disgraceful treatment of God's covenant people, Israel. The previous nine plagues had all been leading to this. None of them had carried any assurance of, nor was it anticipated that they would, in themselves, result in Israel's release from slavery. The announcement of the coming Passover, however, did convey that guarantee and hope, without, moreover, the external involvement of Moses or Aaron. They had been central to the proclamation and fulfillment of the first nine plagues, albeit as conduits in the hand of almighty God. Now, they were to be bystanders like the rest; God alone would be seen to bring about Israel's deliverance. All that had gone before was preparation for this one event; furthermore, the Passover itself was to mark a new beginning for the people of God. So, too, did the initiation of the new covenant by Christ at his final Supper.

The Setting of the Last Supper

By the time of the New Testament, the commemoration of the Passover comprised two parts: the solemn ritual and the satisfying meal. Each part followed a regular pattern:

The solemn ritual

- The cup of consecration is passed around;
- The head of the family performs a ceremonial hand washing, as it is he who presides over the rest of the evening's events;
- Parsley is dipped in salt water and eaten by everyone. The herb represents the hyssop used to smear blood on the doorposts at the first Passover; the salt solution symbolizes the tears of their forbears;
- The first breaking of unleavened bread (that is, the bread of affliction) takes place;
- In response to the question "What does this ceremony mean to you?" (see Exod 12:26), the one presiding over

the meal recounts Israel's history, from Abraham to the circumstances of the first Passover;
- All sing Psalms 113 and 114;
- The cup of proclamation is passed around;
- Everyone washes their hands and gives thanks;
- A sop dipped in a paste of fruit and nuts, called the *charosheth*, is eaten. The paste represents the clay used by the Israelite slaves to make bricks in Egypt. The *charosheth* was often infused with cinnamon sticks, recalling the straw running through the bricks.

The satisfying meal
- The mood relaxes as the gathered group feasts on the roast lamb meal;
- Hands are washed and any bread left over from the ritual part of the meal is finished off;
- A prayer of thanksgiving is offered for the provision of the food;
- The cup of thanksgiving is passed around;
- Psalms 115–118 and Psalm 136 are sung;
- The final cup is passed around;
- Final prayers and praises of thanksgiving are offered.

This was the setting in which the meal of the new covenant, the Lord's Supper, was inaugurated. From this information, it is not difficult to see why the Lord's Supper also became known as the Eucharist, as the Greek noun *eucharistia* literally means "gratitude" or "thanksgiving." Solemn rites demand sober reflection, but true reverence is not enhanced by the absence of thanksgiving and joy.

In the outline above, note that after the meal proper, any uneaten Passover bread was finished off by those not too full to do so. It was apparently at this juncture in the Passover meal that Jesus seized the initiative on the night of the Last Supper. In some way, the fact that this part of the evening had been hitherto meaningless (in the sense that it lacked any of the symbolism of the other features) made his choice of it all the more meaningful. The ceremony had been observed per the tradition, but it had become a ritual devoid of either celebration or commemoration. Now Jesus imposed the covenant ideal in the midst of the social occasion. It is not clear whether he was advocating that the ceremonial aspect be dispensed with thenceforth. It seems more likely that he was effectively saying that whenever future generations would come to this part of the proceedings, the remnant of the bread would represent the remembrance of his broken body. That is, until he took the cup of thanksgiving and gave it an altogether new meaning as well.

Which of Jesus' actions at that Passover meal were premeditated and which spontaneous can only ever be the subject of conjecture. What is clear, however, is the fact that earlier in the day he had implied that what was taking place was all part of the concluding stage of the redemptive plan of the Father (Matt 26:18a). Thus, Christ was not only working to a timetable fixed by God, but—by now, at least—he was also consciously aware of that fact. Not only was his time near in a general sense; his "appointed time" was drawing ever closer as well.

Just as the new covenant fulfilled the old insofar as the old had effectively served its purpose, so too the covenant meal (that is, the Lord's Supper) fulfilled the Passover. In just a few short hours, the symbolism of the Passover meal would be rendered obsolete: the annual slaying of the sacrificial lamb would be superseded by the shed blood of God's Christ on Calvary. In truth, Christ was the focal point of both meals. The Passover pointed forward to him; the Lord's Supper reflects him. In his treatment of John Owen's theology of the covenant meal, Jon Payne concludes:

> Circumcision and the Passover point to the Person and work of Christ as do baptism and the Lord's Supper. They are all signs and seals of the covenant of grace. The former were types and shadows, symbols and signs of the grace of God yet to be fulfilled in Christ. The latter are, according to Owen, signs and seals of the grace of God already fulfilled in Christ. All sacraments, whether they are in the old covenant or the new, ultimately signify that life and salvation are found in God's promises, which are "yea and amen" in Christ Jesus.[2]

We have already looked at the idea of penal substitution in some detail. Nowhere in Scripture is it more graphically symbolized than in the account of this Passover and the institution of the Lord's Supper. The

2. Payne, *John Owen*, 36.

original sacrifice signified that the animal offered had taken the place of the firstborn son of every Israelite household in Egypt; the ultimate sacrifice was to be the Lamb of God, who would die in the stead of fallen humanity, "the righteous for the unrighteous" (1 Pet 3:18). Even the unleavened bread was both symbolic and typical. It symbolized the haste in which the Israelites left Egypt. But it also typified the absolute lack of corruption in the One who, many centuries later, would claim to be the bread of life (John 6:35), influenced by nothing except the fervent desire to do his Father's will and to be about his Father's business.

Note also the apostle Paul's counsel to the believers at Corinth. He does not instruct them to replace the old yeast with a new leaven that is less susceptible to corruption and decay, but to "keep the Festival . . . with bread made without yeast [that is] the bread of sincerity and truth" (1 Cor 5:8).

The Biblical Presentation of the Lord's Supper

Scripture includes four detailed accounts of the Lord's Supper, one in each of the three synoptic gospels and the fourth in the apostle Paul's first letter to the believers at Corinth. Although only Matthew's was eyewitness testimony of the events described, the sources for the other accounts are sufficiently credible as to suggest that they should be accepted without question. A direct relationship between Christ's blood and the new covenant is to be inferred from all four. It has already been observed that integral to the Hebrew word *berith* is the idea of "cutting" a covenant, and that a proper definition of covenant, according to the biblical evidence, is "an agreement administered by blood."[3]

Atonement requires sacrifice, whether by shadow or substance, type or fulfillment. Man has always been incapable of rendering a sacrifice for himself that is sufficient unto the remission of sins, because no man has been personally beyond sin's clutches. Only a substitute could legitimately effect the conditions required for atonement to be made, once for all, and thereby usher in the new covenant. That substitute proved to be the man, Christ Jesus. The hymn-writer put it this way:

> According to Thy gracious word, in meek humility,
> This will I do, my dying Lord: I will remember Thee.
> Thy body, broken for my sake, my bread from heav'n shall be;

---

3. Robertson, *Christ of the Covenants*, 11.

> The testamental cup I take, and thus remember Thee.
> When to the cross I turn my eyes, and rest on Calvary,
> O Lamb of God, my sacrifice, I must remember Thee—
> Remember Thee and all Thy pains, and all Thy love to me;
> Yea while a breath, a pulse remains, will I remember Thee.
> And when these failing lips grow dumb, and mind and mem'ry flee,
> When Thou shalt in Thy kingdom come, Jesus, remember me![4]

Although the synoptic accounts of the Lord's Supper vary in minor details, they simply reflect the confusion of the situation. These variations do not justify the charge that the accounts contradict one another. Luke, in particular, is known for his precision in detail, although he is not quite so pedantic about presenting material chronologically. Thus, the sequence of events in his account differs from others. Luke's order calls for material to be arranged according to type rather than in relation to time.

Some continue to question the setting of the Lord's Supper within the context of the Passover meal, because of the day or date on which it is said to have taken place, and also because of some alleged textual differences between the synoptic gospels and the Johannine account (see John 13). A number of solutions have been proposed with respect to these differences. Some say it might have been a meal anticipating the coming Passover, and thus the meal commandeered some of its elements. Others claim that it was possible to be flexible with the observance of Passover, especially if there was the danger that its ceremony might spill over onto the Sabbath (in Hebrew culture of this period, days were reckoned to begin from the evening of what we, today, would identify as the preceding day).

It is not unreasonable to suggest that our English translations may have, in some measure, masked the truth; i.e., that the clause to which "before the Passover" relates speaks of Jesus knowing about the imminent arrival of his time to depart. The textual evidence is inconclusive. What cannot be denied, however, is the typological relationship between the most notable features of the original Passover event and the circumstances that surrounded it, and the new exodus of salvation to be found in God's true paschal Lamb.

John's omission of an account of the Lord's Supper has proved equally troublesome. Of course, this is not the only occasion where the synoptic and Johannine accounts differ; otherwise, the term "synoptics"

---

4. James Montgomery (1771–1854), *According to Thy Gracious Word*.

would either be unnecessary or would refer to all four gospel accounts. Again, there seems to be no finally irrefutable argument as to why there is no account in the fourth gospel; all we are left with is assumption and educated guesswork. At the risk of contravening the well-known maxim of Ludwig Wittgenstein, "Whereof one cannot speak, thereof one must be silent," my opinion on this matter relates to the date of writing of John's account compared to the others. I am not suggesting that the delay obscured his recollection, but simply that by the time of writing the other accounts were already in widespread circulation. If so, then it is quite conceivable that John thought there was no need to repeat information simply for the sake of presenting a unified message.

Equally arguably, it would not be illogical for Jesus to have celebrated the Passover with his disciples a day earlier than would have been the norm, knowing full well that his availability on the following day was by no means guaranteed. In cases of necessity, such flexibility was provided for within Old Testament guidelines (see Num 9:10–12). However, those who suggest that this provided Judas with evidence of an illegal feast to present to the chief priests seem to be engaging in eisegesis rather than exegesis. Robin Nixon offers the following comment: "There seems to be little doubt that the Synoptic Gospels present Jesus as eating a Passover meal. There is some difficulty in reconciling this with John, but it is possible that there may have been two different calendars in use, and it seems very unlikely that any of the Evangelists would not have accurate information about the dating of the last few days of Jesus' life or that he should feel free to alter it for supposedly 'theological' reasons."[5]

Taken together, then, the accounts of Jesus' final meal with his disciples before his betrayal underscore the following features:

- Jesus' substitutionary self-sacrifice is presented as the guarantee of a coming eschatological banquet (Luke);
- God's salvation is to be made accessible by virtue of Jesus' covenant sacrifice (Mark);
- The provision of forgiveness of sins is assured (Matthew);
- The founding of the church as the universal body of Christ is linked to incorporation into the new covenant (Paul); and
- The self-offering of the Son of God and the incarnation of the Logos are essentially synonymous terms of expression (John).

5. R. Nixon, "Matthew," *New Bible Commentary*, 847.

Summary

Of course, the similarities between Israel's experience of the Passover and that of believers under the new covenant do not begin and end with their respective covenant meals. God's miraculous deliverance of his people from bondage, whence they are guided toward the land of promise under his rule, describes perfectly both Israel's exodus and the believers' redemption from sin's slavery. For the people Israel, the lamb whose blood signaled their freedom from judgment became also the centerpiece of their final meal in Egypt; for Christians, the slain Lamb of God, whose shed blood purchased our atonement, now invites us to feed on him by faith. In the words of David Matthew: "The one Lamb provides both salvation and sustenance."[6]

REMEMBERING THE HEAD, REJOICING WITH THE BODY

The original setting for the Lord's Supper was that of a meal shared among friends: simply put, Jesus and his disciples sat around a table eating food and drinking wine. In biblical times, such fellowship indicated a mutual identification among diners. To socialize in this way effectively said, "I accept you and I acknowledge you." As an aside, this fact alone reveals something of why the religious leaders of Jesus' day were so hostile toward him, for he was unashamed to eat with lepers, tax collectors, the lame, the blind, the socially disenfranchised, the financially impoverished, and many others whom the Pharisees and Sadducees found abhorrent.

Looking Back and Looking Up

The Passover Feast celebrated by the Jewish nation was essentially, but not exclusively, a remembrance, an annual commemoration and reminder of Israel's deliverance from bondage in Egypt. What God had done for the people Israel in the past, however, had both present and future implications, for they were thence bound to him as a covenant people and he to them as a covenant-keeping God.

In the immediate post-Pentecost period of the church, there are many references to fellowship around the meal table, found in such phrases as "breaking of bread" (see Acts 2:46–48). Such occasions often appeared a part of a normal meal. Such was the expression of integrity

---

6. Matthew, *Covenant Meal*, 15.

and fellowship that the whole setting soon became known as the *agapē* meal or "love feast" (see Jude 12). The indications are that, at the beginning of the meal, in accordance with the pattern set at Jesus' Last Supper, there would be a conscious commemoration of Christ's sacrifice, in obedience to his inaugural command: "[Keep on] do[ing] this in remembrance of me" (Luke 22:19). This was clearly not meant to imply a continual reoffering of his sacrifice, rather a perpetual coming to him in faith to feast upon that which had been offered for sins, once and for all (Heb 7:27; 1 Pet 3:18).

We have seen that the Lord's Supper is an occasion for remembrance, for looking back to the source of our salvation. Paul's distinctive teaching on the subject—admittedly set against a backdrop of cavalier abuse—suggests that the covenant meal should in some way proclaim (Greek *katangellō*—"I preach") the Lord's death (1 Cor 11:26). All that is now ours as believers was determined in the Christ-event, central to which was the cross of Calvary, for which we are eternally grateful. However, Jesus' own words are particularly significant here: "Do this in remembrance of *me*" (Luke 22:19; 1 Cor 11:24–25). The Lord's Supper is not just an occasion in which we are reminded of his death. If it were only that, then it would be little loftier than a funeral tea. Howard Marshall illuminates us further:

> The New Testament does not appear to associate sorrow or mourning over the death of Jesus with the celebration of the Supper. [It] was not an occasion for mourning over his death, but rather for rejoicing in his presence and giving thanks for the benefits produced by his death. Whatever may have happened in a later period, the early church remembered at the Supper what the Lord's death had provided rather than grieved over the fact that he had to die.[7]

The Lord's Supper reminds us of Christ's final Passover week, culminating in what the bread and cup represent: his bruised and broken body and his shed blood. The details of the present and future implications are unique and incomparable, in that those who are "in Christ" are people of the new covenant, with God their covenant-keeping Father. For us, however, the Lord's Supper cannot be restricted to remembering Christ's death, without also rejoicing over his subsequent resurrection. It is both the basis of and the inspiration for our worship, as we shall see.

---

7. Marshall, *Last Supper and Lord's Supper*, 153.

We remember that he died and the reasons surrounding his death, but we cannot linger too long on his being dead, for the simple reason that he is now forever alive. Peter Forsyth puts it this way: "Let us get rid of the idea which has impoverished worship beyond measure, that the act is merely commemorative. No church can live on that. How can we have a mere memorial of one who is still alive, still our life, still present with us and still acting in us?"[8]

The redeemed community of God's new covenant people was barely sixty years old when the apostle Paul found himself in a situation where he felt obliged to give instruction on how the true church might be identified. He did so by giving a polarizing description that distinguished the church's members from those not members: It is we who "are the circumcision," he argued, "we who worship by the Spirit of God, who glory in Christ Jesus, and who put no confidence in the flesh" (Phil 3:3). Notice there is no mention of alignment to extra-biblical formulae, denominational constitutions, or attainment of a set pass mark in some apostolically approved, multiple-choice questionnaire. No: worship is the key. But what precisely do we mean by worship? Or, perhaps more to the point: do we all have the same thing in mind when we speak of worship?

There is no doubt that many of those used to an open style of worship would generally dismiss those with a more rigid time of hymn-singing as purveyors of dead works. Similarly, it is not uncommon for the "hymn-sandwich brigade" to trash their more Pentecostal-type brothers and sisters as no more than a bunch of arm-waving, happy-clappy, emotional-to-the-point-of-hysteria jumpers-up-and-down. The truth is that the kind of worship of which Scripture speaks is more about substance than style.

Moreover, if liturgy is to be associated with a set pattern—as it often is—then the so-called open and freer churches that I have frequented over the years have been arguably just as liturgical in their approach as their more traditional counterparts (e.g., praise/worship, prayer, hymn, notices, hymn, sermon, hymn/offering, benediction). I have likewise experienced the more overtly rigid style on a number of occasions when there has been a real sense of the presence of God. The key is undoubtedly heart attitude. But to worship in this way (that is, in the Spirit) does not mean that we commensurately disengage our brains, for elsewhere we are informed that this same Spirit is also the Spirit of wisdom and

---

8. Forsyth, *Church and the Sacraments*, 215.

understanding (Isa 11:2), which we are encouraged to pursue with all due diligence (Col 1:9; Jas 3:13).

As indicated earlier, the dirge-like ceremony of many Communion services is no doubt partly due to an overemphasis on remembering Christ's death and a failure to associate that with his life-giving resurrection. It may also be an overreaction to Paul's criticism of the Corinthian "party spirit." However, the apostolic rebuke was not earned because of any authentic zeal on the part of the Christians at Corinth, but because of impropriety, loutish behavior, and discrimination, all of which run counter to the essence of covenant being expressed in the meal.

The Lord's Supper is peculiarly eucharistic and is known by that title in many church settings. As we have seen, that title has biblical foundation. We give thanks as we partake of the elements (even though some appear to receive it as they would a Christmas gift that fails to excite them). Of course, we must give thanks for Jesus' death, which may well trigger tearful emotions. But we also give thanks to God for his Son's resurrection. It is surely appropriate to do so joyfully.

The original Passover would no doubt have been an immensely tense affair. On subsequent occasions when it was celebrated, it is difficult to imagine that the memory of the slaughtered lamb would have superseded the excitement of the exodus it preceded. For us, it is apposite that we consider the crisis of Calvary, but surely not in such a way as to inhibit our celebration of the empty tomb. The cup of thanksgiving is precisely that: the opportunity to give thanks and to drink thankfully. We both give thanks *for* the cup and *through* the cup. Or as David Matthew concludes: "[The cup of thanksgiving] is both the instrument and the accompaniment of our praise."[9]

Those who claim that belief, unbelief, or disbelief in the physical resurrection of Jesus is neither foundational, on the one hand, nor detrimental to one's Christian faith if it is not present, on the other, have not understood the significance with which it is portrayed in the New Testament. Indeed, Paul affirms that if Christ has not been raised from death, then our faith is futile and sin remains our master (1 Cor 15:12–17). Moreover, and as the apostle here implies, if the testimony of Scripture's contributors cannot be trusted on this point, then can we do other than question the reliability of their evidence elsewhere? It is morally incomprehensible to even consider the possibility that the church

---

9. Matthew, *Covenant Meal*, 112.

could be built upon such a delusion. It is also soteriologically reprehensible to ponder the implications of such a position, given the necessity of the resurrection to the atonement. As Leon Morris reminds us: "Salvation is not something that takes place apart from the resurrection."[10] James Denney puts it this way: "There can be no salvation from sin unless there is a living Saviour: this explains the emphasis laid by the apostle [Paul] on the resurrection. But the living One can be a Saviour only because he has died: this explains the emphasis laid on the cross. The Christian believes in a living Lord who died an atoning death, for no other could hold the faith of a soul under the doom of sin."[11] Or, as the apostle Paul reminded the Roman believers: "[Jesus] was delivered over to death for our sins and was raised to life for our justification" (Rom 4:25). The one is preparatory to—and in many ways incomplete without—the other; the latter cannot be achieved without the former. However, I am not entirely convinced that the idea of Christ's death being the paying of a debt and his resurrection being a receipt of that debt's payment is either particularly helpful or supported by anything other than fanciful notions.

It is not beyond the realm of plausibility that the word *dia* in this phrase (i.e., Rom 4:25) could be translated "because of," in which case the text might read: "He was delivered over to death [because of] our sins and was raised to life [because of] our justification." This would mean that our sin was the cause of his death, an idea which is generally accepted. But was his resurrection the cause of our justification or was he raised because we had been justified by his death and there was, therefore, no further reason for him to be held captive by it?

Commentators are divided on this, largely because it is assumed that the word *dia* must carry the same meaning in both parts of the couplet. It is not necessarily so. The most obvious meaning of the word in this phrase suggests that it does not and that, although Christ was crucified *because* of our sins, he was raised to life *in order to effect* our justification. What may be affirmed with more certainty is that there is surely no more conclusive evidence in Scripture for the doctrine of justification *sola fidei* (i.e., by faith alone) than is to be found here.

The resurrection of Christ is significant for a number of reasons, including these:

---

10. L. Morris, "Resurrection," *New Bible Dictionary*, 1023.
11. Denney, *Death of Christ*, 73.

- It demonstrates that his atoning sacrifice was judged to have been acceptable;
- It ensures our justification;
- It provides the basis for his perpetual mediation on our behalf;
- It paves the way for the coming of the Holy Spirit to sanctify us; and
- It guarantees the believer's personal resurrection and glorification.

Thus, salvation from sin is bought for us by the death of Christ, but its benefits are bestowed upon us by the living Christ. It is at the table of the Lord, therefore, that we are reminded most vividly of his resurrection—the fact that, although he was once dead, he is now alive forever. We do not eat the bread as part of a stale, moldy, maggot-ridden loaf, but as an expression of the life that is ours through "Christ in [us], the hope of glory" (Col 1:27). Similarly, the cup of thanksgiving is exactly that: "participation in the blood of Christ" (1 Cor 10:16), for which we give thanks. There is no room for the façade of religious sobriety around the table of the redeemed, nor indeed for the opposite extreme of contemptuous familiarity. It is essentially a place for rejoicing at the abundant provision of God's covenant grace toward us in Christ Jesus (see Rom 5:17).

John Stott is correct when he asserts that "[i]f the cross is not central to our religion, ours is not the religion of Jesus."[12] My point, however, is that any Christology that so emphasizes the cross of Calvary as to diminish the significance of the vacant sepulcher in a nearby garden is one that is not derived from Scripture's presentation of the facts. Jesus did speak of himself in terms of a sacrificial offering. But he who was condemned on the Friday would also be fully vindicated on the Sunday, demonstrating that his atonement had been found acceptable. The victory had indeed been attained at the cross; but it was endorsed during the period of Christ's burial and confirmed by his subsequent resurrection.

An exclusively resurrection gospel is, however, by the same token equally inappropriate. Christ's resurrection is his being raised from death, the significance of which is governed by the nature, circumstances, and necessity of that death. To place our emphasis on the resurrection of Christ is valid, but it must be acknowledged that we do so only by virtue

---

12. Stott, *Cross of Christ*, 81.

of what it achieves for us in conjunction with the death of Christ. We could never have had his righteousness imputed to us had it not been for the issue of our sinful condition having first been resolved. Thus, by Christ's death we are reconciled to God (Rom 5:10; 1 Pet 3:18); by his being raised to life we "become the righteousness of God" in Christ Jesus (2 Cor 5:21).

The almost universally accepted symbol of Christianity is appropriately an empty cross. It might just as well be a vacant tomb. Those who insist on depicting Christ in the midst of his agonizing crucifixion may well believe that they are remembering and, thus, glorifying the head. When they come to realize that he is no longer dying but is gloriously alive for evermore, they may then begin to rejoice with the rest of the body.

Looking Around, Looking Out, and Looking Forward

One other achievement of the resurrection of Christ is that it provides the basis for the mystical union of believers in relation with him as their head and with each other as the body of Christ. It is vitally important to remember this when we partake of the Lord's Supper: We are not only expressing our covenant relationship with him; we are also acknowledging our covenant membership with each other. Where actual breaking of bread occurs, it is traditionally taken from one loaf. Just as Christ's physical body was broken for us and this breaking was graphically and prophetically symbolized in the first Lord's Supper, so too our celebratory re-enactment of the event now represents the fact that the spiritual body of Christ is whole again (see 1 Cor 10:17).

The new covenant is essentially one that is embraced by individuals, not in isolation, but as part of God's family, the body of Christ (1 Cor 12:12). When we "break bread," we are effectively declaring our oneness with the whole loaf, our togetherness as a spiritual family unit. To share a meal in the biblical sense is to identify with those who are around the table, just as Jesus did (cf. Matt 9:10–11; Luke 7:36–50; 10:38–42). Perhaps this is why the apostle Paul could think of no more potentially restorative judgment for the unrepentant brother at Corinth than that no one should eat with him (1 Cor 5:11). We have already seen how covenants in the Old Testament were usually sealed by the shedding of blood and ratified through a shared meal. How much more, therefore, should the new covenant be instituted and remembered by bread, which represents Christ's body, broken for humanity, and by the cup of wine symbolizing his blood poured out for us (Matt 26:26–28)?

The church is the body of Christ. Library bookshelves are filled with varying opinions as to what the definitive purpose of that body might be. While my convictions preclude me from adhering to many of the principles found in modern Anglicanism, I wholeheartedly affirm the doctrinal legitimacy of some of its Articles of Faith, in particular that the chief end of man is "[t]o glorify God and to enjoy him forever." There are two components to this: glorifying God and enjoying God. However, they are so inextricably linked as to be inseparable, save for the purpose of analysis. As we glorify God, so our enjoyment of him is enlarged and enhanced. Similarly, as we learn to enjoy the Being and presence of Almighty God, our inner sense of his glorification likewise increases. Here, I believe, is a key not to the purpose of the church, but to how the church best operates in fulfilling its purpose. I would define the church simply and essentially as the community of the redeemed. I believe it is at its best when it is also a community of celebration and thanksgiving—a true *koinonia eucharistia*.

As Ernest Kevan has commented: "The table at which you eat is the loyalty to which you are pledged."[13] Although our commitment is principally toward the Lord, the fruit of our vertical relationship will always be conveyed horizontally. In other words, if our heart's desire is to be united with Jesus in vision and purpose, looking forward in eager anticipation to our wonderful reunion at the eternal feast, then we must express covenant love here and now as a public declaration of our commitment to each other. We best demonstrate allegiance to Jesus in our love for one another (John 13:34–35). It is in such a setting that we may expect to see daily growth by the hand of the Lord (see Acts 2:46–47). In the words of David Matthew:

> To draw near to a covenant keeping God has double implications. It brings his covenant blessings closer: love, strength, healing and provision come within easy reach in a whole new way. But the covenant penalties come closer too: we cannot share in the covenant meal in sinful disregard for our fellow-believers and get away with it.[14]

---

13. Kevan, *Lord's Supper*, 46.
14. Matthew, *Covenant Meal*, 103.

The basic hypothesis of this section, therefore, is that any legitimate expression of the Lord's Supper can only be thus identified by the extent to which it effectively communicates the gospel of—and is to be found exclusively in—Christ Jesus as the living head of the new covenant. However, the evangelizing of the faithless should not preclude the edifying of the faithful. Perhaps the fact that many are left unedified is largely the responsibility of those who have failed to give adequate instruction in such matters. So many fail to respond with vigor because they have never been taught the significance of the Lord's Supper and their part in it. The loaf we eat is the bread of life, not the crumbs of lethargy; the vessel we drink from is the cup of thanksgiving, not the chalice of torment. Together, they are the symbols of a communion we share, not of a moment in which I am free to either exercise my individuality or indulge my solitude.

Although it may sound simplistically obvious, the fact remains that the covenant meal is for covenant people, the redeemed community. This is the biblical pattern. Indeed, only the incorporation of pagan traditions and practices has subsequently muddied the issue. Just as the alien was prohibited from eating the Passover meal (Exod 12:43), so too is the Lord's Supper only for those of a truly circumcised heart (Rom 2:28–29; Col 2:11–12).

While continuance of the commemorative communion is commanded, permanence is not implied, for believers are to persist in proclaiming Christ's death—and resurrection—only until he comes again. At that time, what is foreshadowed by the Lord's Supper will replace it—i.e., the Wedding Supper of the Lamb (see Matt 26:29; Rev 19:9). We currently live between these ages and yet are involved in both. We live in this age, but we belong to the next (Heb 6:5). The Supper we currently share is only a sample of what is to come. What gladness there then will be! What depth of fellowship! What an occasion for rejoicing! No conference, rally, or crusade in the world ever came close. And yet we have the opportunity now to experience something of that delight, companionship, and joy—"until he comes" (1 Cor 11:26).

Summary

When attempting to redress a perceived imbalance of emphasis, it is often difficult to avoid going too far in the opposite direction. Lest the reader imagine this to be the case here, let me be quite clear. I am not for one moment proposing that we, as believers, should only remember the head when we consider Christ's death and are similarly restricted to our rejoicing with the body when we contemplate Christ's resurrection. We both remember the head and rejoice with others who are like-minded, whether the primary focus of our attention at any given time is Christ's death or his resurrection. I trust the following diagram will help us to resolve the issue satisfactorily:

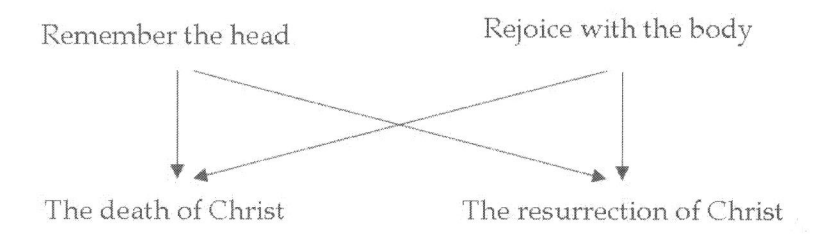

```
Remember the head              Rejoice with the body
       |          \    /              |
       |           \  /               |
       |            \/                |
       |            /\                |
       |           /  \               |
       ▼ ◄────────/    \────────►     ▼
The death of Christ            The resurrection of Christ
```

RECOGNIZING RESPONSIBILITIES

Individuals are primarily members of the church as a matter of their identity in relation to Jesus. However, it is not normal for an individual to grow in Christ outside of healthy, loving, vibrant relationships with other Christians. The very real hazard in overemphasizing personal salvation is that we may devalue the rightful place of the body into which the newly converted are baptized. There is much wisdom in T.C. Hammond's assertion that ". . . no words can express strongly enough the risk of serious loss which dogs the steps of the Christian who has no time for a spiritual "home" in a local community . . . [the Christian] can ill afford to live a detached kind of life . . . if he is to be a successful disciple of Jesus Christ."[15]

Fellowship Based on Relationship

Arguably no word has become more devalued in recent times than the word "fellowship," a word seldom, if ever, employed outside of a Christian context. Thus, it appears that we alone are to blame for robbing it of both meaning and meaningfulness. "Would it be alright if I come by one morning this week for a bit of fellowship?" should suggest

---

15. Hammond, *In Understanding be Men*, 157.

something more weighty than merely the intention to have a banal chat over a bland cup of coffee and a couple of stale cookies. This is especially true given that, biblically, the word speaks of a shared inheritance, a common ministry, and a mutual responsibility. These are not light or insignificant matters.

The word "fellowship" has been defined as "all fellows in the same ship." The Greek noun most commonly translated "fellowship" is *koinonia*, which literally signifies something shared, i.e., something held in common. It may also be translated "communion" (see 1 Cor 10:16; Phlm 6). Although the term "holy communion" usually designates believers coming together to express their covenant relationship with Christ, our common allegiance makes it appropriate for us to understand that such communion is also expressed laterally. Moreover, if it is reasonable to expect that our individual liabilities toward Christ are to be undertaken with sobriety, gratitude, and delight, then surely our mutual responsibilities toward each other should be considered with no less solemnity, thankfulness, and pure joy.

It must also be borne in mind that until at least AD 100, believers in any given locality would meet almost exclusively at one another's homes. There was, consequently, nothing of the ritualism or paraphernalia commonly associated with present-day religiosity. For those first-century Christians, the reality of their salvation was their commitment to Jesus, worked out in relationship with those to whom they were covenantally joined. Scripture teaches that, in some measure, our heart's attitude to Christ is reflected in the way we relate to his people (see Matt 25:40, 45).

In other words, when we say that the church is the redeemed community, the emphasis must fall primarily upon the fact that its members have this in common: they have been redeemed by Christ. However, they are not simply a loose collection of redeemed individuals; rather, they are those who are to be formed into a community of believers. They are thus people in relationship, first with Christ and then with each other.

The significance of the covenant meal is perhaps best encapsulated in the words of the *Savoy Declaration*, formulated by a committee appointed by the British Parliament in 1685. Its members included the likes of William Bridge, Joseph Caryl, Thomas Goodwin, William Greenhill, Philip Nye, and John Owen:

> Our Lord Jesus, in the night wherein he was betrayed, instituted the sacrament of his body and blood, called the Lord's Supper,

> to be observed in his churches unto the end of the world, for the perpetual remembrance, and shewing forth of the sacrifice of himself in his death, the sealing of benefits thereof unto true believers, their spiritual nourishment, and growth in him, their further ingagement [sic] in and to all duties which they owe unto him, and to be a bond and pledge of their communion with him, and with each other.[16]

Indeed, it was because of their utter disregard for this very precept that the Corinthian Christians were so stingingly rebuked. They may well have shared a meal in a corporate setting but, far from *expressing* covenant, that covenant was, in fact, being gratuitously denied. As a result, they effectively brought judgment upon themselves, many having been taken ill and some even dying (see 1 Cor 11:17–31).

Paul's analogous description of the church as the body of Christ is surely no accident. In real terms, it is impossible to relate to an individual's head while simultaneously disregarding the rest of that person's body. As a member of that body ourselves, it is even less feasible. Nowhere is this interrelatedness and sense of mutual responsibility more graphically demonstrated than around the Lord's Table. Such responsibility calls for corporate commitment and familial faithfulness.

One of the things that can be most annoying in everyday speech is the use of unnecessary adjectives, words purporting to bring precision of meaning and clear definition when, in reality, none is needed. "Born-again Christian" is an example—as if there is any kind of Christian other than one who is born again. "Spirit-filled believer" is another. Or how about "redeemed church" or "anointed man of God"? One of the most recent to raise its grotesque head above the pulpit is the call to "whole-hearted commitment." Any commitment that is not wholehearted is really no commitment at all: commitment that is not total is born of compromise.

Scripture also refers to the church as a building, joined together as living stones (1 Pet 2.4–10). The mortar that holds us together is love. We will, of course, be looking at this in more detail in the chapter titled *Covenant Expressed*. It is important to consider the idea here in this context, however, so that we may establish a legitimate foundation in our thinking for what "the fellowship of believers" actually means and entails. The call to express covenant is no mere afterthought or appendage,

---

16. Payne, *John Owen*, 38.

nor should it be presented merely as a good idea to consider, if you can manage it. It is part of our covenant responsibility, just as much as it was expected of and embraced by those in Israel during the period covered by the Old Testament. The major difference is that we are empowered by God's Holy Spirit.

One of the first questions often asked by a new Christian is "How do I read the Bible?" Although I would never condone doing anything with an open—in the absolute sense of the word, i.e., completely unguarded—mind, I would always advocate approaching Scripture with a teachable disposition. The question, however, is more often one of *structure* than *attitude*. There are many reading plans available, though I have never been persuaded by the claims of any. I prefer instead to simply start at the beginning and work my way through to the end. Almost forty years ago, the then-renowned Bible teacher, Ern Baxter, proposed a daily diet of five psalms and one proverb. On the basis that the former are primarily devoted toward God and the latter is directed manwards, he suggested that by using such a scheme for one month, by the end of it we would have learned how the Bible would have us relate covenantally to both God and our fellow man.

Life in the new covenant is one of vulnerability. It calls for believers to be open and prepared to persevere in the midst of pressure, to be consistent where there is conflict and complacency, to seek to serve rather than becoming self-indulgent, and to continue to love where others might choose to opt out. As Terry Virgo points out:

> The New Testament is full of commandments, telling us to do a variety of things for one another. We can only obey these commands and discover their power when we get close enough to handle the discomfort and pain of such encounters.[17]

Unity Maintained by Mutual Acceptance

The unity of the church is a mystical bond effected, not by human endeavor, but by the Holy Spirit of God. Division is both sought and wrought by our enemy, the devil. Thus, believers are not encouraged to attain to unity because, according to Scripture, it has been achieved and is already ours, but to "make every effort to *keep* the unity of the Spirit" (Eph 4:3, emphasis added). Note that unity is not the same as

---

17. Virgo, *Restoration in the Church*, 74.

uniformity; neither is this an argument for unity at all costs. Where there is conflict over issues of truth against heresy, compromise is a poor solution. By way of example: Paul did not counsel the leaders at Corinth to tolerate lascivious behavior for fear that to do otherwise might upset the proverbial apple cart or the status quo. The unity of the Spirit could only be maintained by taking an uncompromising stance against that which sought to bring the gospel into disrepute. However, when genuine repentance was in evidence, forgiveness was quickly proffered. After all, how could any of us be anything but compassionate in such circumstances?

One of the reasons for Paul's strongly worded disapproval of the Corinthians' behavior at the Lord's Table was their self-indulgent gluttony. There is a school of thought, however, that this behavior was largely the product of a legacy of social distinctions (see 1 Cor 11:17–34). If so, the problem is by no means restricted to first-century Palestine. Imagine the scene two thousand years later. A thriving city church of some four hundred members plus embraces a broad sweep of the social spectrum. Among its regular attendees are financial analysts, those on income support, lawyers, supermarket checkout clerks, medical experts, and garbage collectors. Midweek meetings of groups of ten to twelve people are conducted in the homes of members around the city. There, Bible study, prayer, friendship evangelism, and the covenant meal take place in a four-week cycle. Group members who, as indicated above, are of diverse social backgrounds, take turns hosting the covenant meal. The breaking of bread thus sometimes takes place in opulent settings, or in homes that are reasonably comfortable, as well as in more overtly humble surroundings. It is surely not difficult to see how extravagance and show could sit uncomfortably by the side of modesty and financial embarrassment.

The church is clearly not the place for highlighting such differences (Greek *haeresis*) and potential divisions (*schismata*)—the Lord's Table even less so, if that were possible. F.F. Bruce comments: "It was no more possible for the Lord's Supper to be eaten in an atmosphere of social discrimination than it was for the same people to 'partake of the table of the Lord and the table of demons.' The Eucharist could be profaned by faction as certainly as by idolatry."[18]

---

18. Bruce, *1 & 2 Corinthians*, 110.

It is not clear whether Paul's counsel against eating and drinking "in an unworthy manner" (1 Cor 11:27) is to be understood as being directly connected to "without recognizing the body" (v. 29). We cannot even be sure if this "body" refers to Christ's physical body in its salvific significance or if it alludes to the mystical body, the church. (see, however, 12:27.) I think both are possible and equally valid. Similarly, although the emphasis of this section is recognition of our responsibilities to the corporate body of Christ (that is, the church) and its individual members, we must also acknowledge our responsibilities to Christ himself by virtue of what his atoning sacrifice has achieved. Indeed, our duties to the former only exist, *ipso facto*, because of the latter.

For this reason, a wise prelude to partaking of the covenant meal would be a period of self-examination (see 1 Cor 11:27–28). Failure to do so and to take appropriate remedial action for one's wrong actions or inaction can attract divine penalty (v. 29). Regarding the most likely definition of "the body of the Lord" in this context, William Barclay offers the following: "The person condemned is not the person who does not discern that the elements he takes in his hands are the Lord's body . . . but the person who does not discern that Christians are the Lord's body, and must be in unity before they approach the sacrament."[19]

We have seen that the sharing of meals in biblical times signified more than simply eating food around a common table. It was socially significant in that it symbolized mutual acknowledgment and acceptance. In other words, the table was a place of intimate association. This is especially true of the communion table. When we eat bread and drink the cup together, we not only reaffirm our covenant loyalty to Christ, we also graphically identify ourselves as being in covenant commitment with and toward those around the table. To do otherwise is to risk God's judgment (1 Cor 11:30). It is not enough to be related to one another; we must acknowledge our relatedness in the context of godly relationships.

From all that has gone before, we should hardly need reminding that those who have entered into covenant with each other have a responsibility to uphold the conditions of that covenant. This calls for commitment, trust, seeking the good of others with whom we are covenantally attached, bringing godly correction where necessary, sacrificial giving, and possibly even laying down our lives, whether physically or metaphorically, if that is what is called for. Conversely, abrogation of

---

19. Barclay, *The Lord's Supper*, 109.

this responsibility could include disloyalty, betrayal, indiscipline, self-indulgence, and a generally cavalier attitude toward the needs of others.

It would be easy to argue that the Corinthian believers were really nothing more inauspicious than products of their environment. After all, the city had a well-earned reputation as a centre of carnality in the area. However, the root of excusing spiritual apathy on the grounds of cultural lethargy is the same as that which regards the church (both locally and globally) as a thermometer rather than a thermostat. It would also seem that the problem was further compounded by weak leadership, which had failed to deal with the issues before they had the opportunity to become full blown. It might even be argued that the "party spirit" that finally paved the way for their independent streak was encouraged, if not promoted, by the leaders themselves.

The essence of the expression of the new covenant is to be found in interdependent relationship(s). Or, to put it another way, individualism is anathema to Paul's notion of the church as the body of Christ, wherein each member functions in the context of the whole (1 Cor 12:12–62). Over the centuries, and even today, there have been and are those who have appeared to be successful in going it alone. Some have even attracted quite a following, which obviously raises questions about how alone they really wanted to be. Lack of accountability, the "my ministry" syndrome, and exclusively personal religious experiences are the fruit of such independence and readily demonstrate a distinct misunderstanding of what covenant membership actually involves—placing corporate needs before private requirements and giving precedence to mutual vulnerability over egotistical displays of talent or gifting.

Integrity Upheld by the Truth, the Whole Truth, and Nothing but the Truth

Whenever we see the words "function" and "church" in the same sentence, it is usually in the question "What is the function of the church?" Perhaps a more significant question might be "How does the church function?" The analogy employed by Paul of the church as a body of believers suggests that it functions as a living, organic support system. Or, at least, it should do. Of course, Paul is speaking here of the church as the body of Christ in its universal sense. But are there any reasonable grounds to believe that the same principle should not be equally applied to its local expression? This is especially pertinent given that the apostle's words were initially directed to just such a one.

Similarly, much current debate on church growth focuses almost exclusively on increasing attendance. While the issue of growth in numbers is certainly present in the New Testament—most notably in the book of Acts—it seems to emphasize rather the "whole body [being] joined and held together by every supporting ligament, grow[ing] and build[ing] itself up in love, as each part does its work" (Eph 4:16). This is the responsibility we each have, the reality of which is all the more heightened as we come to the Lord's Table to express our covenant commitment to him and to each other. Jim Packer puts it this way: ". . . the New Testament perspective is that God is interested in quality even more than he is interested in quantity. He calls for the evangelizing of the world, but most of all he is concerned that the functioning of the church, the company of the faithful, should always and everywhere bring glory to him as this supernatural life of fellowship with Christ is displayed, lived out, deepened and ripened."[20]

Church leaders clearly carry the burden for supporting the flock entrusted to their care. After all, they will one day be required to give an account as faithful under-shepherds. However, those who are swift to point an accusing finger in the direction of dispassionate pastors or unhelpful elders need also to recognize the volume of evidence in the New Testament for what may only be described as "one anothering." Arguably the most notable and all-encompassing example of this is to be found in Jesus' command to his disciples: "A new command I give you: Love one another. As I have loved you, so you must love one another. By this all men will know that you are my disciples, if you love one another" (John 13:34–35).

Notice whose example we are to follow in this—that of the Lord himself. Notice too the divine imperative—"you must." This is not a matter of choice; it is not a potential extra for the super-spiritual elite amongst us. It is as non-negotiable as it is unconditional. First and foremost, believers have a responsibility to the truth. I am certain that all we who are of an evangelical disposition would agree with that statement. Recent discussions, however, prompt me to qualify it further, for it would seem that what we understand by "the truth" may not necessarily be one and the same. For this reason, I would distinguish between "the truth" (with

---

20. Packer, *Serving the People of God*, 10.

the definite article) and "truth" (without the definite article). I realize this places me in danger of attracting charges of being pedantic, but to my mind "the truth" is not a corpus of doctrine, however valid, but a person. Jesus said, "I am the way and the truth and the life. No one comes to the Father except through me" (John 14:6). Let us, by all means, boast of our holding to the truth, just as long as we are referring to Christ Jesus, our relationship with him, and with others through him.

John Owen is only partly correct when he asserts that "[t]he cause of the death of Christ was sin; the means of the death of Christ was suffering."[21] It is true, but it is not the whole truth, for it does not tell us that the end of the death of Christ was God's satisfaction. Or, to put it another way, the only possible means of God's judicial satisfaction was the sacrificial death of his Son. Those of a Reformed persuasion are swift—and rightly so—to denounce the Roman Catholic Mass on the grounds that it promotes the idea of a re-crucified Christ. But is it any less inappropriate to so obsess about the grave that we effectively keep him there? To paraphrase the words of the angels at the empty tomb: "Why do we persist in looking for the living among the dead and then wonder why so few seem to want to join us in our pursuit? He is not there; he has risen!" (cf. Luke 24:5–6).

Summary

In general terms, responsibility involves both accountability and obligation. This is true whether we have in mind moral, forensic, or natural responsibility (e.g., parenthood). It is certainly no less so in the context of covenant responsibility in the spiritual realm. It seems superfluous to point out, therefore, that responsibility of any kind is essentially about relationships. The fact of mutual responsibility between those joined together in covenant also implies the ability or power to behave in such a way as to effect the best possible outcome for those for whom we are responsible. Thus, our obligation can only ever be to do that which is in our power to do—i.e., that which we have a gift to do. Similarly, the level of obligation to which we may justly be held accountable is governed by the extent of our capabilities. However, it must also be noted that our capacity to perform is significantly increased by virtue of the indwelling of God's Holy Spirit.

21. Payne, *John Owen*, 182.

AVOIDING CURSE, ANTICIPATING BLESSING

Self-examination before partaking of the covenant meal is identified in Scripture not merely as a virtuous exercise, but as a vital expression of our commitment to the Lord and to one another. Taking a few moments to consider if we are fit to receive communion—and being prepared to take appropriate remedial action where necessary—can mean the difference between penalty and profit, curse and blessing. The consequences can range from the tragic to the magnificent. It is, therefore, in our own best interests, both individually and corporately, to judge (Greek *kritikos*—"to give a critical assessment of") ourselves accordingly.

Take a Close Look at Yourself

In the Introduction, we saw that covenant agreements generally consist of the following elements:

- Identifying the parties involved;
- Outlining the terms and conditions;
- Specifying the due penalties and rewards; and
- Signing the deal, usually in blood.

All the divine covenants of the Old Testament followed the same pattern, and the new covenant embraces an identical template. We have seen that curse (Hebrew—*qalal, cherem*; Greek—*katara, anathema*) and blessing (Hebrew—*beraka*; Greek—*eulogia*) are often contrasted in Scripture. This is especially true in the context of covenant and, most notably, in relation to the rewards of disobedience and compliance. Intrinsic to the root of the Hebrew *cherem* in the Old Testament was the idea of seclusion or expulsion from society as the penalty for covenant-breaking. Depending on the nature of the offense, this could very well mean death. Where the seriousness of the transgression did not require such irreversible or drastic consequences, excommunication was not perceived as exclusively punitive, especially given that the intention was the ultimate restoration of the individual(s) concerned. Church leaders who take their guidance from Paul on matters of ecclesiastical discipline will see that this is equally true under the new covenant.

It is similarly significant that, with the giving of the Mosaic law, curses for disobedience were equated with death and the blessings for obedience with life. So, too, may we regard the blessing of God as the capacity to enjoy life to the full, as he intends, whereas to be under his curse—even for a season—is to be devoid of that sense of his presence, which is spiritual death.

I have pointed out elsewhere that judgment is not entirely negative. In fact, judgment itself is simply the process by which we arrive at a decision based upon the evidence available to us. For example, when we choose which radio program to tune in to or television channel to watch, we have subjected all the options—including the one we finally favored—to our judgment. Of course, to judge ourselves is not without built-in subjectivity and concomitant frailty. For this reason, the criteria we use should not be based upon personal feelings, possible excuses, or potentially legitimate reasons for failing in our duty. Speaking of the final judgment at the end of the age, Bruce Milne asserts that "[t]he basis of judgment will be man's response to the revealed will of God."[22] When Christians judge themselves or others, or make general moral decisions, the standard should be precisely the same. Paul reminded the Corinthian believers that if they had judged themselves, they would not come under external judgment. In much the same way, although self-control (Greek—*enkrateia*) does not render self-examination unnecessary, it should also ensure a positive outcome.

The immediate context of Paul's counsel to the Corinthians is that, having examined themselves, the believers may then eat. In other words, there seems to be no suggestion that anything discovered upon examination could prevent their participation in the Lord's Supper. There are a number of possible reasons for this, none of which is entirely conclusive. John Owen, for example, emphasizes the need for solemn preparation in order that the covenant meal may be approached in an appropriate manner. He may well be right. From my own experience, I have found that a distinct lack of formality has generally been the breeding ground for extreme familiarity, even contempt. Equally true, however, excessive zeal for the ceremonial has often tended toward a ritualistic pomp, relegating the true essence of covenant (that is, relationship) to the periphery of the eucharistic expression. We must, of course, respect the presence of God in our midst. As his covenant sons and daughters, however, it behooves us to bathe in his splendor rather than to cringe before his might (see Ps 66:3).

---

22. B.A. Milne, "Judgment," *New Bible Dictionary*, 641.

To my mind, the most plausible rendering of the text of the passage would see the basic etymological sense of the Greek word retained: The verb *dokimazō* translated "to examine" in most English translations (see, e.g., 1 Cor 11:28) means literally "to approve" (it is used primarily of metals that have been refined). Thus, we must consider if there are any known impurities that might otherwise hinder our participation in the covenant meal. Any found should be resolved immediately if that is both possible and practicable. If not, the individual should determine within him or herself before God to do so at the earliest opportunity. He or she is then free to share in the elements with a pure conscience. There is no suggestion, however remote, that people should abstain from receiving upon having found faults within themselves. The only caveat I would endorse to this principle is in the case of those for whom it is a condition of church discipline. Of course, if it is known in advance that there are unsettled issues, it begs the question why they have not been considered and put right prior to coming to the Lord's Table. This may well be covered by what John Owen describes as "preparation."[23]

It is not the intention of this work to imply that God is incapable of dispensing justice without the use of some outside agency. The weight of evidence in the New Testament, however, does suggest that very often his preferred *modus operandi* is to do so through the local church, usually its leaders. This is true of both curses and blessings. A word of caution, and comfort: Those who find themselves part of a fellowship whose leaders are particularly weak in this area must not think that either their sin will go unpunished, on the one hand, or that their gifts and talents will be left unnoticed, on the other. God is more than capable of personally rectifying such situations.

Avoiding the Penalty for Covenant Transgression

The basic hypothesis of this book is that God considers covenant a very serious matter indeed. I believe he has chosen to invest himself in it as the basis upon which he reveals himself to the created order. To accept the terms and conditions of the proffered covenant agreement and subsequently to break them is a similarly solemn affair. It is not so much that the tragedy is worsened in the context of the covenant meal as that the sense of its reality is somewhat heightened. The consequences for those

---

23. In Payne, *John Owen*, 127–154.

at Corinth, says Paul, was frailty, general ill health, and even premature death (1 Cor 11:29–30). It is naturally possible that those so afflicted could have been the victims of their own gluttony, and that their ailments were linked to an abused digestive system. However, it is equally possible that this was not the case. The evidence is inconclusive either way and, therefore, largely immaterial. The suggestion has also been made that some progression might be inferred from the text, implying that a candidate might be "elevated" from one level to another if the warnings of the current "stage" have not been sufficiently heeded. This seems more than a little fanciful and is difficult to maintain from the evidence we have here. I am once again reminded of my former college professor's maxim: "Where Scripture is silent, it is sagacious not to speculate."

What can be affirmed from Scripture, however, is the number of incidents where individuals, or even groups of people, have lost their lives, apparently before their time, because of some episode of serious covenant-breaking. In the previous chapter (1 Cor 10), Paul went out of his way to remind the Corinthians of some of these episodes in Israel's illustrious history (vv. 7–10). Impatience, grumbling, divisiveness, independence, and especially idolatry and immorality are all cited as being harbingers of a premature death.

Idolatry may be defined as the worship and/or reverence of that which is not God. Many of the Christians at Corinth would have been all too familiar with the handmade "gods" of wood and stone associated with the pagan sacrifices of their day. In clear breach of their covenant obligations, the people of Israel of old consistently yielded to the temptation to embrace the "gods" of the nations they had conquered, found themselves living near, or within whose boundaries they were presently exiled. It would appear from the pages of the New Testament that many first-century believers had failed to learn the lessons of their forebears' past.

But idolatry cannot be consigned exclusively to the pages of history. Even in our own day, it is to be found in the cult of celebrity: the eulogizing of the talentless by the mindless. And neither is the church exempt from idolatry. Personality preachers, rock-star-featured worship leaders, image-conscious evangelists, and those driven by charisma rather than *charismata*—all point to a breed of Christianity that has allowed itself to pay homage to that which is not God. It is my firm conviction that Christians who have permitted themselves to become enticed by the gods of the age, whether that be in the form of the latest fashion accessory, their local sports hero, the new "in" television program, or the "must-have" religious icon, would do well to hear again Elijah's counsel from Mount Carmel: "How long will you waver between two opinions? If the Lord is God, follow him; but if Baal is God, follow him" (1 Kgs 18:21).

Having already pointed out that to sin sexually is to sin against one's own body, Paul reminds the Corinthians about the sexually immoral behavior of their predecessors and what it cost them (1 Cor 10:8). The body of Christ and the body of the Christian have this in common: God resides in both of them by his Holy Spirit (see 1 Cor 6:19; Eph 2:19–22). Thus, an act of impurity of this nature is, by extension, an act against the larger body of believers to which we all belong, and an offense against the temple of the Holy Spirit. Dare we think that we can commit such an offense and share the elements of the Lord's Supper without inviting serious consequences upon ourselves? Even the Old Testament prophets considered such duplicity to be folly (Jer 7:9–10).

Of course, it is true that idolatry and immorality are vices to be shunned by Christians at all times. They are character traits unworthy of Christian believers. Why, then, should the point be particularly emphasized in the context of the covenant meal? This is an interesting question that merits closer inspection. We have already noted that the significance of the elements lies in what they symbolize. This is also true of the meal itself and, as such, brings into sharper focus certain characteristics that elsewhere might not be subject to such scrutiny. In the words of David Matthew: "The covenant meal is a dangerous place for hypocrites."[24] When outward expressions of loyalty and identification are betrayed by a heart attitude of unfaithfulness and dissociation, then we can be sure that our secret will not remain one for very long. Judas may have been the first to discover this; he most certainly was not the last.

We cannot expect to be excused where Corinth was chastened. Neither should we have cause to consider ourselves to be necessarily beyond the reaches of such recklessness. In a strange way, however, there is some ground for thanksgiving that the profanity of the Corinthians afforded the opportunity for apostolic correction from which we may all benefit. Indeed, given that this is the most exhaustive teaching we have on the Lord's Supper in the whole of the Bible, we are left only to wonder

---

24. Matthew, *Covenant Meal*, 119.

how such revelation might have come to us had it not been for the failure of the early church in this regard.

Paving the Way for the Blessing of God in the Here and Now . . .

Appropriate covenant conduct not only enables us to avoid potential curses that might otherwise come our way; by embracing our responsibilities and living aright, we are entitled to anticipate the blessings of the Lord. Again, the sense of this reality is particularly intensified as we share the covenant meal, the determining factor being the attitude with which we receive it. Do we recognize the Lord's body, not only in remembrance of the physical torture Jesus endured on the cross, but also in the metaphysical sense of our siblings in Christ? Moreover, what kind of blessings ought we to anticipate? Well, thinking laterally for a moment, if illicit behavior wrought frailty and death for our predecessors, then it seems reasonable to imagine that righteous conduct might bring health and life. This was certainly true of Israel of old. On leaving Egypt's borders, God made this promise to the people, through Moses: "If you listen carefully to the voice of the Lord your God and do what is right in his eyes, if you pay attention to his commands and keep all his decrees, I will not bring on you any of the diseases I brought on the Egyptians, for I am the Lord who heals you" (Exod 15:26). According to the psalmist, that is precisely what happened:

> [The Lord] brought out Israel, laden with silver and gold, and from among their tribes no one faltered. Egypt was glad when they left, because dread of Israel had fallen on them . . . He brought out his people with rejoicing, his chosen ones with shouts of joy; he gave them the lands of the nations and they fell heir to what others had toiled for—that they might keep his precepts and observe his laws. (Ps 105:37–45)

Of course, this is not to promote the unbiblical notion that all personal sickness is the product of individual sin, nor the equally unorthodox idea of a so-called "prosperity" gospel. But God's justice and goodness should neither be overlooked nor underestimated when coming to the Lord's Table. Palmer Robertson puts it this way: "Each time a group of believers in Christ celebrates the Lord's Supper, they rejoice in their current experience of the blessings of the new covenant because of their fellowship with God achieved by the 'blood of the covenant.'"[25]

Regarding the covenant meal as a means of grace, David Matthew also makes a valid point when he says that "[t]he [Lord's] Supper . . . becomes a means of grace only to those who have already been 'strengthened by grace.' In other words, we receive grace from the Lord's Supper when we first bring grace to it."[26] The sacraments are symbolic insofar as they point to something greater than themselves. But this in itself does not necessarily mean that they are thereby prevented from also functioning as means of grace. Those who claim that they are do not always do so on the basis of the revelation of Scripture, but as a reaction—one might even say, overreaction—to some prevailing heresy or other. Note again Paul's words to the church at Corinth: "Is not the cup of thanksgiving for which we give thanks a *participation* in the blood of Christ? And is not the bread we break a *participation* in the body of Christ?" (1 Cor 10:16).

The word the NIV translates as "participation," the KJV renders as "communion." The original Greek, however, is *koinonia*, which literally means "having in common," "partnership," or "fellowship." In this context, surely the sense of *koinonia* is in identifying with, recognizing, and demonstrating the reality of our mystical union with Christ and, by virtue of that fact, our spiritual union or common bond with other believers.

In many current church circles, the word "fellowship" is either much maligned because of abuse or has become devoid of real meaning or value by way of its misuse. It must not for that reason, however, be removed or allowed to disappear from our vocabulary. Rather than respond negatively to its distortion, it would be far more beneficial for us to restore it to its original meaning. *Koinonia*, as we have seen, means "fellowship," with the emphasis being on things shared. John Stott gives perhaps the most lucid definition when he asserts that "[i]n particular, *koinonia* bears witness to three things we hold in common. First, it expresses what we *share in* together (our common inheritance); secondly, what we *share out* together (our common service); and thirdly, what we *share with* each other (our mutual responsibility)."[27] Can there be any greater blessing or state of blessedness in this life?

25. Robertson, *Christ of the Covenants*, 299.
26. Matthew, *Covenant Meal*, 153.
27. Stott, *Living Church*, 96.

My understanding of Scripture informs me that fellowship is integral to the concept of communion; my experience as a Christian over the past thirty-some years tells me that this fellowship is seldom realized. Our togetherness with Christ should never be devalued or diminished. But if our togetherness in Christ with others is allowed to be effectively sacrificed on the altar of some perceived notion of "the alone" coming to "the Alone," then we must seriously question whether we have an appropriate appreciation of what the Lord's Supper both symbolizes and signifies. In the words of Jim Packer:

> The communion table must bring to us a deeper realization of our fellowship together. If I go into a church for a communion service where not too many folk are present, to me it is a matter of conscience to sit beside someone. This togetherness is part of what is involved in sharing in eucharistic worship in a way that edifies.[28]

The Christian walk is essentially and precisely just that—a journey. The first step toward becoming a Christian is motivated by God's saving grace. While that—and that alone—is sufficient to affirm our eternal destiny, access to eternal life (Greek *zōē aionios*) as a qualitative experience in the here and now requires that we constantly and consistently draw from God's sustaining grace. Doing so, in turn, nurtures within us a gracious disposition, by faith (Eph 2:8).

. . . and in the Age to Come

While it is true that coming to the Lord's Table in a spirit of covenant faithfulness enables us to anticipate the temporal blessing of God, it is equally true that we look forward with eager expectation to eternal blessings. There will come a "time" when time as we know it will cease (this is not to suggest that eternity will necessarily be timeless). Thence, the Lord's Table as we celebrate it will be rendered superfluous: "Whenever you eat this bread and drink this cup, you proclaim the Lord's death until he comes" (1 Cor 11:26). The consummation of this age and the commencement of the next will also be celebrated by a covenant meal of sorts, participation in which is to be a blessing in itself: "Blessed is the man who will eat at the feast in the kingdom of God" (Luke 14:15).

---

28. Packer, *Serving the People of God*, 50.

The fact that there is to be a wedding supper naturally presupposes that a marriage has taken place. The bridegroom and his bride are the Lamb and the church—Jesus and the redeemed community. As individual members of that committed body, believers are to be adorned in garments that they have previously prepared for themselves (Rev 19:7–8). Even in the Old Testament, natural Israel was spoken of as being joined to God in matrimonial terms (see Isa 62:4–5; Jer 2:2). Having violated the covenant by indulging in spiritual adultery, it was left to the prophet Hosea to speak as God's mouthpiece concerning the fulfillment of his purpose through the new covenant: "I will betroth you to me forever; I will betroth you in righteousness and justice, in love and compassion. I will betroth you in faithfulness, and you will acknowledge the Lord" (Hos 2:19–20).

There is arguably no more powerful imagery in Scripture than this, simply because there is no more potent intimacy of relationship than the joining of two people in the union of marriage. It is an image that the apostle Paul takes up when he compares the Bible's initial reference to marriage with the ultimate fulfillment of that union, Christ and his church (Eph 5:31–32). Indeed, Paul saw it as part of his apostolic commission to prepare those under his charge for the blessed day when they would be presented "as a pure virgin" to Christ, their husband (2 Cor 11:2). Although the Wedding Supper of the Lamb is rightly to be perceived as a celebratory feast of the joining of bride and groom in perfect union, it is also but the beginning of a wonderfully blessed marriage relationship. Just as human marriage was always intended to be an exclusive relationship of growing intimacy and developing recognition between two people, so too will eternity be an occasion for the increase of Christ's government (Isa 9:7) and an ever-growing sense of appreciation in respect of his covenant faithfulness, power, and love.

Arguably, one of the major blessings forthcoming at the end of the age is the receipt of our resurrection bodies. At that time, we will finally and forever be free from the decaying limitation imposed upon us by our first father's breaking of God's creational covenant with him. Moreover, the whole of the created order will also participate in this release from the frustration of unfulfilled potential (see Rom 8:19–21). The greater blessing, however, is undoubtedly to be the experience of the undiminished, unchangeable, and uninterrupted presence of our God.

The original Passover meal was eaten by the Israelites in preparation for the journey they were about to take to a known destination. The route they opted for might not have been the one God intended; the path they chose may even have placed them in greater natural peril than would otherwise have been the case. The generation that set out did not make it to the Promised Land, but the covenant people of God did receive their inheritance—and with great joy. As God's new covenant people, we too look forward to a known destination, eagerly anticipating the blessings that await us there. Our route will largely be governed by choices we make along the way. Some will be good and godly; others may not be. But we will arrive to claim the blessings of our inheritance.

In these days, when God is restoring a sense of covenant to the church, we can no longer remain satisfied to merely go through the motions of attending church services or participating in church-related activities once, twice, or three times a week. We are being challenged more and more to live in the reality of what we confess to be true. The covenant meal is symbolic of a depth of oneness within the covenant community. We are increasingly hungry for spiritual reality at both personal and corporate levels. No longer are men and women of God content to simply talk a good sermon; they are beginning to break out into the realm of living epistles (see 2 Cor 3:2).

SUMMARY

Over the years, I have known both the extreme privilege and profound displeasure of experiencing the Lord's Supper in many different ways. The experience of those around me has also ranged from detached duty to enchanted enjoyment. Sadly, there have been far too few occasions when I could honestly say that meaningful covenant was expressed. Equally tragic is the fact that the historical record of the church paints an all-too-similar picture. Even during times when there was perhaps more tangible fervor for God's word, the issues were clouded by partisanship, and no effort was made at resolving them by a principled study of the scriptural facts. Theological treatises and debates produced far more heat than light, primarily because the main proponents were not so much defenders of the faith as protectors of their denominationally conditioned version of it. Surely, the Lord's Supper deserves better.

We have seen in this chapter that, although the covenant meal is largely symbolic, it is by no means exclusively so. The sense of the reality that it signifies is heightened both by the solemnity of the occasion and the sobriety of our union with Christ and with each other. The experience of God's love for us in Christ is no more real at the Lord's Table than it is away from it, though the sense of it—or feeling, if you will—most certainly is. So, too, our covenant commitment toward that part of the family of God with whom we break bread. The kind of love that Christ commands of us is of the same essence as that he has reserved for us (see John 13:34; 15:12, 17; 1 John 3:23). His love is not a merely sentimental sloppiness; it always finds practical expression.

Partaking of the covenant meal may invoke a tearful response. If so, let our tears be tears of joy and wonder rather than sadness and morbidity. Allow it to become a time where faith is renewed, weariness is overcome, sensitivities to the spirit of the occasion are heightened, and the body of Christ is once again infused with and enthused by its corporate objective—to give thanks to the Lord Jesus. It is, after all, his Supper.

5

Covenant Expressed

By now, surely one issue has become crystal clear—our God is a God of covenant. Moreover, as has been intimated throughout this text, it is my conviction that covenant can only properly be understood in terms of relationship. Indeed, perhaps it is for this reason that Jesus identified these as the two greatest commandments: "Love the Lord your God with all your heart and with all your soul and with all your mind and with all your strength" and "Love your neighbor as yourself" (Mark 12:28–31). Paul echoed the sentiment in his exhortation to the believers at Rome: "Let no debt remain outstanding, except the continuing debt to love one another, for he who loves his fellow man has fulfilled the law. The commandments," he adds, "are summed up in this one rule: 'Love your neighbor as yourself'" (Rom 13:8–9).

Lateral covenant and fellowship are so closely linked as to be almost indivisible. For example, the business arrangement between James, John, and Peter (Luke 5:10) might loosely be described as a covenant of sorts, but their mutual relationship is as co-"fellowshippers" (Greek *koinonoi*). They had a common interest (i.e., fishing) in which they jointly participated (the business), presumably in accordance with predetermined terms and conditions that spelled out potential benefits and penalties. No doubt there was also an agreed objective to which each party subscribed and contributed. (It is admittedly unlikely that their enterprise would have been ratified by blood, although some kind of sign would in all likelihood have sealed their agreement.)

I have remarked before that a covenant is essentially an agreement between two parties of not necessarily equal stature. Peer covenants too were not uncommon during the period covered by the Old Testament; indeed, Scripture records several such agreements, a selection of which we shall consider shortly. I believe it has been necessary first to look at the divine covenants as ideal models upon which to base our own notions of lateral covenants, rather than the other way around. After all, how we relate to one another as Christians must surely emanate from our relationship with Christ, and not vice versa.

In this chapter, we will begin by looking at three examples of peer covenants in the Old Testament: those between Abraham and Abimelech, Jacob and Laban, and David and Jonathan. We will then consider in more detail precisely what it means to be a new covenant people, before finally looking at the implications for us as Christians in the twenty-first century, especially in terms of covenant loyalty.

OLD TESTAMENT EXAMPLES

Here we are at last: the final chapter. Having looked for the most part at the theology of covenant and its implications in general terms, we must now turn our attention to the practical application of all that has gone before. One of the most productive elements of discipleship is exemplary conduct. We learn best when we see the principles we are being taught expressed in the attitude and behavior of others. Of course, we can also learn by mistakes, our own and those of others close to us—and the Old Testament is rich in instruction! Those who dismiss the witness of the Old Testament as of no value for the Christian have failed to not only understand the Augustinian epithet that "the new is in the old concealed, the old is in the new revealed"; likewise, they do not appreciate the wisdom of the apostle Paul's counsel: "These things happened to them as examples and were written down as warnings for us, on whom the fulfillment of the ages has come" (1 Cor 10:11). Let us look at a number of cases from the Old Testament, therefore, and see how they might speak to us down the centuries.

Abraham and Abimelech (Gen 21:22–34)

The treaty between Abraham and Abimelech is significant for more than its value as an example of lateral covenant. The names of the two contributors are especially worthy of our attention, for Abraham means "father of many/the multitudes" (though his original name, Abram, means "exalted father") and Abimelech means "my father, the king." Integral to the root of both names is the originally Aramaic word, *abba*, which denotes a sense of warm intimacy, as well as filial respect. Thus, fatherhood played an important role in the implications of this particular covenant, something that may not be immediately apparent from the text. Moreover, Abimelech was the king of Gerar in Philistia, a tract of land that—etymologically, at least—would later become known as Palestine. Could it be that we have evidence here of an ancient pact between Israel and Palestine from almost four thousand years ago?

The nature and purpose of the covenant agreement between these two prominent characters was the mutual recognition of respect, trust, and integrity. Given the circumstances of their initial introduction, this is quite a surprising turn of events. Abraham arrived at Gerar after the incident at Sodom and Gomorrah. Whether God's judgment there had conditioned his approach in any way is difficult to say, but there was obviously some reason, born out of fear, that he chose to suggest that he and Sarah were not man and wife, but merely siblings (Gen 20:2). Only the protective hand of God prevented Sarah's defilement at the hands of her royal host (v. 3). Furthermore, it was only Abimelech's blamelessness that held steady the divine judgment that might otherwise have come his way (vv. 5–7).

Some have commented with wondrous incredulity at the prospect of Abimelech's attraction to Sarah, especially in view of her apparent age at the time. However we resolve the matter for ourselves—and Scripture affords us precious few clues—we must remember that she is presented as a woman of singular beauty, by divine providence yet of child-bearing capability, and both she and her suitor were instruments in the hands of an omnipotent God, used to teach a sober lesson to Abraham, her husband.

A short time later, there was a dispute, contested by Abraham and some of Abimelech's servants, over the ownership rights of a certain well (Gen 21:25). Abimelech denied any knowledge of his servants' actions, and a covenant treaty was established between the two at a place thereafter called Beersheba. Beersheba means "well of the oath" (*sheba* also sounds like the Hebrew for "seven," possibly referring to the number of ewe lambs given by Abraham as a token of his innocence (vv. 29–31)).

The word *be'er* has a number of shades of meaning, though they each generally refer to the sinking of an artificial shaft in order to either provide access to underground water or to act as a cistern in which to catch and store falling rainwater. Britain's climate is such that it makes it impossible for us in this country to comprehend the lengths to which some biblical characters would go to retain their well rights (see Gen

1:25). I suspect the same is true of many places in the United States. In more arid environments, however, wells were—and to a certain degree, still are—so important as to be a much-cherished inheritance.

Geographically, Beersheba (i.e., the town that was built near the site of the well) became the southernmost point in Israel. Hence its use in the common phrase "from Dan to Beersheba" (see Judg 20:1; 1 Sam 3:20; 1 Kgs 4:25) in much the same way that people in the UK might say "from John O'Groat's to Lands End" [sic!] or that North Americans might say "from sea to sea." During the period of Israel's settlement, Beersheba acquired further significance, as it lay directly on the major trade route to and from Egypt. The present town of Be'er Sheva is situated some fifty miles south-west of Jerusalem, with the Mediterranean to the west and the Dead Sea to the east.

There are essentially two Hebrew words translated "oath": *shebua* and *'ala*. Whereas the latter is linked to a verb that means "to pronounce a curse," the former and its derivatives convey a more general meaning of "a solemn promise." The binding nature of oaths is so highly regarded in Scripture that to violate them could have potentially fatal consequences (see Ezek 17:16; Acts 5:1–11). This, of course, corresponds with the seriousness with which the Bible regards the breaking of covenant.

From this and the other evidence we have already considered, it might be presumed that a binding oath is a significant feature of the covenants in the Bible. A more detailed analysis, however, reveals that the relationship between the two is so close and the defining boundaries so indistinct that it might be more appropriate to speak of "oath" and "covenant" in almost synonymous terms. In some ways, it is like the canonization of Scripture. The early church fathers did not invest authority in what we now regard as the New Testament so much as they recognized the inherent authority already invested in the documents that comprise it. So, too, the binding oath is not so much a feature that ratifies the covenant as it is a means of expressing that the formalization has already taken place.

Of course, it is true that not all covenants in the Old Testament unequivocally mention the existence of an oath being sworn. This, however, only serves to fuel the argument that at some level the words "oath" and "covenant" are transposable. As Palmer Robertson points out: "The formalizing process of oath-taking may or may not be present. But a covenantal commitment inevitably will result in a most solemn obligation."[1]

---

1. Robertson, *Christ of the Covenants*, 7.

The covenant between Abraham and Abimelech effectively declared the intention of each to protect the other's posterity. As a people group who inhabited the land promised to Abraham's descendants, it is worth mentioning that the Philistines were never completely driven out by the Israelites, despite God's command to wipe out all of Canaan's inhabitants. In some cases, this was a clear act of stubborn defiance and, in others, the product of unwise alliances. In the case of the Philistines, however, the suggestion that it may have been in recognition of Abraham's earlier covenant with Abimelech is not entirely without possible warrant. The fact that the Philistines themselves consistently failed to give the covenant the same level of honor (e.g., Judg 10) did not in itself negate the covenant obligations of Abraham's descendants.

Abraham had embraced the covenant agreement that God had presented before him; this did not, however, preclude the possibility of other peer agreements. The inevitable caveat, of course, is that the terms and conditions of the latter were restricted by the established parameters of the former. Indeed, it might even be argued that it was God's choice of Abraham as a covenant partner that made him such a highly prized asset for others to court. Despite his guile on their initial meeting, Abraham must have been generally regarded as a person of integrity. The fact that his faith in the living God was so amply rewarded may also not have gone unnoticed by others, especially those who showed signs, however remote, of acknowledging that same God (see Gen 20:4, 17; 21:22–23).

Jacob and Laban (Gen 31:22–25)

If the covenant between Abraham and Abimelech is the etiology for an ancient agreement between God's people and Philistia, then that between Jacob and Laban offers the origin of a similar contract between Israel and Aram. Just as we saw that this was a possible reason why the Philistines were never completely driven out of Canaan, the same may be said of Israel's reluctance to entirely overthrow the Arameans. It might even be argued that the personal relationship between the two covenant individuals serves almost as an allegory of the relationship between the two people groups represented by each man.

The lateral expression of the new covenant, which we shall consider later in this chapter, is founded upon common purpose, common objectives, a common head, and more than a little mutual trust. If anything, the covenant established between Jacob and Laban was an example of precisely the opposite. Each had a deceitful disposition and had spent years prior to the arrangement in view seeking only to hoodwink and outmaneuver the other. In fact, it is probably not too much of an exegetical stretch to suggest that the covenant between them was born more out of weariness at constantly wondering what the other might be up to, rather than a genuine desire to promote the other's well-being.

The condensed version of the background to the covenant is this: Jacob had served his uncle, Laban, for twenty years because he loved Laban's youngest daughter—this after being duped into taking her older sibling in marriage, against his wishes. He had tended his uncle's flocks for little reward and, even in this, Jacob found Laban to be duplicitous and self-centered. Finally, Jacob decided to move on, but did so in a dishonest manner. Laban was not happy. Whether it was the thought of no longer having access to his daughters and grandchildren, or the prospect of seeing a source of cheap labor disappear from sight, we can only surmise. When Laban caught up with Jacob, a prolonged exchange of views ensued, and the two parties finally reached partisan agreement. Each called upon God as his witness, and they set up a cairn of stones to mark the occasion. Carl Schultz points out the significance of the stones: "It was common practice to set up a [stone] as a sign that a treaty had been established between two households or nations . . . On both sides, appeal is made to the deity as a witness, showing that the covenant is unalterable. Moreover, as in the case at Sinai, Jacob and Laban offered a sacrifice in the mountain and shared a common meal."[2]

This last comment seems to be supported by the fact that the covenant was forged at a place called *Galeed* by Jacob and *Yegar Sahadutha* by Laban. In each of their respective languages, Hebrew and Aramaic, the meaning is the same: "witness heap." Some have even suggested that the choice of Galeed by Jacob was an idiomatic play on words over the name of the place to which he initially fled from Laban—Gilead. However, there is nothing in the text to add weight to such a proposition. A more substantial inference might be drawn from the fact that the pile of stones thereafter served as a testimony to the act. The pile served as a witness just by being; it didn't have to actually do anything other than remain *in situ*. A salutary lesson, perhaps.

Rather more can be made of its secondary name, Mizpah, the basic meaning of which is "watchtower." The root *mizar* means "hill"; it seems obvious to suggest that the ideal tactical positioning for a watchtower

---

2. C. Schultz, "Covenant," *Theological Wordbook*, 128.

would be at a place of natural elevation. As mentioned earlier, some suggest that Jacob and Laban were not really agreeing to act as each other's protector, but were rather calling God to witness from on high their promise that they would not actively pursue the other's harm. In effect, it was a non-aggression pact. It might even be said that the oath sworn between them was not so much a mutual blessing as a joint caution against future hostility.

Subsequently, the name Mizpah appears in the Old Testament in reference to a number of sites, ranging from a Benjamite town near Jerusalem (Josh 18:26) to a place in Moab where David's parents sought refuge during their son's persecution by Saul (1 Sam 22:3). None of these may be identified with Galeed with any degree of certainty, though the principle behind the meaning of the name can be maintained in each case. There is also mention of a Mizpah in the apocryphal works as the place where Judas Maccabaeus convened a gathering of his warriors in order to seek God's guidance prior to confronting the Seleucid army (1 Macc 3:46).

As we saw in the covenant between Abraham and Abimelech, so too Jacob and Laban bound themselves to their agreement by the swearing of an oath (Gen 31:52). However, Meredith Kline makes the valid point that "Laban [identified] Nahor's and Abraham's God in a Terahite syncretism (v. 53; cf. 12:1), but Jacob [invoked] God by a name related distinctly to the Abrahamic covenant."[3] John Calvin makes the same point. Although the translation belongs to the mid-nineteenth century, the general sense of it remains comprehensible.

> It is indeed rightly and properly done, that Laban should adjure Jacob by the name of God. For this is the confirmation for covenants; to appeal to God on both sides, that he may not suffer perfidy to pass unpunished. But he sinfully blends idols with the true God, between whom there is nothing in common. Thus, truly, men involved in superstition are accustomed to confound promiscuously sacred things with profane, and the figments of men with the true God. He is compelled to give some honour to the God of Abraham, yet he lies plunged in his own idolatrous pollution; and, that his own religion may not appear the worse, he gives it the colour of antiquity. Meanwhile, Jacob does not swear superstitiously. For Moses declares that he sware [sic] only by the "fear of Isaac."[4]

3. M.G. Kline, "Genesis," *New Bible Commentary*, 105.
4. Calvin, *Genesis*, 181.

In essence, the witness heap was a memorial cairn. As such, it served a two-fold purpose: It was both a mechanism to remind people that something significant had taken place there and a reminder of what actually had taken place. In ancient Hebrew culture, it was not as uncommon as we might think to associate important events with inanimate objects (see also Josh 4:4), though it is equally clear that they were only ever intended to serve as symbolic references to the fact that God himself was the true witness of their appeal.

The stone pillar was also a spiritual landmark in the life of Jacob. It was effectively a pillar of separation. He might even be charged with further deceit in agreeing to the terms and conditions of the covenant treaty, given that he appears to have had absolutely no intention of crossing Laban's path anyway. That said, however, it is not beyond the bounds of possibility that Laban was fully aware of that fact.

David and Jonathan (1 Sam 18:1–4)

The relationship between David and Jonathan has often been cited as the prime example of covenant expressed between two peers—and not without good cause. Those who seek to sully the image with suggestions of sexual impropriety do so without any legitimate biblical warrant. The exchanging of robes can be more legitimately understood as a symbol of Jonathan conceding his rightful claim to the throne than as a prelude to physical familiarity. Theirs was a model of homo-sociality, not a paradigm of homoeroticism. As Jerry Landay writes: "The friendship of Jonathan and David was the embodiment of the sheer love of man for man, an intimacy based on shared experiences and dangers . . . a kind of intuitive trust that transcends the taint of ambition, jealousy or the claim of sex."[5]

They were friends, but their friendship was built on a firmer foundation than merely common likes and dislikes. It was forged in the furnace of divine purpose and proved in the crucible of difficult circumstance. Theirs was a covenant of godly brotherhood. It was a covenant perfect in its inauguration and almost ideal in its expression: almost, but not quite. In the preamble to the passage in which Jonathan and David exchange covenant oaths, we see a familiar covenant word: *chesed* (1 Sam 20:14), commonly translated "loving kindness." The NIV translates it "unfailing kindness," pointing to its enduring nature. Leonard Brockington

---

5. Landay, *David*, 36.

observes that "[l]ove and loyalty are the very essence of any relationship based on a personal covenant; in Hebrew these two aspects are bound together in the single word *hesed*."[6]

Most importantly, the covenant that existed between David and Jonathan did not involve just the two men; it was built on a triangular relationship. In the first book of Samuel we read: "May the Lord be between you and me forever" (1 Sam 20:23). This was the basis of their unity. They were one in purpose and knit together in motivation because they were joined in spirit by the Spirit of God. After the covenant between David and Jonathan was initially established (1 Sam 18:3), Scripture describes a number of subsequent episodes in which they renew their pact (e.g., 20:16–17; 23:18). This should not suggest that the original agreement had been violated in any way or was in need of urgent appraisal, rather that circumstances afforded opportunities for them to reaffirm their pledge to one another. The final occasion is touched with both poignancy and irony. Not only is it the last-recorded instance of a meeting between them; the context suggests that Saul's search for David was a frustrated pursuit, and yet Jonathan appears to have had not the slightest difficulty locating his closest friend.

Throughout the narrative that features David's endurance of Saul's hostility, Jonathan seeks to bring peaceful resolution to the situation. His name is a shortened version of Jeho-Nathan, which literally means "God has given." He was certainly a divine gift to David, and would have been to his father, too, if only Saul had suspended his pride long enough to unwrap its contents. We have seen that, in terms of divine covenant, Jonathan himself is not without christological typology. The gap between the righteousness of David and the sinfulness of Saul required a mediator inextricably and covenantally linked to both parties. Sadly, the more Jonathan sought to bring peace to his father's spirit, the angrier his flesh became.

When considering the peer covenant between Abraham and Abimelech, we noted that God's covenant with Abraham did not preclude the possibility of his entering into other covenant treaties, provided they did not exceed the parameters of the divine covenant. The ultimate tragedy for Jonathan was that he died fighting alongside his father (1 Sam 31), David's sworn enemy. There is, of course, a natural sense of allegiance and commitment to one's own bloodline, both expected and

---

6. L.H. Brockington, "1 and 2 Samuel," *Peake's Commentary*, 327.

to be expected. But when the demands of that loyalty impinged upon the conditions of a covenant agreement freely entered into, then the latter should have superseded the former.

Jonathan's declaration that God's hand was upon David as the divinely appointed successor to Jonathan's father, Saul, was all the more remarkable given that, as the king's eldest son, he himself was the natural heir to the throne. Although Scripture presents him as a valiant warrior (1 Sam 13, 14), it is for his loyalty to David that Jonathan is perhaps best remembered. On one occasion, he put his own life in jeopardy (19:1–20) rather than renege on the pact into which the two had entered, even apparently excusing himself from his father's two missions against David, the first at En Gedi (24:1–2) and later at Hakilah (26:1–2). But it was at Mount Gilboa that Jonathan sacrificed his life, when his filial duty finally gained the upper hand over his fealty to David (31:2).

After Jonathan's death alongside his father and brothers on the battlefield, there was a strange mixture of emotions in Israel. Those who had remained faithful to David saw the opportunity for his kingship to finally be extended throughout the land. Even some who had been close allies of Saul's house during his lifetime recognized God's hand upon David, and throughout the course of events that ultimately brought about their sovereign's downfall. Some of Saul's men remained defiant and intended to carry on as before: "The king is dead. Long live the king!"—but a king from the same dynastic line. Others knew that David was divinely favored and feared the worst.

Mephibosheth was Jonathan's son. He was five years old when his father, grandfather, and uncles lost their lives at Jezreel. His nurse either knew nothing of David's covenant with Jonathan or imagined that its conditions were only valid as long as they both remained alive. Consequently, she panicked. In her haste to protect the boy's life, he fell and his feet were crushed. Thereafter he lived as a cripple in the wilderness, ever fearful of being hunted down and discovered. At this stage, it seems that David was not even aware of Mephibosheth's existence. When he found out, he sent a chariot to Lo-Debar, east of the Jordan River, for him. As he heard it approaching, Mephibosheth thought it could mean only one thing: he, too, was about to die. Only when he met the king face-to-face did he learn the truth. He was to be the beneficiary of David's covenant with his father, Jonathan: his inheritance was restored and he received the king's favor and protection (see 2 Sam 9).

The lessons we might learn from the account in Scripture of the covenant between David and Jonathan are many and wondrous. Those that draw one person may be completely different from those that draw another person. Three I believe to be of paramount importance are these:

- True friendship that perseveres is possible between men;
- The criteria for true friendship are that those concerned are selfless, righteous, and evince a servant disposition; and
- Given that true friendship was possible in the light of comparatively limited revelation, should it not be more common under the illumination of the new covenant?

It comes as no surprise to discover that David is almost universally acknowledged as the greatest king to rule over God's covenant people, Israel. It should be equally unsurprising to learn that Jonathan is ranked by many as one of the most self-denying characters in Jewish history. Edward White has the following to say:

> This covenant evidenced one of the finest friendships in history. All through the centuries the love of Jonathan and David has symbolized that unselfish fraternal feeling that should characterize the true relations of men with an exalted, common purpose in life, and their relation became the foundation for many of the best known fraternal organizations.[7]

It is said that a true friend is someone with whom we can be ourselves. I would put it more exclusively than that: friendship of this kind is the only secure environment in which we may be ourselves without fear of reprisal, misrepresentation, or betrayal. I thank God that there are those who provide that for me and—I hope—I, too, for them. I also give thanks to God that the best of these amongst men is, in fact, a woman—my wife. May that always be the case. Also, may my circle of friendships of this kind continue to increase, as the days go by, rather than diminish.

Summary

We have looked at three examples of personal covenant relationships in the Old Testament. They each teach us something, even if it is how *not* to apply the principles of creating lateral covenants. Of course, their

---

7. White, *Law in the Scriptures*, 166.

very nature restricts the lessons they are able to provide. The covenants we have looked at between Abraham and Abimelech, Jacob and Laban, and David and Jonathan were all exclusive and, therefore, by definition, limited in their scope. In the remainder of this chapter, we shall be looking at how we may best express covenant laterally, not in exclusive terms, but as co-members of the all-inclusive new covenant.

We are joined together because we are one in Christ. And yet within the parameters of that inclusivity, there will be those with whom we have a special bond. God will draw alongside us those with whom we share a mutual recognition of gift and function; a reciprocal responsibility to ensure, to the best of our abilities, that the divine potential in each other is maximized; and a sense of common loyalty that always seeks the best possible outcome even if, on occasion, that calls for brutal honesty.

A NEW COVENANT PEOPLE

As we draw toward the overall conclusion, the next two sections of this chapter will focus on the new covenant people and how they express their covenantal loyalty. Of course, it goes without saying that the new covenant people consists of all those and only those who truly belong to the church of Jesus Christ, in accordance with the stipulations recorded in Scripture. It should be equally obvious that, for most of us, the opportunity to create and participate in lateral covenants will be limited to the local church of which we are a part. It must also be pointed out, however, that our covenant obligations toward those outside of that structure are not thereby diminished. Other Christians with whom we enjoy fellowship on a less-frequent basis, whether because of distance, conflicting schedules, or other natural circumstances, remain our covenant brothers and sisters in Christ. Whether we see each other several times a week, twice a year, or once every blue moon, the depth of relationship is the same because it is built on a firmer foundation than frequency of fellowship.

A Community of Believers

We have seen that the noun usually translated "church" in English Bibles is the same word used in the Septuagint for the Hebrew word *eda* or "congregation"—i.e., the Greek word *ekklēsia*. It is a compound of two words, the preposition *ek* and a nominal form of the verb *kaleō*, meaning "to call out for a specific purpose or those of like mind."[8] In terms of etymological definition, there appears to be such a close link between *ekklēsia* and the verb *sunagō* (literally "to assemble") and its cognate, *sunagogē*, (a word used both of the place of assembly and the people therein assembled) that one is almost tempted to use the English words "church" and "synagogue" interchangeably.

If the premise behind the subtitle of this book is valid, then it behooves us as believers to demonstrate that fact to a watching and largely ignorant world. What I mean is this: If covenant truly is the basis of God's self-disclosure, then the foundation of the way Christians reveal God in Christ should be as a covenant-keeping people. In an age where individuality is encouraged and independence promoted, the Scriptures continue to testify to the hallmarks of arguably the most successful period in the history of the church thus far. "They devoted themselves to the apostles' teaching and to the fellowship, to the breaking of bread and to prayer. Everyone was filled with awe, and many wonders and miraculous signs were done by the apostles. All the believers were together and had everything in common" (Acts 2:42–44).

There seems little evidence—other than by inference—to suggest that the wonders and miracles were only made possible by their devotion, and I would certainly not wish to present it as a formulaic condition. However, it would seem reasonable that those who bemoan the apparent lack of the sense of God's almighty presence might at least consider a more diligent approach to the study of his word, genuine care and compassion, regular opportunity for partaking of the Lord's Supper, and prayer according to the pattern of Jesus' clear and distinct instruction on the matter.

By definition, then, the church is the redeemed community, that is, the company of all true believers. No other definition has biblical warrant. In reality, its temporal function must be perceived in relation to the eternal purpose of God. In AD 325, the Council of Nicaea concluded that the marks of this redeemed community, its identifying characteristics, are visible unity, sanctity, catholicity, and apostolicity. We are one because we are so in Christ. Not only does this reality release us from the necessity of trying to achieve unity, it also demonstrates that it would have been beyond our capacity to do so outside of Christ. Our sanctification, too, is guaranteed by virtue of a life given over to the leading of the Holy Spirit. The church is universal in view of its being unrestricted

---

8. See Vine, *Expository Dictionary*, 75–76.

by time, place, race, culture, or denominational allegiance. The church is apostolic in the sense that we are built on the foundation of, and devote ourselves to, the teaching of the early apostles.

If the vertical aspect of our covenant relationship is that of sons in relation to their Father, then the horizontal implications of the same covenant are that we relate to one another as members of a family. It is perhaps significant how seriously the apostle Paul seemed to regard those first seeds of denominationalism at Corinth: "Is Christ divided?" (1 Cor 1:13). No amount of ecumenical endeavor or striving to bring the multi-faceted tribes together could—or yet, still can—produce unity in the faith. Many might be willing to find common ground in terms of fellowship, breaking of bread, and prayer, but the foundation for all of these must surely be a return to true apostolic instruction (Acts 2:42).

It is perhaps noteworthy that in the environment of a lateral covenant such as is described in Acts, evangelistic fruitfulness seems not to have been a major difficulty. In response to their holding to the teaching of the apostles, engaging regularly in fellowship, breaking bread together regularly and informally, and considering prayer to be the naturally supernatural means of Godward communication, others were divinely added to their number on a daily basis. This should really have come as no surprise. After all, Jesus had promised that when he was lifted up, he would draw all men to himself (John 12:32). What better way to exalt the risen Lord than to display the true marks of discipleship in a measure of love that extends beyond the parameters of "I'll remember to pray for you, brother." Dismissing the plea for help from those to whom we are joined, with a glib "just trust the Lord, sister," fails to recognize, let alone acknowledge, that we may be the ones the trusted Lord opts to use in order to minister to that need.

The apostle Paul employs many metaphoric images to convey the idea of the church as the new covenant people of God. In relation to its worshipfulness, it is a building (Eph 2:21); in respect of its corporate nature, it is a body (Rom 12:4–5; 1 Cor 12:12–27); with reference to the sanctification process of the Holy Spirit upon its members, it is a bride (Eph 5:25–27). And so, under the new covenant, the redeemed community of God is a praising people, a mutually interdependent people, and a people of whom it may rightfully be said, "They are a work in progress." In the words of Howard Snyder: ". . . according to the New Testament, the church is a charismatic organism, not an institutional organisation."[9]

9. Snyder, *Problem of Wineskins*, 157.

Covenant Expressed 169

The significant feature of any living organism is development. This is no less true when considering the church in either its universal or local aspects. The difficulty in our understanding arises, however, in view of the fact that, today, church growth is spoken of almost exclusively in terms of an increase in numbers. The scriptural position is quite different. Although being "added to" was a prominent characteristic of the New Testament church, more distinctive still was coming—or rather, being brought—to maturity.

Maturity has absolutely nothing to do with age, very little to do with experience, and everything to do with the acceptance of responsibility. Our English word means, among other things, "to be complete in natural development." Biblically, we might say that it means to be spiritually perfect. This, of course, will not be fully realized until the sanctification process is complete, but it is a work in progress. God's ideal for his church is that it ultimately comes to maturity. In some respects, the measure of the whole is governed by the level of its constituent parts. This means that his purpose for you and me as individual members of the new covenant is that we each become fully developed Christians. At the moment, that may seem a distant objective, but he has not left us unequipped for the task. As Paul so lucidly reminds us: "It was [Christ] who gave some to be apostles, some to be prophets, some to be evangelists, some to be pastors and teachers [in order] to prepare God's people for works of service, so that the body of Christ may be built up until we all reach unity in the faith and in the knowledge of the Son of God and become mature, attaining to the whole measure of the fulness of Christ" (Eph 4:11–13).

The Old Testament book of Proverbs has traditionally been divided into three parts for the purpose of analysis:

- Chapters 1–9: Early life/youthfulness
- Chapters 10–24: Early adulthood
- Chapter 25–31: Maturity (when experience has wrought wisdom)

The nineteenth-century Anglican expositor, Charles Bridges, lauds it in these words: "[The book of Proverbs] is . . . a guidebook and directory for godly conduct. The details of the external life, in all the diversified spheres, are given or implied with perfect accuracy, and with a profound knowledge of the workings of the human heart."[10]

10. Bridges, *Proverbs*, xii–xiii.

The fear of the Lord is truly the beginning of knowledge (Prov 1:7), but having absolute trust in him as a covenant-keeping God (22:19)—that trust expressed in character-building loyalty to others who have discovered the same truth (27:17) and justice for the socially dependent (29:7; 31:8–9)—surely indicates that one has moved a considerable way in the journey toward maturity. Therefore, unity of faith plus personal knowledge of the Son plus absolute fullness of Christ equals maturity. And we accomplish it by recognizing, identifying, and making room for the valid expression of the tools God has placed at our disposal to effect personal, interpersonal, social, and cultural change. But it all begins with the very simple step of embracing the lateral covenant, an acknowledgment that I need you and you need me.

Under One Head

It is Christ's headship—and that alone—which gives the church its unity. Constitutional conformity can neither achieve such unity nor, indeed, maintain it. True oneness is organic, not organized; it is expressed as life in accordance with the Spirit, not the letter (2 Cor 3:6).

The kingdom of God is a subject for another time. In this context, however, it is appropriate to remind ourselves that covenant people relate to each other by virtue of first submitting to the kingdom rule of God in their lives. In other words, we identify with one another as members of the body of Christ, having him as our common head. We express our oneness in him in accordance with the principles of his kingdom (that is, the kingdom over which he is king). Otherwise, our capacity to communicate the gospel is severely hampered. The message of the kingdom must be seen to be true experientially, not only believed to be true by virtue of fine-sounding arguments or convincing dogma.

The church is essentially an agent of no other kingdom but Christ's. It is not a tool for denominationalism, much less a weapon with which to browbeat those who—unwittingly or otherwise—stand outside its borders. It is, as we have seen, the body of Christ on earth, comprising the redeemed. Although, when viewed separately, these are redeemed individuals, the Bible speaks of the church only in the context of a redeemed corporate entity, whether that is in its local or universal expression. Whichever it is we have under consideration, each may be spoken of as a single organism. The local church is one body *in* Christ; the universal church is one body *under* Christ. Of course, in real terms, the converse is equally true. However, local churches are usually—according to the biblical pattern—*under* Christ by virtue of their submitting to local delegated leadership. There is no such appointed intermediary for being *in* Christ.

There are many differences between the church universal and the church local. These include tangibility, visibility, sphere of expression, sense of belonging, level and frequency of fellowship, accountability, witness—and the list goes on. But the differences, such as they are, exist only in measure, not in essence. The catalogue of common traits is far lengthier. Indeed, it would be true to say that the universal church is not so much made up of the total number of local churches in the world, but that the latter is a geographically defined manifestation of the former. Thus, the body metaphor is aptly applicable to both.

In terms of natural physiology, a body can only be in one of two possible states. It can either be entirely dead or it can be both living and dying (by degrees, of course). It cannot be only living without some semblance of mortal decadence taking place. The same is true—in relative terms, at least—of the body of Christ. If it is not dead, then it is both living and dying. Whereas the rate of growth and decay in a natural body is continually regressive from the point of birth (that is, moving toward death), the opposite is true of the body of Christ, as moral decadence progressively gives way to sanctified righteousness.

My long-favored definition of the church is simply that it is "the redeemed community." However, I recently stumbled across this definition of Jim Packer's, which seems particularly appropriate in the current context: ". . . the New Testament idea of the church is reached by superimposing upon the notion of the covenant people of God the further thought that the church is the company of those who share in the redemptive renewal of a sin-spoiled creation, which [renewal] began when Christ rose from the dead."[11]

Thus, against those who claim that certain local expressions of the church seem to be dead, I would argue two things. First, if it is a legitimate local expression, there will be features that are compatible with both living and dying, however remote the former may seem to be. Second, not everything that identifies itself as church necessarily *is* church. Unless it is defined in accordance with biblical standards, it may well be simply a gathering of individuals with certain religious proclivities. Remember, the church, whether universally or locally considered, is essentially and

---

11. Packer, *Serving the People of God*, 6.

necessarily "the company of those who share in the redemptive renewal of a sin-spoiled creation," brought together in Christ as members of the new covenant. Any collection of people that falls short of this biblical standard fails to meet the requirements of what Scripture calls "church."

In order for this new covenant people to be truly effective—both corporately and as individuals—such a radical transformation is called for that only new birth will suffice. Fallen humanity is tainted with sin. This manifests itself overtly in areas of self-interest, egocentricity, and the promotion of a philosophy that is encapsulated by a "looking-after-number-one" approach to life. If these sins do not receive the fatal blow they deserve at conversion, they will continue to dog us throughout our Christian experience. This is surely what Jesus had in mind when he said, "If anyone would come after me, he must deny himself and take up his cross and follow me. For whoever wants to save his life will lose it, but whoever loses his life for me and the gospel will save it" (Mark 8:34–35).

Taking up our cross (note, not Christ's) has little, if anything, to do with endurance; it is all about executing the death sentence on any desires we may have that are based on perceived "rights." Perhaps it is for this reason that the newness of life of which Scripture speaks can only commence with the burial of the old self in the rite of baptism (see Rom 6:4).

Presentation, not Pretence

As discussed in the preceding chapter, individuals are primarily members of the church as a matter of their identity in relation to Jesus, although their normal growth in Christ requires participation in healthy, loving, and vibrant relationships with other Christians. It is critical that we do not overemphasize individual salvation to the detriment of the legitimate place Scripture accords the corporate body into which the newly converted are baptized. I am particularly indebted to Charles Haddon Spurgeon for his observation that "those who go about and speak lightly of church fellowship, and would have all Christians maintain themselves in separateness from the churches, do mischief, and are unwittingly the agents of evil; for the church is, under God, a great blessing to the world; and union with the church is intended to be a method of confession which is not to be neglected."[12]

12. Charles Haddon Spurgeon, from a sermon delivered at The Metropolitan Tabernacle on 19 July 1863.

Christian living under the new covenant is a life of exposure. It often requires of us that we persist when others might more readily surrender, be unswerving in situations where it might be easier to feign satisfaction, look for opportunities to be of service rather than to be waited on hand and foot, and carry on loving when others might choose to leave well enough alone. The church will not fulfill its purpose at the hands of bedside Baptists, settee Salvationists, Pentecostal party-poopers, charismatic couch potatoes, or Methodist ministries from the maisonette (with apologies for any offense caused both to those mentioned and to others who may feel left out). On fifty-four separate occasions, the writers of the New Testament instruct us how we, as Christian believers, should treat one another (in the Greek word *allelōn*); it is always in the context of social interaction. For those first-century Christians, the reality of their salvation was to be found in their commitment to Jesus as expressed in relationship with those to whom they were covenantally joined. Scripture teaches that we, too, reflect our attitude to Christ in the way we relate to his people (Matt 25:40, 45).

The basis of Paul's theological position was his conviction in a corporate, mature church, brought to perfection by each part working for the mutual edification of the whole, in love. Such a vision does not allow for a church with either dismembered or artificial limbs, much less for those who would seek to actively work against one another. Covenant relationships are organic in the sense that they are not maintained according to electoral constitution, but by the sharing together of a common life and purpose. The outworking of covenant means that there are both tangible privileges and clearly defined responsibilities within the church as a whole, and in its local expressions. Contributions of gift, ministry, finance, and prayerfulness are balanced by being submitted to godly overseers, whose function it is in God quite simply to "oversee." It is they who are responsible for the welfare of the flock entrusted to their care (1 Pet 5:3). Or, as the writer to the Hebrews puts it: "they keep watch over you as men who must give account" (13:17).

Church discipline is a valid expression of church government. The New Testament may not be as precise as some would like it to be with regard to the administration of chastening, due in no small part to the fact that it was never intended to formulate a hard-and-fast set of rules. For this reason, Paul offers little more than principles or guidelines to ensure that, as far as is practicable, the glory of God as seen through his church is maintained (2 Cor 6:14–7:1), that the church remains pure (1 Cor 5:6; 11:27), and that any offenders are dealt with in a manner aimed primarily at their ultimate restoration (5:5; 2 Thess 3:14). Any discipline required should ideally be preventative where, in the milieu of loving relationships, the local administration will suffice in keeping the unity of the Spirit without the need to resort to judicial measures.

The maturity God seeks in us, he has purposed to be effected through edification, exhortation, and admonition. It is a delight to him when we begin to show signs of living in secure relationships instead of in fear, loneliness, and introspection. Life is also a pleasurable experience for those so freed. For some years, I was bound by the "loner" tag, branded by many as an antisocial, independent, individualistic rebel. The truth was that I longed to relate and only chose not to for fear of being hurt yet again. But, oh, the joy of being released by God's Spirit into the good of what I was created for. He has broken down the barriers of mistrust and replaced them with arms of love, fellowship, togetherness, oneness, warmth, correction, godly discipline, and encouragement—the congenial benefits of covenant.

New covenant people may be identified by certain distinctive features, which distinguish them from those who are not new covenant people. Jesus provided some clues to his closest followers when he said: "You are the salt of the earth . . . You are the light of the world" (Matt 5:13–14). This is not to imply that unbelievers are wholly incapable of having a positive influence on society or doing ethically good works. Some of the religious leaders of Jesus' own day were eminently capable of that, but he nevertheless insisted that citizenship in the kingdom of God consisted of those whose righteousness surpassed that of the Pharisees and the teachers of the law (v. 20). True righteousness is not about merely keeping commandments. That was what lay at the root of the old covenant's impotence—it evoked an externally ritualistic approach that was not the product of an inner spiritual condition. Christian righteousness is not achieved by a fresh attempt to live by the rule book, but by a new birth (John 3:16), which must be preceded by the death of the old self.

Biblical corporeity is essential to the concept of covenant. The very idea of covenant presupposes a people who can exercise that covenant. Throughout the Old Testament history of Israel, we see that their obligations were not only manifested in how they related to Yahweh, but in what ways this was worked out laterally amongst themselves. God's purpose for his people has not changed: they should be a covenant-keeping people. The major differences are that now, since the Christ-event, the covenant stipulations are no longer inscribed on tablets of stone, but are indelibly etched on our fleshly human hearts (see Jer 31:31–34), and the Holy Spirit thus enables us to comply as a delight instead of a duty.

If one of the characteristic traits of new covenant people is a deeper level of righteousness, then another is a wider expression of love. It is not just that the measure of commitment toward our friends and relatives is more intense, but that the parameters extend to include even those who are habitually hostile toward us (see Matt 5:43–44). The Pharisees had taken a lateral exegesis of the Hebrew Scriptures to the extreme. Nowhere had they been commanded to hate their enemies, only to love their neighbors (Lev 19:18). Jesus reinstated the original intention of God's heart and gave it renewed application. In effect, he was saying: "Your neighbor is not just the one with whom you have much in common, find agreement in matters of theology, or just generally enjoy being around; your neighbor is your fellow man, irrespective of the presence or otherwise of common likes or dislikes." The love of the Father is all-encompassing. The Son of God does only what he sees his Father doing. In us, too, there should be a family resemblance.

All of these acts must be rooted in the fact that we are in Christ. Otherwise, they are simply good deeds that are as much use as filthy rags (Isa 64:6). They become effective because our commitment to righteousness; our concern for the unsaved, the needy, and the socially outcast; and our higher ideals are born of our relationship to Jesus. Thus, we need to understand precisely what he meant when he spoke of himself as the vine and of us as the branches (John 15:1–8). In order to accomplish this, we must first rid our minds of what we think he said and consider the actual words. For years, I have thought of this particular text along the lines of his being the trunk and we the branches (that is, bits added on, but emanating from) or that he is the root and we are the branches (that is, connected somehow, but separated by the eminently more spiritual). But he is the vine: root, trunk, and branches; we are not simply loosely attached to him as a tag would be, nor related by a third party: we are part of him. He is not simply joined to us; he actually is in us. Indeed, this is the hope of glory (Col 1:27).

One of the most effective initiatives for church expansion in the UK over the past thirty years or so—and more recently throughout the world—has been the Alpha course. Part of its success is no doubt due to its overtly non-denominational stance, which makes it ideally suited for effortless adaptation. The emphasis on friendship evangelism in a non-threatening environment is another positive feature. The fact that God seems to have set his seal of approval on it should not be underestimated either. One of Alpha's early thought-provoking discussions bears the title *Christianity: Boring, Untrue, Irrelevant?* The aim is to debunk the myth, or at least to argue that, although one's experience of it may well have been all of these things, that need not necessarily be the case.

The fact that many churches convey their particular brand of Christianity in a way that is far from riveting—with little sense of genuine conviction, and utterly unrelated to the realities of life—must surely be beyond dispute. If I can see that as a believer, little wonder that the unregenerate tend to find us so unappealing. Now, it is all very well and good to argue that God is capable of reaching out to the lost, or unchurched, or unelect, or whatever noun sits more comfortably within your denominationally developed vocabulary, but we are called to be witnesses. As I mentioned earlier, this may only consist of being, but it is being in such a way that demonstrates all that is good about Christianity.

Playing the blame game about how the current situation came about is largely unproductive. Only living our lives as vibrant and true covenant believers, who fulfill the covenant in ways relevant to our socio-cultural settings, will suffice, and only lives that are governed by the Holy Spirit of God will ultimately prove effective.

Summary

So, new covenant people are marked by a deeper sense of commitment to moral standards than were adherents of the old covenants—as well as by wider parameters for the expression of godly love. They should also be noted for loftier objectives. To a world that rewards not just the ambitious, but those who are ruthlessly so (to the point of not allowing anything or anyone to stand in their way), the words of Jesus seem diametrically opposed: "Seek first [the Father's] kingdom and his righteousness" (Matt 6:33a). The kingdom of God is not a geographical location or the final destination of the redeemed; it is the rule of God in action. As the Lord's Prayer intimates, the coming of God's kingdom is essentially synonymous with his will being done on earth as it is in heaven (v. 10). Wherever godly principles dictate the agenda, there is the kingdom of

God. It is true that Jesus' words are not an advisory; they are a command. However, they also end with a promise: "and all these [other] things will be given to you as well" (v. 33b). What other things? Those things—such as what we eat, drink, or wear—that we are not to prioritize over seeking to honor God in all that we think, say, and do (v. 31).

COVENANT LOYALTY

The *Concise Oxford Dictionary* defines loyalty as "the state of being . . . true or faithful (to duty, love, or obligation)." In New Testament terms, the closest equivalent noun is related to the Greek *pistos*, a verbal adjective signifying faithfulness, trustworthiness, or reliability, all of which are implied by the essence of covenant. Indeed, so integral to the concept of covenant is loyalty that disloyalty might be deemed tantamount to the breaking of covenant. Strictly speaking, of course, such qualities exist perfectly in God toward us, and a significant measure is required of us toward him. However, in the context of lateral covenant, a certain degree of person-to-person loyalty is surely also to be expected. We will look at these in four distinct areas: honor, confrontation, forgiveness, and provision.

Honor—No Hint of Betrayal

There is a subtle distinction between libel and slander, though both may give rise to legal action. In simple terms, a libelous act is one in which a defamatory statement is made in written or published form, while slander is a spoken assertion that is damaging to a person's reputation. What libel and slander have in common is that they are false representations. In Scripture, however, not only is there no reference to libel (for obvious reasons), there is likewise no suggestion that a defamatory remark made has to be proved to be inaccurate. It can be true and still be regarded as slander. The main verb employed by the writers of the New Testament is *blasphēmeō* and its cognates, from which we obtain our English word "blaspheme." It usually denotes "taking the Lord's name in vain," but its actual meaning is "to speak evil against," without any specified object—it could be anyone. Other English translations render it "to rail," "revile," or "speak calumny against."[13]

---

13. Vine, "Report," *Expository Dictionary*, 954.

Perhaps an English word closer in meaning to the original would be "gossip," although this tends to dilute the seriousness Scripture assigns such ill-conceived conduct. This is especially true in view of the Greek noun translated "slanderer," *diabolos*, which surely identifies the action with its true source. Indeed, so convinced was the apostle Paul of the ungodly nature of speaking ill against a fellow-believer that he advocated the relinquishing of all social ties with the perpetrator: "You must not associate with anyone who calls himself a brother but is . . . a slanderer . . . With such a man do not even eat" (1 Cor 5:11).

Therefore, part of our covenant loyalty toward other Christians is to maintain a measure of honor toward them in what we say about them. We are likewise covenantally obliged to preserve the same level of honor on their behalf in relation to what we hear said about them by others. This does not necessarily mean merely defending them in their absence. After all, it might reasonably be argued that a false defense is as illegitimate as an erroneous accusation. As implied earlier, the integrity or otherwise of the allegation is not the issue in question; it is the potential to damage the reputation of the brother or sister in Christ, irrespective of whether his or her demeanor or behavior warrants the charge.

The word "honor" has sadly become devoid of its true meaning in the understanding of many, largely by virtue of constant misuse or abuse. There are no degrees of honor, any more than there are of commitment. To speak of "wholehearted commitment" is to imply that it is possible to be anything less than fully committed. Similarly, partial honor does not exist. A perceived honor that fails to withstand the test of costliness is not really honor at all. But neither can honor be forced. If it does not exist naturally—though admittedly it is of supernatural origin—then the kind of honor displayed will not be the product of loving trust, but more likely of fear.

Genuine honor is not motivated by the potential for favor in return. This is true even if the possible benefactor is of divine origin. To think "I must honor this person because he or she has an influential circle of contacts" is bad enough, but is it really any worse than the conviction that we remain honorable toward God in the hope of eternal reward? What truly is our motivation—relationship or self-centeredness? Also, what precisely do we mean by honor? Or, perhaps more to the point, what do we envisage it means to honor? Defending the indefensible is certainly not part of the scope of honor. Indeed, I would argue that it honors an individual far more to point out the errors of his or her ways than to turn a blind eye to them or even excuse such behavior. As the writer of the Proverbs reminds us: "Wounds from a friend can be trusted, but an enemy multiplies kisses" (Prov 27:6).

The basis of our honor can provide a clue. Our friends are usually—if not exclusively—those with whom we have much in common. We may also come to count as friends those with whom we rejoice over our differences but, more often than not, friendship begins with a shared purpose, mutual interests, and/or familiar understanding. It is easy to like those who are most like us. Imagine the following: Stan supports a different football team than I do, but we are still each sufficiently passionate about the sport to enjoy a healthy debate about the state of the national game. His political views are surprisingly similar to mine, as are his musical tastes, his appreciation of single-malt whisky, his sense of humor, and his love of vintage motor cars. Not only that, but Stan's comprehension of events at the consummation of the age, discussed over a dram or two of *Caol Ila*,[14] is remarkably close to how I see them unfolding.

Joe, on the other hand, could hardly be more different. He cannot understand the apparently pointless obsession with sport, *per se*; he is at a loss to comprehend how people could possibly dare to call themselves "Christian" and vote anything but Conservative; any melody written after 1910 is not worthy of the assignation "musical;" and "Christians and alcohol? Don't you read your Bible, brother?" Similarly, as far as Joe is concerned, humor is a frivolous waste of time and effort, designed by the devil to keep believers from the Lord's work, while transport is merely a means of getting from one set of crusade meetings to another. As for the end time, "what is now veiled will be revealed when God chooses for it to be so."

And then someone asks for your opinion about each of them. "Well, I've always liked Stan. From the very first time I was introduced to him, I just knew, it was almost like a prophetic insight that here was a true brother in Christ, upon whom the Spirit of God rests in abundant measure. And I have not been proved wrong, have I, Ethel? In fact, if anyone were to ask me to name one Christian of the many I have come across in the past thirty-odd years who epitomizes the essence of a true believer according to the biblical pattern, then Stan's your man."

---

14. A brand of single-malt whisky.

"And Joe? Ah! I wish you hadn't asked me about Joe, really. Now, I'm sure he means well. It's just that . . . well . . . he doesn't seem to get it. I don't know if he had a difficult upbringing, or if there's some hidden secret lurking in his closet, but there's just something not quite right about Joe. In fact, between you and me—and I only mention it for prayer and because I'm really concerned that he truly embraces the gospel—I think he's seriously in need of spiritual counseling; if not, some medical attention. I mean, it's unnatural, isn't it, Ethel? It's not as God intended us to be."

I repeat: it is easy to like those who are most like us. In effect, we are really smiling at the reflection in the mirror, only to find that, amazingly, it smiles back at us. But does this also affect our sense of honor? Or should there be a different criterion? At the risk of incurring allegations of impersonal detachment, I would suggest that our sense of honor—in this context, at least—should be motivated, not by the individual in question, but by his or her standing as a valid and vital member of the body of Christ. After all, the honor, loyalty, and commitment of which we speak are our covenant honor, covenant loyalty, and covenant commitment, of which Jesus is the basis and foundation.

As far as its members are concerned, the practical application of the whole of the new covenant is perfectly summed up in just one commandment: "Love one another" (John 13:34). The context shows that this is also the most powerful means of identification: "By this all people will know that you are my disciples" (v. 35). Consequently, the converse can have one of two possible conclusions:

- If you do not love one another, people will not know that you are my disciples; or
- If you do not love one another, people will know that you are not my disciples.

It is unclear which would be the more accurate. Perhaps the best policy would be to not stray into such areas of uncertainty, i.e., by simply loving one another. But what does this mean? Well, as John Stott rightly points out: "the practical consequences [are] both negative and positive."[15] On the one hand, such love ensures that we do not defame, dishonor, despise, or disregard our covenant brothers and sisters in Christ; on the other hand, it provides the basis for mutual respect, edifi-

---

15. Stott, *The Living Church*, 99.

cation, encouragement, forbearance, prayerfulness, and godly admonition where necessary.

Confrontation—No Offense Given or Taken

One should not imagine that the principles governing what we say about each other or tolerate being said by others negate our covenant responsibility to confront and challenge when called upon to do so. What we say emanates from what we are, for it is "out of the overflow of the heart [that] the mouth speaks" (cf. Mt 12:34; Luke 6:45). Therefore, if we truly have our fellow-believers' best interests at heart, we will look for opportunities to edify and not be afraid to rebuke. Of course, there will be varying degrees of willingness to speak to situations within the covenant family, where our freedom to voice concerns is in no small part determined by how close we are to one another. It is much easier, for example, to both give and receive correction where there already exists a firm foundation of mutual acknowledgment and acceptance than where such a platform is flimsy. There is little value in attempting to drive a ten-ton truck over a bridge made of straw.

A number of passages in Scripture speak to the issue of how we are to deal with troublesome issues within the covenant family. Many are contained within the book of Proverbs; however, the major principles are outlined by Jesus in Matthew's gospel account. First, Jesus implies that our coming before God is in some way dependent upon such issues not remaining outstanding (Matt 5:23–24). He then goes on to suggest that the matter be satisfactorily resolved in private wherever possible and that the primary motivating factor should be the continued spiritual well-being of the other party (see 18:15).

The word used in older English translations to describe this function is "admonition." It attempts—albeit imperfectly—to translate the Greek *nouthesia*, a compound of two words meaning literally "to put in mind." Thus, Vine posits that *nouthesia* is "the training by word, whether of encouragement or, if necessary, by reproof or remonstrance."[16] Although some denominations might make this directive exclusively the province of church leaders (see Acts 20:31; 1 Cor 4:14; Titus 3:10), the New Testament is not so prescriptive (see Rom 15:14; 1 Thess 5:14; 2 Thess 3:15).

Again, confrontation must not be regarded as necessarily an antonym of concord. In most cases, positive confrontation can be the har-

---

16. Vine, *Expository Dictionary*, 22.

binger of true spiritual harmony. The only caveat that I would add—and it is an admittedly large one—is that we ensure that the reasons we have for challenging certain issues are genuinely because we believe that the testimony of Jesus has been, is being, or is in danger of becoming seriously hampered, and not that we are seeking conflict simply because our private expectations have been compromised in some way. Does the issue really contravene God's clearly revealed word, or merely our culturally, socially, or politically polarized understanding of it? Our personal values can form an important and appropriate touchstone, provided we don't seek to impose them on others with the suggestion that "thus says the Lord . . ." Also, can we be absolutely sure that our decision to confront someone now is not itself in conflict with God's timing for the issue to attain a more satisfactory conclusion?

A distinction must also be made between "speaking the truth in love" (Eph 4:15) and simply loving to speak the truth, irrespective of the consequences. The context of Paul's counsel suggests that it does not mean having a serene look on our face as we tell our brother in Christ that he is grotesquely overweight, or mustering up our most angelic persona as we instruct our sister that she has the complexion of a recently used rugby field. The tongue has the power of life and death (Prov 18:21); apparently, there is no middle ground. In other words, its capabilities are exclusively either edification or destruction, building up or tearing down. It is possible to speak the truth in love with no positive effect, but that does not mean that there will be no effect at all. Therefore, it behooves us to give careful consideration to what we are about to say; some words once on the tip of our tongue would have been better left there. Let the words of the apostle James be our guide: "Everyone should be quick to listen, slow to speak and slow to become angry . . . if anyone does not keep a tight rein on his tongue, he deceives himself and his religion is worthless" (Jas 1:19, 26).

There are many potential grounds for conflict, including different experiences, a clash of values, varying opinions, and diverse backgrounds. Where these are the only basis of conflict, perhaps tolerance is more advisable than conflict. After all: "As iron sharpens iron, so one man sharpens another" (Prov 27:17). Sometimes, tension can be created by a perceived threat to one's identity. It seems to me that the recent and growing obsession with the cult of celebrity is born of a crisis of identity. That this fixation has invaded the Christian domain is clear—in the extent to which leadership status and clamoring for titles has become more important than fulfilling functional roles—and appears to bear out my suspicion. It is notable that Jesus was so conscious of who he was, and what he had come to do, that he was completely at ease taking on even the most menial of tasks, such as washing the disciples' feet (see John 13:3–5).

It is also said that Jesus was meek and gentle (2 Cor 10:1). This should not be regarded as weakness or a *laissez-faire* attitude toward inappropriate behavior. Neither should it be forgotten that this same meek and gentle Jesus was not averse to dealing with ungodly impropriety wherever he encountered it, even if that was in the temple courts (Matt 21:12–13). Where God's honor is at stake, confrontation may be ultimately inevitable.

To many people, confrontation does not come easy—nor should it. Just as we are more likely to accept correction from those whom we trust have our best interests at heart than from a total stranger, so too we should feel more than a little uncomfortable accepting rebuke from those who revel in the nickname of "Conflict Charlie" or "Gordon the Grumpy."

Perhaps one reason why we tend to steer clear of confrontation is because we have little idea of how to confront someone except through anger. Let us be quite clear about this: love should not only be the *motivation* for the confrontation, it should also provide the *platform* for the confrontation itself. God challenges us over certain issues because he loves us, not because he feels like letting off heavenly steam every so often. Similarly, to abstain from confrontation for fear of potentially causing hurt is really to abdicate our responsibilities. It might even be considered an abrogation of the restored image of God in us.

Godly confrontation is not to be confused with the (un)spiritual gift of discouragement. But neither should the equally devout trait of forbearance and confrontation remain mutually exclusive. Jesus was both charitable and challenging, long-suffering and confrontational, and he is supposed to be our role model. For us, the whole sanctification process involves God the Holy Spirit illuminating those areas of our lives that are most in need of being dealt with so that we may become increasingly Christ-like (1 Thess 4:3–8; 5:23).

Forgiveness—No Score to Settle

Our understanding of the biblical concept of forgiveness has become muddied, because the conventional treatment is that forgiveness is simply being "let off" for some misdemeanor on the grounds that it is relatively insignificant. Forgiveness in Scripture, on the other hand, takes full account of the seriousness of the offense and is released on the basis of two important features: the gracious disposition of the forgiver and the indisputable sense of remorse on the part of the one to be forgiven. Just as sin is essentially a breach of covenant, so too is forgiveness for sin based upon God's covenantal grace toward the sinner and the sinner's repentance for having violated his or her covenantal obligations. David Augsburger of Fuller Theological Seminary asserts that "forgiveness is the mutual recognition that repentance of either or both parties is genuine and that right relationships have been restored or achieved."[17]

In terms of the subject before us here, we too are expected to maintain the lateral covenant between our brothers and sisters in Christ to the best of our spiritual capacity. Note again that Scripture does not suggest that we do this; it mandates that we do. "Bear with each other and forgive whatever grievances you may have against one another. Forgive as the Lord forgave you" (Col 3:13).

There are two very small but significant words that help us understand the dynamics of our forgiveness toward others. They are the words that show us how we are to love others: the words are "as" and "so." Each has a vast array of uses. When employed together in this way, however, they simply mean "in precisely the same manner as such and such, do so and so." Consider the following, therefore: "As I have loved you, so you must love one another" (John 13:35). "As the Lord has forgiven you, so you also must forgive" (Col 3:13 (ESV)).

How does the Lord forgive? He does so on the basis of Christ's finished work, activated by repentance on our part, and without further recollection of the violation of the covenant. Forgiveness absorbs pain, just as love conquers enmity. It was the grace of God in Christ that enabled him to forgive, and it is the grace of Christ in us by the Holy Spirit that empowers us to conduct ourselves in exactly the same way.

Forgiveness lies at the heart of the gospel message. It is accessible to all by faith through repentance. Forgiveness between brothers and

---

17. D. Augsburger, "Forgiveness," *New Dictionary of Christian Ethics*, 389.

sisters in Christ should be similar. It should always be available to those who express authentic sorrow for their actions and commit to a redirection of life. Faith, too, is in evidence, for it is what binds us together as covenant family members.

The interesting thing is that Scripture does not seem to be overly concerned with apportioning blame regarding the breakdown of fellowship. Thus, wherever the fault seems to lie, it is always our responsibility to seek restoration (cf. Matt 5:23–24; 18:15–17). This applies even if you were initially in the wrong, have sought forgiveness, and the other party has not responded favorably to your conciliatory gesture. The aim is not to demonstrate a point; it is to win back your brother or sister. If he or she proves to be ungracious, then he or she alone is responsible before God for that attitude.

Even if those who have caused us hurt do not repent, we can still be released from the burden of leaving the situation unresolved by making it clear that we continue to hold out the hand of forgiveness. We are able to do this in the full knowledge that justice will finally prevail simply because God is just (2 Thess 1:6). In this, too, we follow Jesus' example as one who silently endured because "he entrusted himself to him who judges justly" (1 Pet 2:23).

In general terms, unrepented sin is undoubtedly the greatest stumbling block to both corporate church growth and individual Christian maturity. More specifically, however, I would suggest that the mantle of shame falls rather easily around the shoulders of those who do not forgive. The unwillingness to forgive cripples, twists, deforms, stunts, deprives of sleep, increases blood pressure, gnaws away at our insides, reminds us of long-past hurt, feeds pride, forces innocent bystanders to choose sides against their better judgment and, worst of all, it pleases the devil. That alone should cause us to sign up for a gap year of forgiving everything and everyone we can think of who has hurt us.

Similarly, the willingness of my brothers or sisters to forgive my hurtful comment, inappropriate behavior, or flagrant disregard for their well-being requires that I am truly sorry for such conduct, and that I thence move on in the good of having been forgiven. The basis, of course, is love, out of which emanates trust. Trust will no doubt have been damaged to some degree, but the readiness to forgive on the part of the injured party suggests that it might yet be restored. As the ones who have been forgiven, we too need to respond positively by trusting that the forgiveness on offer is as genuine and as unconditional as is God's forgiveness toward us.

My personal experience is such that the single most difficult obstacle to overcome in this area is not so much being able to forgive others as knowing how to embrace forgiveness for ourselves. A cavalier lack of recognition of having caused offense will obviously hinder the possibility of any restoration of relationship, but so too will the incapacity to appropriately deal with the issue of guilt. Of course, this is further exacerbated by the enemy's constant taunts that we are unworthy of any hope of forgiveness. So who do we believe: him or our loving, heavenly Father? This is why it is so important to realize the basis of true forgiveness. Whether it is divine forgiveness, offered by God, or forgiveness among peers, among believers, the grounds are essentially, constantly, and reassuringly the same: the atonement of Christ, whereby we are genuinely set free without repercussions. God has decreed it so in his role as eternal judge, and the devil cannot take the matter to any higher court on appeal.

Love is the key to all four elements being considered in this section. Nowhere will this be more apparent than in the area of forgiveness. We have already seen that when Jesus commanded the early disciples to love one another, it was to love as he had loved them. The expression of Jesus' love for us all met its zenith at the cross. It was a love that was extreme, a love that was ultimately self-sacrificing, and a love that was forgiving to the uttermost. Is our love for the family of God as intense? In terms of forgiveness, it certainly needs to be. Otherwise, dare we really expect to receive the Father's forgiveness for ourselves (see Matt 6:14–15)?

Provision—No Debt Outstanding

The apostle John was convinced that the witness to the love of God in us is our willingness to share with those in need (1 John 3:17–18). This love was so much in evidence in the early church that Scripture records—as if for our consideration—that "there were no needy persons among them. For from time to time those who owned lands or houses sold them, brought the money from the sales and put it at the apostles' feet, and it was distributed to anyone as he had need" (Acts 4:34–35).

I have had the immense privilege of being both benefactor and beneficiary on a number of occasions over the years. It is said that it is more blessed to give than to receive (Acts 20:35). We demonstrate our covenant loyalty to those of the household of faith by ensuring that we take advantage of every opportunity to do them good (see Gal 6:10). This does not mean, however, that to be the recipient of a gift is totally devoid of blessing, especially if the gift has been unsolicited except in private prayer. Insofar as the new covenant effectively restores the image of God in us—within certain parameters, of course—then surely we should expect to see a measure of his munificence replicated in us. The testimony of Scripture seems to indicate that man is not essentially narcissistic, but has become so as a product of the fall. It might reasonably be argued, of course, that it was Adam's self-centeredness that caused him to fall in the first place. However, that in itself does not necessarily mean that his egotistical proclivity was essential to his being. Far from it, in fact. God saw what he had created and commented that it was very good (Gen 1:31).

As with other virtues, beneficence is also capable of gross misappropriation. Can we always guarantee, for instance, that our concern for others is not in some way governed by selfish ulterior motives? This has certainly been my experience of those heavily committed to the so-called "prosperity teaching." Books, instruction manuals, seminar DVDs, and propaganda downloads on the principle of sowing and reaping abound. This is not to say, of course, that there is anything inherently wrong with the principle of sowing and reaping. How could there be? It is, after all, a principle with some biblical warrant (see Matt 13:1–23; Gal 6:7). In fact, many of us have learned—often by the long and painful route—that what we receive from being part of God's covenant body is in some way commensurate with what we are first of all prepared to give to it. And this is by no means restricted to financial matters. The New Testament writers also make it clear that it is not a question of how little we can get away with giving. If the grace of the Macedonian churches of the apostle Paul's experience is anything to go by, then it will require the giving of our very selves (see 2 Cor 8:1–5). Just in passing, let me remark that the level of urgency in their grace of giving (v. 7), which was so intense that they begged to be allowed the privilege (v. 4), is something that I have not encountered as a Christian. I suspect few have.

The question is: What is our motivation? Are we truly sowing in God's kingdom so that an abundant kingdom harvest might be reaped? Or do we see it as some sort of divinely appointed investment plan with material benefits?

In any case, we are not giving what is ours. When we gave our lives to Christ, it was an act that included all that we are and have, whether that be talents, gifts, means, or resources (Matt 25:14–29). From that point on, we became mere stewards of these things. As such, we are expected to manage all that has been entrusted to our care faithfully (1 Cor 4:2). Scripture gives some clear indicators about how we should contribute toward the needs of others:

- Secretly (Matt 6:1–4); if we publicize the fact, that in itself will be our reward;

- In proportion to our means (Mark 12:41–44); the amount we give is relatively unimportant; what we are left with, however, is hugely significant;

- With due care and consideration (1 Cor 16:2); our giving should not be a spur-of-the-moment decision or an impulsive emotional response; and

- With gladness (2 Cor 9:7); there is no such thing as reluctant generosity.

The lust for money is powerfully destructive (1 Tim 6:10). This teaching is not exclusive to the New Testament. God's judgment against Israel was delivered, in no small measure, because the people had so distanced themselves from the essence of their covenant responsibilities toward others. Through the prophet Amos, he decried their actions: "They sell the righteous for silver and the needy for a pair of sandals. They trample on the hands of the poor as upon the dust of the ground and deny justice to the oppressed" (Amos 2:6-7).

For those who are troubled by consumerism, the god of the age, there is arguably no more disarming technique than to give. Giving strips materialism of its power immediately. Unfortunately—though perhaps also unsurprisingly, given the pervading influence of sin—there are those within Christendom who preach a message of giving only to feed, fund, and finance their own covetous, insatiable appetites. "Give to the work," they say, but they fail to define "the work" as the annual golf club membership, the Aston Martin or BMW that will soon occupy the pastor's private parking space, or the "essential" solid oak study, featuring bookshelves with leaded glass doors so that we can all marvel at the unparalleled beauty of the library it houses. And Jesus says to us all: "Where your treasure is, there will your heart be also" (Matt 6:21).

The relationship we have with material objects says much about how seriously we regard our covenant relationship with God and others. This is not to say that wealth in itself is inherently sinful. Far from it. The question is: How tightly do we hold on to what we have? The answer—the nature of a godly attitude—is surely to be discovered in Paul's words: "I have learned to be content whatever the circumstances. I know what it is to be in need, and I know what it is to have plenty. I have learned the secret of being content in any and every situation, whether well fed or hungry, whether living in plenty or in need" (Phil 4:11–12).

The level of commitment required of us—in terms of releasing and embracing forgiveness toward and from one another, being comfortable in confronting issues in others and having them challenged in us, meeting others' needs and honoring our brothers and sisters in Christ—cannot take place within a structure of simply attending meetings, however regularly, however Spirit-filled those gatherings might be. Meeting others' needs and honoring our brothers and sisters in Christ can only take place within a framework of covenant family—the redeemed community of God.

The binding component in all of this—and much more besides—is *agapē*, godly love. This is *the* commandment of the new covenant (John 13:34–35). The fact that Christ issued a command—he did not make a recommendation—is especially significant. The love we are called upon to show others must neither depend on or be dictated by subjective feelings. In other words, it is not the fruit of our emotions but an act of the will. How else could we possibly be expected to love our enemies (Matt 5:44)?

SUMMARY

Scripture tells us about a number of peer covenants. The most significant of them, even in the Old Testament, were those grounded on a more firm foundation than merely a mutually beneficial agreement between two otherwise disinterested parties. We looked at several cases in point: Abraham, the man noted for his faith, was able to faithfully enter into covenant with Abimelech because his faith was rooted in a covenantally faithful God. The relationship between David and Jonathan, much heralded throughout history as the epitome of brotherly love, endured under the utmost stress simply because both men were committed to a greater covenantal purpose under God. Even the covenant between Jacob and Laban, though engineered out of common mistrust rather than reciprocal philanthropy, was largely effective because the supplanter was willing to lay down his habitual tendencies for the sake of God's covenantal honor.

We also looked at the new covenant people as a community under the headship of Christ. This is not a passive concept. Nor is it one that has a neutral effect on those who stand outside its parameters. The people of God are a testimony, whether we choose to be so or not. Non-believers will judge believers by whether they honor their covenant responsibilities, irrespective of the fact that the non-believers would probably not speak of the matter in those terms.

Within the new covenant, lateral relationships of the David and Jonathan ilk require openness, loyalty, and integrity, and they involve more than a little risk. While it is possible to remain satisfied with the apparently threat-free experience of knowing only superficial acquaintances, I am once again reminded of the words of the late Dr. Martyn Lloyd-Jones, albeit spoken in a different context: "The great danger is that we should be content with something that is altogether less than that intended for us."[18]

Covenant loyalty can often involve making uncomfortable decisions. There will be times of hurt, when we are prone to be both misunderstood and misrepresented. But no problem is beyond satisfactory resolution when we take into account the fact that we are blood relations, called out of our old way of life, and into a family in its truest sense. Let the Psalmist have—almost—the final word:

> How good and pleasant it is when brothers live together in unity! It is like precious oil poured on the head, running down on the beard, running down on Aaron's beard, down upon the collars of his robes. It is as if the dew of Hermon were falling on Mount Zion. For there the Lord bestows his blessing, even life for evermore. (Ps 133)

---

18. Lloyd-Jones, *Joy Unspeakable*, 16.

Conclusion

WHEN I FIRST CONSIDERED collating the material for this book, my aim was essentially two-fold: to establish and—where necessary—reaffirm the essential nature of the concept of covenant, and its implications as the basis of God's relationship with humanity. It was necessary to keep certain objectives in mind:

(1) To evaluate the major covenants of the Old Testament;

(2) To assess the key features of the new covenant in the light of the above findings;

(3) To examine closely the relationship between law and grace in the context of the new covenant;

(4) To identify the biblical significance of the covenant meal for believers; and

(5) To propose practical ways of expressing covenant laterally on the basis of the biblical record.

Chapter 1 looked briefly at God's covenant agreement with six individuals: Adam, Noah, Abraham, Moses, Phinehas, and David. Although each was momentous in its own right, the singular merits of each covenant were superseded by their value in the context of Old Testament revelation, i.e., the pedagogical development of each covenant from the one that preceded it.

Even then, however, the true significance of those covenants can only be fully appreciated in the light of the new covenant fulfillment by Christ, discussed in chapter 2. Here we saw that Adam's lost image of God was fully restored in mankind, or at least potentially restored; the coming of Jesus also offered the possibility of a new beginning for all who would step into the ark of God's provision. Real Abrahamic sonship is not dependent upon natural descent, but is the exclusive claim of those who exercise the same measure of faith he did. Where Moses effected Israel's deliverance from natural bondage in Egypt, so Christ liberated us all from the bonds of the devil and his hordes; and the priestly and kingly covenants under Phinehas and David, respectively, were filled out to their fullest potential through Christ's ushering in of a new and dynamic royal priesthood.

Chapter 3 offered a more in-depth look at the relationship between law and grace under the terms and conditions of the new covenant. I argued, contrary to common misrepresentation that, although the law's penal requirements have been fully met for us by God's grace toward us in Christ Jesus, this fact does not absolve us of the responsibility to honor God by upholding the law. Misunderstanding about this issue is rife. Some of this may be excused by the fact that Scripture's application of the word itself is not as universal as we might expect it to be. At its most basic, however, the law of God is simply the will of God expressed in forensic terminology. As the redeemed community of believers, can there be any justifiable reason for not wanting to be obedient to the revealed will of God?

The fourth objective was achieved in chapter 4, when I considered a number of different aspects of the covenant meal. As one of only two legitimate, new-covenant sacraments, we saw that it, too, is rooted in the Old Testament, namely in the Passover Feast. By taking time to remember the head, i.e., Christ, as per biblical instruction, only then are we able to fully rejoice with the body. As partakers of the meal, we must embrace certain responsibilities in order to avoid the curses and in anticipation of the blessing of our covenant God. Whatever we call it, covenant meal, Eucharist, breaking of bread or holy communion, the Supper belongs to the Lord and should be regarded as essentially his.

Finally, chapter 5 sought to apply the principles of all that had gone before. The previous chapters had been leading up to the central question of chapter 5: In the twenty-first century, how should Christian believers express, between and among themselves, the covenant of which they are all a part? Again, we looked at Old Testament examples for clues. The general theme of the concluding section of this chapter was covenant loyalty, viewed from four angles: mutual honor, potential confrontation, the releasing of and liberation brought about by forgiveness, and reciprocal provision.

All in all, then, I believe that the overarching aim of this work has been fully satisfied. The standing of the concept of covenant is not only validated by Scripture; I believe it is absolutely indispensible to our growth into maturity as believers. It has shaped our past, molds us in the present, and has the capacity to determine our future. Whether it will do so is in some way dependent upon how earnestly we learn the lessons of Scripture. Do we have eyes to see and ears to hear? If so, we can ill afford to ignore the evidence provided by God in relation to this most wondrous of subjects. It is, after all, the basis of God's self-disclosure.

Bibliography

Albright, William F. *Archaeology and the Religion of Israel*. Baltimore, MD: Johns Hopkins, 1953.
Alt, Albrecht. *Essays on Old Testament History and Religion*. Oxford: Blackwell, 1968.
Atkinson, David J. and David H. Field, eds. *New Dictionary of Christian Ethics and Pastoral Theology*. Leicester, UK: InterVarsity Press, 1995.
Barclay, William. *The Lord's Supper*. Louisville, KY: Westminster/John Knox, 2001.
Baxter, J. Sidlow. *Explore the Book*, Vol. 4. Grand Rapids, MI: Zondervan, 1960.
Berkhof, Louis. *Systematic Theology*. Edinburgh: Banner of Truth, 1988.
Black, Matthew and H. H. Rowley, eds. *Peake's Commentary on the Bible*. London: Thomas Nelson, 1962.
Bolton, Samuel. *The True Bounds of Christian Freedom*. London: Banner of Truth, 1978.
Bridges, Charles. *Proverbs*. Geneva Series of Commentaries. Edinburgh: Banner of Truth, 1998.
Bromiley, Geoffrey W. *International Standard Bible Encyclopedia*, Vol. 3. Grand Rapids, MI: Eerdmans, 1986.
Bruce, Frederick F. *1 & 2 Corinthians*. The New Century Bible Commentary Series. Grand Rapids, MI: Eerdmans, 1982.
Brunner, Emil. *The Mediator: A Study of the Central Doctrine of the Christian Faith*. Translated by Olive Wyon. London: Lutterworth, 1952.
Bullinger, E. W. *Number in Scripture: Its Supernatural Design and Spiritual Significance*. Grand Rapids, MI: Kregel, 2003.
Calvin, John. *Genesis*. Geneva Series of Commentaries. Edinburgh: Banner of Truth, 1992.
Campbell, Kenneth M. *God's Covenant*. Nutley, NJ: Presbyterian & Reformed, 1974.
Campenhausen, Hans von. *The Formation of the Christian Bible*. London: A. & C. Black, 1972.
Dabney, Robert L. *Systematic Theology*. Edinburgh: Banner of Truth, 1985.
Davies, Eryl W. *Numbers*. The New Century Bible Commentary Series. London: Marshall Pickering, 1995.
Davis, John J. *Biblical Numerology: A Basic Study of the Use of Numbers in the Bible*. Grand Rapids, MI: Baker Academic, 1968.
Denney, James. *The Death of Christ*. London: Hodder & Stoughton, 1911.
Douglas, James D., ed. *New Bible Dictionary*. Leicester, UK: InterVarsity Press, 1992.
Douglas, Mary. *In the Wilderness*. Oxford: Oxford University Press, 2001.
Dumbrell, William J. *Covenant and Creation: An Old Testament Covenantal Theology*. Carlisle: Paternoster, 1984.
Elwell, Walter A., ed. *Encyclopedia of the Bible*, Vol. 1. London: Marshall Pickering, 1990.

Ferguson, Sinclair B. and David F. Wright, eds. *New Dictionary of Theology*. Leicester, UK: InterVarsity Press, 1993.

Forsyth, Peter T. *The Church and the Sacraments*. London: Longmans, Green & Company, 1917.

Gaffin, Richard B., ed. *Redemptive History and Biblical Interpretation: The Shorter Writings of Geerhardus Vos*. Phillipsburg, NJ: Presbyterian & Reformed, 2001.

Golding, Peter E. *Covenant Theology*. Ross-shire, UK: Mentor, 2004.

Grudem, Wayne A. *Systematic Theology*. Leicester, UK: InterVarsity Press, 1994.

Guthrie, Donald and J Alec Motyer, eds. *New Bible Commentary*. Leicester, UK: InterVarsity Press, 1992.

Hammond, Thomas C. *In Understanding be Men*. Leicester, UK: InterVarsity Press, 1979.

Hansen, G. Walter. *Galatians*. New Testament Commentary Series. Leicester, UK: InterVarsity Press, 1994.

Harris, R. Laird, et al., eds. *Theological Wordbook of the Old Testament*, Vol. 1. Chicago, IL: Moody, 1981.

Hendriksen, William. *Galatians*. New Testament Commentary Series. Edinburgh: Banner of Truth, 1990.

———. *Matthew*. New Testament Commentary Series. Edinburgh: Banner of Truth, 1989.

———. *Romans*. New Testament Commentary Series. Edinburgh: Banner of Truth, 1982.

———. *Survey of the Bible*. Darlington, UK: Evangelical, 2003.

Hodge, Archibald A. *Outlines of Theology*. Edinburgh: Banner of Truth, 1991.

Hodge, Charles. *Systematic Theology*. Philipsburg, NJ: Presbyterian & Reformed, 1992.

Jensen, Irving L. *Jeremiah and Lamentations*. Chicago, IL: Moody, 1974.

———. *Survey of the Old Testament*. Chicago, IL: Moody, 1978.

Johnson, Paul. *A History of the Jews*. London: Weidenfeld & Nicolson, 1987.

Jordan, James B. *Through New Eyes: Developing a Biblical View of the World*. Brentwood, TN: Wolgemuth & Hyatt, 1988.

Keil, Carl F. *The Prophecies of Jeremiah*, Vol. 2. Grand Rapids, MI: Eerdmans, 1968.

Kendall, R. T. *Worshipping God*. London: Hodder & Stoughton, 2004.

Kevan, Ernest F. *The Lord's Supper*. Darlington, UK: Evangelical, 1982.

Ladd, George E. *A Theology of the New Testament*. London: Lutterworth, 1975.

———. *The Gospel of the Kingdom*. Grand Rapids, MI: Eerdmans, 1990.

Landay, Jerry M. *David: Power, Lust and Betrayal in Biblical Times*. Berkeley, CA: Ulysses, 1998.

Larkin, William J. *Acts*. New Testament Commentary Series. Leicester, UK: InterVarsity Press, 1995.

Liefeld, Walter L. *Ephesians*. New Testament Commentary Series. Leicester, UK: InterVarsity Press, 1997.

Lloyd-Jones, D. Martyn. *Expository Sermon on 2 Peter*. Edinburgh: Banner of Truth, 1999.

———. *Joy Unspeakable*. Eastbourne, UK: Kingsway, 1985.

———. *Studies in the Sermon the Mount*. Leicester, UK: InterVarsity Press, 1960.

———. *The Law: Its Functions and Limits*. Edinburgh: Banner of Truth, 2001.

———. *The New Man: Commentary on Romans Chapter 6*. Edinburgh: Banner of Truth, 1979.

Marshall, I. Howard. *Last Supper and Lord's Supper*. Carlisle, UK: Paternoster, 1997.

———. *1 Peter*. New Testament Commentary Series. Leicester, UK: InterVarsity Press, 1991.

Matthew, David. *The Covenant Meal*. Leicester, UK: Harvestime, 1988.

McComiskey, Thomas E. *The Covenants of Promise: A Theology of the Old Testament Covenants*. Leicester, UK: InterVarsity Press, 1985.

Morris, Leon. *The Apostolic Preaching of the Cross*. Grand Rapids, MI: Eerdmans, 1988.

Murray, John. *The Covenant of Grace*. Phillipsburg, NJ: Presbyterian & Reformed, 1992.

Noth, Martin. *Numbers*. Old Testament Library Series. London: SCM, 1968.

Osborne, Grant R. *Romans*. New Testament Commentary Series. Leicester, UK: InterVarsity Press, 2004.

Packer, James I. *Celebrating the Saving Work of God*. Carlisle, UK: Paternoster, 2000.

———. *Serving the People of God*. Carlisle, UK: Paternoster, 1998.

Payne, Jon D. *John Owen on the Lord's Supper*. Edinburgh: Banner of Truth, 2004.

Pink, Arthur W. *The Divine Covenants*. Grand Rapids, MI: Baker, 1973.

Rad, Gerhard von. *Genesis*. London: SCM, 1961.

Rendtorff, Rolf. *God's History: A Way Through the Old Testament*. Philadelphia, PA: Westminster, 1969.

Ridderbos, Herman N. *The Epistle of Paul to the Churches of Galatia*. London: Marshall, Morgan & Scott, 1976.

Robertson, O. Palmer. *The Christ of the Covenants*. Phillipsburg, NJ: Presbyterian & Reformed, 1980.

Scroggie, W. Graham. *Know Your Bible: Analytical Volume 1—The Old Testament*. London: Pickering & Inglis, 1960.

Slemming, Charles W. *The Bible Digest*. Grand Rapids, MI: Kregel, 1968.

Snaith, Norman H. *The Distinctive Ideas of the Old Testament*. London: Epworth, 1944.

Snyder, Howard A. *The Problem of Wineskins: Church Structure in a Technological Age*. Leicester, UK: InterVarsity Press, 1975.

Stedman, Ray C. *Hebrews*. New Testament Commentary Series. Leicester, UK: InterVarsity Press, 1992.

Stott, John R. W. *The Cross of Christ*. Leicester, UK: InterVarsity Press, 2008.

———. *The Living Church*. Leicester, UK: InterVarsity Press, 2007.

Taylor, Vincent. *The Atonement in New Testament Teaching*. London: Epworth, 1963.

Vine, William E. *Expository Dictionary of New Testament Words*. Iowa Falls, IA: Riverside, 1975.

Virgo, Terry. *Restoration in the Church*. Eastbourne, UK: Kingsway, 1985.

Wallis, Arthur. *Living God's Way*. Eastbourne, UK: Kingsway, 1984.

———. *The Radical Christian*. Eastbourne, UK: Kingsway, 1982.

Walvoord, John F. *The Millennial Kingdom: A Basic Text in Premillennial Theology*. Grand Rapids, MI: Zondervan, 1983.

Watson, Thomas. *A Body of Divinity*. Edinburgh: Banner of Truth, 1983.

White, Edward J. *The Law in the Scriptures*. St Louis, MO: Thomas Law, 1935.

Woodall, Christopher. "A Race in Need of Redemption: The Necessity, Reality and Benefits of the Atonement." MA dissertation, Potchefstroom University for Christian Higher Education, 2001.

Young, Edward J. *The Study of Old Testament Theology Today*. Cambridge, UK: James Clarke, 2004.